Simon's Saga for the SAT* I Verbal

by Philip Geer

BARRON'S

*SAT is a registered trademark of the College Entrance Examination Board,
which does not endorse this book.

All inquiries should be addressed to:
Barron's Educational Series, Inc.
250 Wireless Boulevard
Hauppauge, New York 11788
http://www.barronseduc.com

Library of Congress Catalog Card No.: 2002016320

International Standard Book No. 0-7641-2200-2

Library of Congress Cataloging-in-Publication Data
Geer, Philip.
    Simon's saga for the SAT I verbal / Philip Geer.
        p. cm.
    ISBN 0-7641-2200-2
        1. Scholastic Aptitude Test—Study guides. 2. English language—
Examinations—Study guides. 3. Universities and colleges—United States—
Entrance examinations—Study guides. I. Title: Simon's saga for the
SAT I verbal. II. Title.

    LB2353.57 .G44 2002
    378.1′662—dc21   2002016320

Printed in the United States of America

9 8 7 6 5 4 3 2 1

Acknowledgments

Song lyrics in Episode 22 from "Golden Rays" and "Moon in D" by Geoff Geer,
Copyright © 1998 by Geoff Geer. Reprinted by permission from Geoff Geer.

L. 151–2, 160–1 from THE ODYSSEY OF HOMER by RICHARD LATTIMORE,
Copyright © 1965, 1967 by Richard Lattimore. Reprinted by permission of
HarperCollins Publishers Inc.

Dedicated To

My son Geoff, for Axel's song and all the
wonderful music through the years.
-How can I sing it, except like this . . .

My son Dan, for being a great friend.
See you on 20 meters.
-VK6YDJ, this is 9V1AV . . .

My wife Sue, for everything.
-Remember?

Lincoln and Marina at Marima Cottages,
Pemberton, Western Australia,
for their karri forest retreat that
gave me the peace to write.

Wayne Barr and Marcy Rosenbaum at Barron's,
for believing in Simon.

About the Author

Philip Geer lives in Singapore where he directs Mentaurs, an educational consultancy that prepares students for the SAT I, SAT II, GRE, and other standardized tests. From 1978 until 2001 he taught English at the junior college level for the Singapore Ministry of Education. When he is not conducting test-preparation workshops or writing books such as *Simon's Saga*, he enjoys traveling and learning about different cultures.

You can contact the author at simon@mentaurs.com to give your comments on *Simon's Saga* and visit the website at *www.mentaurs.com* to learn more about building your verbal skills for the SAT I.

CONTENTS

Preface

Welcome to the world of *Simon's Saga*. I wrote this book to help students learn a lot of the difficult words they need to know to do well on the SAT I. There are many ways to increase your vocabulary, but one of the best is to see how a large number of words are actually *used* in writing. *Simon's Saga* teaches you 820 essential words in a story about the adventures of a group of college students.

As you read *Simon's Saga*, you'll be in good hands. In addition to teaching you all those words, Simon and his friends will help you to become familiar with important ideas in fields such as psychology, sociology, philosophy, political science, astronomy, and mythology that are discussed in SAT reading passages. All *you* have to do is read the episodes and then do the exercises.

Enjoy the story. And good luck on the SAT.

Philip Geer

"The two basic stories of all times are Cinderella and Jack the Giant Killer—the charm of women and the courage of men."

— *F. Scott Fitzgerald*

Episode 1

Welcome to College

Hi, I'm Simon. Welcome to college. I'll be your guide—sort of your **mentor**. You'll see what college is like from the student's point of view—the inside story. You'll meet my buddies and hang out with us. We're having a barbecue later on and some of the coolest people on campus will be there.

Before we meet my friends and start to party, we'd better get some boring, **mundane** stuff out of the way. See, in college, if you want to have fun, you first have to do some really serious work. And to get into a good college like mine, you'd better have a pretty good SAT score.

How do you get a good SAT score? Well, for the verbal part, the most important thing you need to know is those **bizarre** words they're always sticking into the test. Do you know what a **charlatan** is? No? Don't worry, when I was in high school I didn't either. (It means a "fake.") In fact, there were an awful lot of words that I didn't know. So, I was pretty worried back then. How was I going to learn all those words so I could get a decent SAT score?

Luckily, my best buddy happens to be a genius. His name is Axel. We go way back together—to first grade, in fact. But I'll tell you more about that later. Anyway, Axel is a very **discerning** guy. He had recognized how weak my vocabulary was years before I did. He tried to get me to improve it, but I wasn't interested. So, in twelfth grade Axel really got on my case. He told me that my weak vocabulary would be **deleterious** to my academic future; in other

1

words, it would hurt my chances of getting into a decent college. I became kind of **morose** when I realized that I would have to study long lists of words. But with Axel's help I did. And here I am. It was no **aberration**. There was no **chicanery** involved. It was just good old-fashioned hard work that did the trick. One month, six hours a day, memorizing long, boring lists of words. Whew!

Now, I'm a pretty OK guy. I mean, I give some thought to the people around me. Since I find **cognition** a somewhat **tedious** process, I figured other people might too. I said to myself, "Why not give the students coming up a break? Why should they have to go through one month of **unadulterated** misery as I did?" So, I had an idea. (It's rare, but it happens **sporadically**.) I thought, why not fire up the word processor and crank out a little **didactic** tale to help people like you learn the words without having to give up all your fun? I got my friends together and they agreed to help. Together, we have a **prodigious** vocabulary.

Another thing before we start: I really want you to do well on the SAT. So read these little episodes and have a great time. My friends and I have done a lot of the work for you. But here's a flash—you'll have some pretty heavy lifting to do too. I mean, I could open up your head and pour the words in, but that wouldn't be cool.

Have you noticed that I've been using some pretty unusual words? *These are the vital SAT words you have to learn.* They're all in bold. (**Like this.**)

Here's the drill: If you don't know a word, just check out the list at the end of each episode. This gives you the **denotation** of the word *as it is used in the episode.* It also gives you other meanings if it's really critical that you know them. All of these words are the ones the guys in Princeton, New Jersey who dream up the SAT assume to be part of a good student's **lexicon**.

The deal is, we'll pause the action for a little while after each episode. When this happens—you're on! Just look at each word in bold, check out its definition, and see how it's used in the story. When you think you've got it nailed, do the exercises at the end of the episode.

If you do OK, just keep going. If you don't do so well, you should go back for a little retooling. Read the story again and review how the words are used. Then, it's up to you to check out where you went wrong on the exercises.

Now, if you find yourself going back a lot to check out the words, don't worry. There's no **ignominy** in forgetting the meanings of words. Even Dr. Miller, my English professor, says he sometimes forgets words he's learned. But he doesn't let it get him down. That's because he's also picking up new words every day—really **arcane** words like "makimono." (Don't worry, the SAT test isn't that tough; but just for the record, a makimono is a Japanese art scroll.)

Would you like a hot tip? Get your hands on the most complete dictionary you can find. My roommates and I keep a **gargantuan** one on our kitchen table in the house so we can look up words we meet in our travels. Pretty **eccentric**, right? Yes, but it's amazing how fast your vocabulary improves if you look up words you don't know. And once you've seen a word a few times and looked it up, you'll really start to remember it.

Well, it's time for you to get to work. It would be great if you could get this **pedestrian** stuff out of the way so we can get to know each other better. I'll just hang out and wait for you to finish. Hey, I know the thing looks a little **daunting**, but I think the meanings are quite **explicit**. Just take it one episode at a time and, before you know it, you'll have learned an incredible number of new words. To be precise, you'll learn 820 words, the core of a college-level vocabulary you need for the SAT.

Oops—just one last thing I forgot to tell you: The SAT words in all of the episodes are also listed together in alphabetical order at the back of the book. See, I use many of the words I've taught you in each episode later in the **saga** so that you learn how they're used in different ways and to help you remember them. So, if you're reading along and come across a word you don't know that's not in bold, check it out in the list at the back. You've probably learned it in an earlier episode but it's kind of slipped your mind. But that's OK. As I said before, forgetting a few words happens to the best of us.

So, now you know the drill and where you fit into the picture. Yeah, you've got some work to do—I can't deny that. But, as I said, stay cool. You can handle it. Listen, if I can write this book, you can learn some words. Have fun!

Definitions

1. **mentor** N. wise advisor
2. **mundane** ADJ. typical of the ordinary (also: worldly as opposed to spiritual)
3. **bizarre** ADJ. strikingly unusual; fantastic
4. **charlatan** N. fake
5. **discerning** ADJ. perceptive; showing insight and judgment
6. **deleterious** ADJ. harmful
7. **morose** ADJ. ill-humored; sullen
8. **aberration** N. something different from the normal or usual
9. **chicanery** N. trickery; fraud
10. **unadulterated** ADJ. absolutely pure
11. **sporadically** ADV. occurring irregularly
12. **cognition** N. mental process by which knowledge is acquired
13. **tedious** ADJ. boring; tiring
14. **didactic** ADJ. instructional; teaching
15. **prodigious** ADJ. enormous (also: extraordinary)
16. **denotation** n. direct meaning of a word
17. **lexicon** N. vocabulary
18. **ignominy** N. great personal dishonor or humiliation
19. **arcane** ADJ. known only by a few; obscure
20. **gargantuan** ADJ. huge

21. **eccentric** ADJ. odd; deviating from the normal
22. **pedestrian** ADJ. ordinary; commonplace
23. **daunting** ADJ. frightening; intimidating; discouraging
24. **explicit** ADJ. very clear; definite
25. **saga** N. prose narrative

Simply Simon

Think you know the words? Then prove it! Choose the *best* word to fill in the blank in each of the sentences below.

aberration   mentor   mundane   chicanery

lexicon   sporadically   morose   arcane

unadulterated   bizarre

1. If you study hard and don't do well on a test, you shouldn't become _____; keep working hard and you'll probably do a lot better on the next one.

2. One thing I really respect about the teachers here is that they will tolerate no _____ when it comes to assignments; you have to be completely honest or you're out.

3. Axel doesn't like to spend a lot of time thinking about _____ things such as what he should wear or eat.

4. I like food that is _____ by preservatives or artificial coloring.

5. Axel once tried to explain some of the _____ mysteries of calculus to me.

6. Every student should have a/an _____ who can give him or her advice on academic matters.

7. One thing I've learned in college is that what is _____ to one person might be the most normal thing in the world to somebody else.

8. Axel is such a genius that it's a/an _____ when he doesn't know something.

9. The astronomy club has been observing an object that they believe appears _____ over a thousand-year period.

10. I was encouraged when I heard that you need to have only a/an _____ of 3,000 words in order to understand 80 percent of what you read.

Making Sense

Indicate whether or not each of the words in **bold** makes sense in the sentence. If it makes sense, put Y (Yes); if it doesn't make sense, put N (No).

1. I don't mind if a book is **didactic**, but I don't like it if the author seems to be trying to teach you something. ____

2. Axel says that the work of most scientists is not noticed by the public, and that only a few scientists achieve **ignominy** through winning awards such as the Nobel Prize. ____

3. A good dictionary gives accurate **denotations** of words. ____

4. Once, as a prank, I got a guy who was a complete **charlatan** to go to an advanced physics seminar; he spouted nonsense about black holes and superstrings for fifteen minutes before Professor James, the head of department, asked him to identify himself. ____

5. Albert Einstein had such a **pedestrian** mind that he came up with many startling new insights into the workings of nature. ____

6. Pollution in an environment can be **deleterious** to creatures that live in it. ____

7. A good scientist must be careful not to give an **explicit** account of her findings so that others can learn from them. ____

8. Getting a good grade in math is a **daunting** task for me since math has always been my weakest subject. ____

9. I'm a typical **eccentric**; nearly everything I do is perfectly normal. ____

10. Axel says that atoms are so **gargantuan** that they can be observed only through powerful microscopes. ____

Match It

Match each of the following words to its meaning.

1. ignominy	a. intimidating
2. cognition	b. perceptive
3. deleterious	c. ordinary
4. pedestrian	d. dishonor
5. saga	e. enormous
6. didactic	f. harmful
7. prodigious	g. instructional
8. daunting	h. narrative
9. eccentric	i. process of acquiring knowledge
10. discerning	j. odd

Axel Speaks

Greetings! I believe that you are now ready for something more intellectual. Choose the *best* word to fill in the blank in each sentence.

1. It was not basic research, nor even applied science, but applied technology that—through _____ production of weapons and other materials—gave the United States and its allies victory in World War II over an enemy that was in many ways their superior militarily.

(A) tedious

(B) explicit

(C) prodigious

(D) steady

(E) pedestrian

2. Remarkable advances in molecular biology have made it possible for doctors to diagnose certain genetic _____, such as Down's syndrome, before a person is born.

(A) diagnoses

(B) aberrations

(C) mentors

(D) difficulties

(E) denotations

3. The ozone layer has made life possible on Earth by shielding it from the extremely _____ effects of ultraviolet radiation from the sun.

(A) deleterious

(B) arcane

(C) mundane

(D) disturbing

(E) complex

4. The question of whether a work of art should be _____ or whether its function is to merely entertain is an important issue in literary criticism.

(A) admirable

(B) eccentric

(C) realistic

(D) didactic

(E) explicit

5. Even at speeds close to that of light, travel to a nearby star system, such as Alpha Centauri, would take about four years—a/an _____ undertaking.

(A) didactic

(B) pioneering

(C) unadulterated

(D) pedestrian

(E) daunting

Answers on page 442.

And now, on with the story.

At the Library

How did you do on the exercises? Pretty good? Keep it up.

Hey, I promised to introduce you to my friends, didn't I? Let's take a look and see who's around the house. Generally, people are pretty **quiescent** around here on Saturday morning. No one besides me seems to be conscious. I guess my roommates must be snoozing, catching up on their Zs after last night's **revelry**.

You might be wondering why a fun-loving guy like me is the only person up so early. The deal is, I'm a football player and I've got a really *major* game today, so I decided to lay kind of low last night. That's why I'm having this **novel** experience of being the only one up so early. Actually, I enjoy the peace of the morning.

But you see, this game is HUGE. I don't like to exaggerate, but if we win, it's bowl time—Gigantic Bowl Time! Lose, and we're off to one of those dinky little bowls you watch only if there's absolutely zilch on the box. So, you can see why I don't want to lose to Big State University. Those guys are really good. But I know we won't **squander** this chance. We'll win and be ranked among the top teams in the country at the end of the year.

I've got this little **ritual** I do every Saturday morning before a game. I know it sounds a little weird, but I **perambulate** around the campus and, eventually, I find myself at the stadium. While I'm walking, I go through the game plan, the coach's strategy for the game, in my mind. Basically, I get my head focused. When you're the quarterback you're the

11

head honcho. (Oops. Dr. Miller, my English professor, says "head" is **redundant** because honcho means "the head dude.") You are expected to have every play down cold.

Now, you don't have to be exactly **prescient**, but you do have to have some serious **foresight** because you never know what those guys on the other team are going to throw at you. One busted play could change the outcome of the whole game. Coach Wilson and his assistant coaches have showed us some great ways to limit the ability of State's front four to get to me before I can throw the ball. These strategies should help us to **sustain** our drives on critical third down situations.

I think I'm talking too much football. I get pretty **garrulous** when I sound off about football. Shall we perambulate a little?

Did you know that a lot of those old Greek philosophers liked to **peregrinate**, thinking and **expounding** on their ideas? Pretty interesting, huh? I learned that in my philosophy class. Some of them who followed Aristotle's teachings were actually called **peripatetic** because they discussed philosophy while they were walking around. Sort of like me, right?

Anyway, there I go, **digressing** again. I've strayed from the thread of this little story. OK. Let's see where our little ramble has taken us. Here's the library. It's not exactly my favorite place to hang out, but I don't hate it. I'm no **bibliophile**, but I do have tremendous respect for the scholars who spent endless hours studying and writing all those **tomes** in there. Some **pundits** say that books are **obsolescent** because this is the information age, but I think they have a pretty **tenuous** case. I mean, there's little evidence to support it. People will always like books—even guys like me. You see, the Internet is OK for sending **missives** to your girlfriend, but for research (yep, even I can't avoid having to take a peek at some data occasionally), nothing beats the good old library.

Anyway, let's see if the chief book honcho is around.

"Hey, Dr. Larsen. Great to see you!"

"Hello, Simon. Are you here to borrow some books or to study?" Dr. Larsen laughed. "Or are you here to check out the girls?" he asked.

"Now, Dr. Larsen, you know I'm one of your regular customers. I'm always coming here to stock up on the latest books. Your **caricature** of me as a guy who's just interested in scoping out girls is a **travesty** of the truth."

"Wow. Your vocabulary has certainly improved since your freshman year, Simon. Maybe you actually are acquiring **erudition** here."

"My **predilections** certainly have changed, Dr. Larsen. I've abandoned my **puerile** pursuits for **loftier** ones. In consequence, my taste in the reading material that I like to **peruse** has become quite intellectual."

"Nicely put, Simon," Dr. Larsen replied. "You certainly have become more **articulate**."

Simon beamed. "Thank you, Dr. Larsen," he said. "You know, while I'm here I think I'll look for that new translation of Plato's *Republic*. It's supposed to be absolutely *amazing*."

"Ah, yes," Dr. Larsen said. "I read Professor Hall's review of it. An excellent choice, Simon. I see that your interests really have become more **sophisticated**. Let me see, I think it should be right here on the new acquisitions shelf. I'll just take a look at ... ." Dr. Larsen broke off. He was looking at Simon, who was staring past him, wide-eyed, at something over in the reference section.

DEFINITIONS

1. **quiescent** ADJ. still; inactive
2. **revelry** N. boisterous festivity
3. **novel** ADJ. new or original
4. **squander** v. to waste
5. **ritual** N. detailed procedure regularly followed (also: the prescribed form of conducting a ceremony)
6. **perambulate** v. to stroll

7. **redundant** ADJ. unnecessarily repetitive; exceeding what is necessary
8. **prescient** ADJ. having knowledge of events before they occur
9. **foresight** N. concern with respect to the future (also: the ability to foresee)
10. **sustain** V. to maintain (also: support; uphold; undergo)
11. **garrulous** ADJ. very talkative
12. **peregrinate** V. to wander from place to place
13. **expound** V. to explain by presenting in detail
14. **peripatetic** ADJ. moving from place to place
15. **digress** V. to stray from the main topic
16. **bibliophile** N. book lover
17. **tome** N. book (usually large and scholarly)
18. **pundit** N. authority or critic
19. **obsolescent** ADJ. becoming obsolete (for example, no longer used)
20. **tenuous** ADJ. weak; insubstantial
21. **missive** N. letter
22. **caricature** N. exaggerated portrait
23. **travesty** N. highly inferior imitation
24. **erudition** N. deep learning
25. **predilection** N. preference; disposition
26. **puerile** ADJ. childish; immature
27. **lofty** ADJ. elevated in nature; noble
28. **peruse** V. to examine
29. **articulate** ADJ. speaking in clear and expressive language
30. **sophisticated** ADJ. having worldly knowledge or refinement (also: complex)

Simply Simon

Think you know the words? Then prove it! Choose the *best* word to fill in the blank in each of the sentences below.

missive   perusing   quiescent   sustain

predilection   novel   revelry   expounds

foresight   squander

1. Although I don't have a/an _____ for cooking, I certainly enjoy eating good food.

2. A student with _____ can plan ahead so that she has enough time to complete all of her assignments.

3. After several months of getting pretty bad grades during my freshman year, I decided to adopt what was for me a/an _____ approach to academics—I studied regularly.

4. If you get a/an _____ from the Dean of Students, you can be pretty sure that it contains either really good news or really bad news.

5. After a big victory, my teammates and I enjoy a bit of _____ .

6. _____ a high-quality newspaper tells you a remarkable amount of stuff about the world.

7. It annoys me to see a student _____ the opportunity to acquire an education.

8. Professor Chandler, my political science professor, often _____ on the topic of globalization.

9. Spring is my favorite season because so much life that was _____ in the winter becomes active again.

10. Reading about the lives of important people in a particular subject helps me to _____ my interest in that area.

Making Sense

Indicate whether or not each of the words in **bold** makes sense in the sentence. If it makes sense, put Y (Yes); if it doesn't make sense, put N (No).

1. Our team has a little **ritual** we go through before each game: each player shakes hands with all the coaches and thanks them for all the hard work they put into preparing us for the game. _____

2. It's a good idea to use as much **redundant** language in your assignments as you can so that your teacher doesn't have to read through a lot of unnecessary stuff. _____

3. Some educators say that the blackboard and whiteboard are **obsolescent** teaching aids that soon will be seen only in museums. _____

4. There's a guy in my political science class who's so **garrulous** that sometimes it's difficult for other students to get a chance to talk. _____

5. **Digressing** too much from the main theme in an essay is generally a bad idea because it makes it hard for the reader to follow your argument. _____

6. Some political **pundits** argue that presidential campaigns are too long. _____

7. Dr. James won a Nobel Prize for his **tenuous** research in the area of quantum mechanics. _____

8. A good **caricature** of a person gives a fair and balanced view of that person. _____

9. A professor is almost by definition a person of considerable **erudition**. _____

10. The search for truth is one of humanity's most noble and **puerile** pursuits. _____

Match It

Match each of the following words to its meaning.

1. perambulate   a. book lover

2. prescient   b. stroll

3. peregrinate   c. noble

4. peripatetic   d. book

5. bibliophile   e. having knowledge of events before they occur

6. tome   f. moving from place to place

7. travesty   g. speaking in clear and expressive language

8. lofty   h. wander from place to place

9. articulate   i. highly inferior imitation

10. sophisticated   j. having worldly knowledge or refinement

Axel Speaks

Greetings! I believe that you are now ready for something more intellectual. Choose the *best* word to fill in the blank in each sentence.

1. If the view that humankind originated in Africa and then dispersed around the world is correct, physical differences in groups of people arose as they evolved to adapt to varying conditions they faced in their _____ .

(A) encounters

(B) aberrations

(C) propulsion

(D) generation

(E) peregrinations

2. According to psychologists, people are born with a tendency toward either introversion or extroversion that can be modified to some degree by conscious choice and social influence, but the underlying _____ will remain dominant.

(A) travesty

(B) generality

(C) predilection

(D) exaggeration

(E) similarity

3. As was their usual practice, the Romans adopted the god Dionysus from Greek mythology and called him "Bacchus"— from which we get the word bacchanalia: riotous, drunken _____ .

(A) revelry

(B) erudition

(C) prosperity

(D) rashness

(E) missives

4. The Canadian literary critic Marshall McCluhan must have been _____ when he coined the term "global village" in the 1960s, well before modern communications had become nearly as widespread as they are today.

(A) prescient

(B) articulate

(C) didactic

(D) wise

(E) imaginative

5. Although there are many _____ systems in the space shuttle, it is still possible that both the main system and the back-up system could fail, resulting in a catastrophic failure.

(A) tenuous

(B) unusual

(C) basic

(D) obsolescent

(E) redundant

Answers on page 443.

And now, on with the story.

Episode 3

The Flirt

"Wow! Hey, Dr. Larsen, who's that?"

Dr. Larsen turned around and looked. Now he knew what had so suddenly attracted Simon's attention. "The blonde?" he asked.

"Yeah."

Dr. Larsen sighed. "Still the same old Simon, I see," he said. "She's a freshman. A regular in here. She's a very **diligent** student. An art major." Dr. Larsen said. He paused. "Hey, wait a minute. Aren't you still going with Jaz?"

Simon gazed longingly at the girl.

"Jaz? What? Oh yeah, Jaz. Of course," he said. "Hey, but cut me some slack, Doc. Just because I'm going with someone doesn't mean I've suddenly gone blind!"

Simon was silent, admiring the girl. Suddenly, he smiled broadly. "And you know, come to think of it, a little chat can never do any harm. I guess I'm just a naturally **affable** guy."

Simon strolled over to where the girl was sitting, intently reading a very big book.

"Hi," he said.

The girl looked up. "Hello," she said.

"I'm Simon. I just happened to notice the book you're perusing and I felt I just had to come over and ask about it. It's one of my favorites. It's an absolute classic."

The girl gave him an odd look. Simon tried to see the title but he couldn't quite make it out.

21

"I hope you don't take this as a **gambit** by me to pick you up," said Simon.

The girl laughed, but seemed rather **circumspect**. After all, she had never met Simon.

"I thought you were reading one of my all-time favorites, *The Complete Dialogues of Plato*."

"No, it's just the course directory."

"That's fascinating! So, are you deciding what to take next semester?"

"Yeah."

"If I may be allowed to **speculate**, you're an art major, right?"

She smiled. "Pretty good. Your **conjecture** is accurate. How **astute**. How could you tell?"

"Oh, just a lucky guess." Simon gave her one of his famous smiles.

The girl smiled back at him. Bingo! So far so good, Simon thought. Smooth sailing. This is a piece of cake. And then, for some **inexplicable** reason, he violated, in one moment, two of his own **cardinal** rules: one, *never* **embellish** your line—keep it simple, sincere, and direct; two, focus *completely* on the job at hand. Perhaps he had grown overconfident; perhaps, for some reason, he was off his game just the tiniest bit. Whatever the reason, he did it.

"Maybe it's because you tickled my **aesthetic sensibility**," he said.

The girl looked blankly at Simon. "*What?*" she said. She was thinking: *Such* a pity. He's *such* a hunk. The guy's not only a total babe, she thought, he's *astoundingly* good-looking. A real Adonis. Like the picture they had shown her in art history last week. Yes, too bad. But *nothing* is worse than lame. A lame Adonis. Yuck.

As Simon watched the girl's face, he saw that her look of blankness was turning to a look of something closer to disgust. Her expression seemed to say, "*Tickled my aesthetic sensibility?* Is this guy *weird* or something?"

Simon **admonished** himself for his **pretentious** and **pedantic** language. Sometimes all these **exotic** words just seemed to come tumbling **spontaneously** out of his mouth. (*Three years ago, Axel said that he would make sure the words were* **inscribed** *in my memory*, Simon thought. *I guess he succeeded. Now I can't get rid of them.*)

Unfortunately, this time they had come out of his mouth at a very **inopportune** moment. This girl must think I'm a complete weirdo, Simon thought. And one thing he knew for sure—girls did not like weird. *Different*, maybe—but not weird. OK, he thought, if anybody can pull this one out, it's you. *Just get back to the playbook.*

"I mean," he said, "you kind of *look* like an art major."

She smiled slightly.

That's better, Simon thought. She seemed to like that. Not fancy, but at least it bought some time, and if there was time, there was hope, however **forlorn**.

Definitions

1. **diligent** ADJ. making a persistent and painstaking effort
2. **affable** ADJ. friendly
3. **gambit** N. carefully considered strategy
4. **circumspect** ADJ. cautious
5. **speculate** V. to conjecture
6. **conjecture** N. conclusion reached without complete evidence
7. **astute** ADJ. keen in judgment; shrewd
8. **inexplicable** ADJ. difficult or impossible to explain
9. **cardinal** ADJ. of foremost importance
10. **embellish** V. to add details to make more attractive (also: adorn)
11. **aesthetic** ADJ. pertaining to beauty or art
12. **sensibility** N. refined awareness and appreciation in feeling

13. **admonish** v. to reprimand
14. **pretentious** ADJ. making an extravagant show; ostentatious
15. **pedantic** ADJ. having a narrow concern for book learning and technicalities
16. **exotic** ADJ. strikingly unusual
17. **spontaneously** ADV. occurring apparently without cause
18. **inscribed** ADJ. written
19. **inopportune** ADJ. ill timed
20. **forlorn** ADJ. nearly hopeless (also: sad and lonely; destitute)

Simply Simon

Think you know the words? Then prove it! Choose the *best* word to fill in the blank in each of the sentences below.

circumspect   inopportune   cardinal   admonished

sensibility   pedantic   embellishes   gambits

affable   inexplicable

1. One of my _____ rules of life is, "Don't worry about what you can't do anything about."

2. Studying the works of some of the great writers has made my literary _____ more mature.

3. My Aunt Joan asked for a raise at a/an _____ time; the company she works for had just lost a lot of money.

4. It is _____ to me that more students don't become involved in politics.

5. I became more _____ about criticizing other people after I realized I was far from perfect myself.

6. A good storyteller often _____ the events she's narrating to make them more interesting to her listeners.

7. Dr. Larsen once _____ me for talking too loudly in the library.

8. In high school I tried a lot of _____ to avoid doing work.

9. A successful politician is generally a/an _____ person who mixes easily with many different types of people.

10. I like professors who can explain complex subjects without being _____ .

Making Sense

Indicate whether or not each of the words in **bold** makes sense in the sentence. If it makes sense, put Y (Yes); if it doesn't make sense, put N (No).

1. In discussions in English class I often argue for the view that literature cannot be purely **aesthetic** but must concern itself with social and moral issues. ____

2. I enjoy **exotic** foods such as hamburgers and hot dogs. ____

3. If she is very **diligent** in her work, a highly intelligent student will probably flunk out of college. ____

4. I don't like to wear **pretentious** clothes; generally I just wear a pair of jeans and a polo shirt. ____

5. Science is based solidly on the absolute certainties of reason, evidence, and **conjecture**. ____

6. Professor Chandler said that my analysis of the decline of communism was so **astute** that he felt it was only fair to give me a "D" for it. ____

7. In history class we've seen that nothing happens **spontaneously**; there's a cause for every event that takes place. ___

8. Our team was completely **forlorn** after learning that we'd been voted one of the best teams in the country. ___

9. The astronomer Carl Sagan often **speculated** about the possibility of intelligent life existing in other parts of the universe. ___

10. Some day I'd like to see my name **inscribed** on the Heisman Trophy honoring the nation's best football player. ___

Match It

Match each of the following words to its meaning.

1. pedantic	a. keen in judgment
2. embellish	b. conclusion reached without complete evidence
3. astute	c. having a narrow concern for book learning
4. admonish	d. cautious
5. aesthetic	e. making a persistent and painstaking effort
6. circumspect	f. add details to make attractive
7. exotic	g. difficult or impossible to explain
8. conjecture	h. pertaining to beauty or art
9. diligent	i. strikingly unusual
10. inexplicable	j. reprimand

Axel Speaks

Greetings! I believe that you are now ready for something more intellectual. Choose the *best* word to fill in the blank in each sentence.

1. The paintings of the French artist Eugène Delacroix illustrate the romantic interest in the primitive and the _____, as well as its interest in nature and belief in humanity's inborn goodness.

(A) dated

(B) pedantic

(C) ridiculous

(D) exotic

(E) public

2. Astronomy has developed in modern times from a largely _____ field to one that has created models of the universe based on the laws of physics and on observations such as the velocity of the galaxies.

(A) aesthetic

(B) sophisticate

(C) quiescent

(D) speculative

(E) arcane

3. Like the seventeenth-century English philosopher John Locke, Communist educators believe that a young child's mind is a *tabula rasa* (that is, a blank slate) on which they can _____ the values of their philosophy.

(A) expound

(B) inscribe

(C) caricature

(D) embellish

(E) create

4. The question of whether form should follow function or function should follow form—that is, should purely artistic considerations be subordinate to utilitarian ones—is one of the enduring issues in _____ debate.

(A) didactic

(B) traditional

(C) aesthetic

(D) explicit

(E) cognitive

5. In the early nineteenth century, prominent scientists such as Charles Lyell and Charles Darwin were puzzled by the sudden disappearance of species from the fossil record because their view of this record was _____ on the assumption prevailing at the time that the earth had existed for only several thousand years, a period of time that did not seem to allow time for species to become extinct.

(A) explained

(B) sustained

(C) misconstrued

(D) predicated

(E) admonished

Answers on pages 443–444.

And now, on with the story.

SIMON IN COMBAT

"Do art majors have a certain *look* or something?" the girl asked. She did not seem happy. In fact, Simon thought, she looks sort of annoyed.

Simon was dazed. It was getting *worse* instead of better. Now, apparently, she was being *sarcastic*! His strongest instinct was to flee. But Simon was not a coward. He had never fled a battle before. **Sarcasm**, he knew, was a hazard of the battlefield. It came with the territory. If he was going to flirt, he had to be able to take hostile fire. Ridicule was a harsh weapon, but a **legitimate** one that a girl could **deploy** if some jerk was trying to bug her. It was a female **prerogative**. But for one so young and so pretty to be so unkind .... She seemed to be toying with him, reeling him in and then letting him out. As much as he hated to give up on this dazzling girl, he would, he realized, have to withdraw from the field as gracefully as he could.

"I ..., I ...," Simon stammered.

Suddenly, the girl's **countenance** was transformed. The most glorious smile Simon had ever seen illuminated her face. Simon saw beams of light streaming from her eyes. She was **incandescent**, radiating love. Simon stared in wonderment at the girl. Surely, he thought, this was an angel come to show me **clemency** in the middle of battle. He was too stunned to speak. All he could do was wait for whatever came next.

The girl put her hand on top of Simon's and looked up at him. "I'm sorry," she said. "That came out the wrong way. I'm afraid I'm not very good at this." And then she took her hand and held his forearm, gently squeezing it. As she held his arm, she looked up, into Simon's eyes, and smiled again. For a moment, Simon was transported into some **supernal** realm far from Earth.

"So what are you here for, some research?" she asked.

"Luckily," he said, "I'm all caught up on my work." *With a little help from my friends*, he thought. He recalled Axel helping him with his last political science paper— "Globalization: **Benign** Trend or **Malignant** Growth in the Body Politic?" It amazed Simon how **comprehensive** Axel's knowledge was. The guy seemed to know *everything*. He was an astrophysics major, but he could help anybody in any field from history to chemistry. What a debate that paper had **engendered** after he had given a summary of it to the class!

"I'm just browsing, trying to pick up something interesting." He paused, smiled, and then said, "To read."

"That's really good," the girl said. "I mean, that you're all done with your work."

"Yeah, so I've got loads of free time," Simon said.

"Oh, that's *great!*" the girl exclaimed.

Simon smiled broadly. Everything was back on track. Now all he had to do was decide where they should go after the game—he and this amazing young woman.

But suddenly the girl was no longer smiling. She was now very serious, peering closely at Simon's face. Simon felt uncomfortable. Under the gaze of those intelligent blue eyes, he felt a little like an insect being examined. Here we go again, Simon thought. Either this girl finds me completely **charismatic** or she is filled with **disdain** for me. I know some people are fickle, but this is ridiculous. Once again, he waited for the girl to pass her **verdict** on him.

The girl cocked her head fetchingly to one side. She continued her examination of Simon, gazing intently at him. "Wait a *minute*," she said finally, "aren't you the *football* player?"

Simon looked a bit **sheepish**. "Yeah," he admitted. "I throw the old pigskin for our alma mater."

"And pretty good, too, from what I've heard," she said.

Simon thought it should be "pretty *well*." Sometimes he became rather pedantic.

"Aren't you like an *all-American* or something?" The girl was now becoming quite **animated**.

He gave her his best "aw shucks, it's really nothing" look. "Yeah, I guess I do OK."

"Hey, I saw you throw that game-winning pass on TV last year against State. It was into some really fierce coverage, and with the blitz on too. Ten seconds left on the clock. You kept your cool, sidestepped that safety who was trying to blindside you, read the coverage, waited for a passing lane to open, and *zip*—right between two of the best defensive backs in the conference. That pass had to be *perfect*. And it was." She gazed at Simon like he was a demigod.

Simon's eyes narrowed. This girl was pretty unbelievable, he thought. She was totally **alluring** and she talked football like the defensive coordinator at Miami.

"So, when's the next game?" she asked. She batted her eyelashes and ran a hand through her hair. She continued to gaze fondly at Simon.

Simon felt his knees becoming weak. He struggled to catch his breath. "Breathe deep...breathe deep... ," he said to himself. "Be cool."

After several moments Simon looked at his watch and said, in the most casual tone he could, "Kick-off is in exactly three hours and eleven minutes."

"Of *course!*" she exclaimed. "It's the big game against State!"

"Hey, I've got a great idea," Simon said. "Maybe after the game you and I ..." He stopped talking. He saw that the girl was no longer looking at him. Her eyes were focused on something behind him. On her face was an **enigmatic** expression. She was gazing at something past him, over his shoulder. Slowly, almost **furtively**, Simon turned his head.

1. **sarcasm** N. scornful remark
2. **legitimate** ADJ. in accordance with established standards; reasonable
3. **deploy** V. station systematically over an area
4. **prerogative** N. exclusive right or privilege
5. **countenance** N. facial expression
6. **incandescent** ADJ. shining brightly
7. **clemency** N. kind or merciful act; leniency or mercy
8. **supernal** ADJ. heavenly; celestial
9. **benign** ADJ. harmless (also: kind)
10. **malignant** ADJ. highly injurious
11. **comprehensive** ADJ. thorough
12. **engender** V. to cause; produce
13. **charismatic** ADJ. having great personal magnetism or charm
14. **disdain** V. to treat with scorn or contempt
15. **verdict** N. finding of an authority
16. **sheepish** ADJ. embarrassed; bashful
17. **animated** ADJ. lively
18. **alluring** ADJ. very attractive
19. **enigmatic** ADJ. deeply puzzling; mysterious
20. **furtively** ADV. sneakily; stealthily

Simply Simon

Think you know the words? Then prove it! Choose the *best* word to fill in the blank in each of the sentences below.

deploy   engenders   sarcasm   alluring

comprehensive   verdict   enigmatic   countenance

disdain   charismatic

1. It is the policy of the United States to _____ nuclear weapons only if it is absolutely necessary.

2. A friend of mine who is a drama major performed in a play recently in which the characters spoke only in _____ utterances that left most of the audience baffled.

3. My western civilization course gave me a/an _____ survey of the development of our civilization.

4. Poverty sometimes _____ unrest in society.

5. My political science teacher says that most successful leaders have _____ personalities that attract people to them.

6. After I applied for the special studies program in world politics I waited nervously for two weeks for the _____ of the program's committee.

7. Jaz is so naturally _____ that she doesn't have to use makeup.

8. A person who cheats on an assignment is dishonest and should be treated with _____ .

9. It is amazing how quickly a teacher's _____ can change from sunny to cloudy and back again.

10. My psychology professor described _____ as a form of verbal aggression.

Making Sense

Indicate whether or not each of the words in **bold** makes sense in the sentence. If it makes sense, put Y (Yes); if it doesn't make sense, put N (No).

1. Professor Chandler, my political science professor, has gone to several developing countries as an observer to help ensure that elections were **legitimate** expressions of the people's will. ____

2. The sun is the most **incandescent** object in the solar system. ____

3. Some people believe that angels exist in a **supernal** realm. ____

4. In a political science paper on the effects of globalization on developing countries I reached the conclusion that globalization has had a number of **benign** effects that have significantly damaged such countries. ____

5. A good leader must look **sheepish** at all times in order to project an air of authority. ____

6. There's nothing more relaxing than a long, **malignant** party with all of your friends. ____

7. Under the Constitution it is the president's **prerogative** to veto legislation passed by Congress. ____

8. My physics teacher in high school loved explaining concepts to the class and often became so **animated** that the students in the front row had to hunker down to avoid being struck by his flailing arms. ____

9. I'm the type of guy who likes to move around campus **furtively**, stopping to talk to everyone I meet. ____

10. Studies have shown that there is a great variation among judges in the extent to which they show **clemency** to people that have been convicted of crimes. ____

Match It

Match each of the following words to its meaning.

1. benign	a. deeply puzzling
2. charismatic	b. thorough
3. enigmatic	c. highly injurious
4. legitimate	d. place systematically
5. comprehensive	e. having great personal magnetism
6. engender	f. heavenly
7. supernal	g. exclusive right
8. malignant	h. harmless
9. deploy	i. reasonable
10. prerogative	j. cause

Axel Speaks

Greetings! I believe that you are now ready for something more intellectual. Choose the *best* word to fill in the blank in each sentence.

1. Since solar energy drives most of the chemical and biological processes that _____ and sustain life, it can be said that the source of life on Earth is the power generated by hydrogen in the Sun.

(A) prohibit

(B) engender

(C) allow

(D) admonish

(E) encourage

2. The _____ of the leader of the country generally assumes more importance in the fascist system than in the democratic system because fascism is normally founded on a "cult of personality."

(A) kindness

(B) charisma

(C) countenance

(D) prerogative

(E) voice

3. Psychology makes use of insights from other social sciences, such as anthropology and sociology, to gain a/an _____ view of human mental processes in relation to environment and culture.

(A) comprehensive

(B) historical

(C) circumspect

(D) prescient

(E) tenuous

4. The space shuttle was designed to reduce the cost of placing payloads in orbit around the earth by being reusable; although the shuttle has had many notable successes, NASA found that the savings compared to using conventional vessels were not as great as expected, and so recently has begun, once again, to _____ its rocket launchers.

(A) encourage

(B) admonish

(C) engender

(D) deploy

(E) embellish

5. Recent observations have shown dolphins to be, at times, far from _____ ; sometimes they viciously attack humans and even kill their own young.

(A) benign

(B) enigmatic

(C) gracious

(D) charismatic

(E) supernal

Answers on pages 443–444.

And now, on with the story.

A Narrow Escape

"Hey, Jaz! Great to see you! What are *you* doing here?"

Jaz looked fixedly at Simon. She does not seem particularly **ebullient**, Simon decided.

"So, Simon, you must be here doing some research for the game," Jaz said, glancing at the girl.

Oh boy, Simon thought, *this could be trouble*. Though she could sometimes be quite **acerbic**, his girlfriend seldom resorted to sarcasm. When she did, it meant she was **volatile** and might become **bellicose** at any moment. He had to **mollify** her—and quickly! He felt like he was standing on the edge of a very deep **ravine**, and he was about to fall into it. Yes, he had to act with **alacrity**. Now, if there was one thing Simon was good at, it was keeping his cool under pressure, whether it was gargantuan hulks trying to tear off his head on the football field or his girlfriend trying to cramp his style.

"I was just answering some **queries** this scholarly young woman had about what courses she should take next semester," Simon said. "She wants to know what the most interesting courses are and how they're taught." He glanced at the girl, who remained **impassive**, except for the slightest trace of a smile on her face. This should **appease** Jaz, he thought. Jaz never tired of discussing **pedagogical** topics.

Jaz brightened and looked at the girl. She smiled. *That was a close one*, Simon thought.

"Oh, Simon knows all about the syllabus of practically every course on campus," Jaz said.

The girl looked impressed. "Wow!" she said. "You must be quite the scholar. That's really helpful."

Simon practically glowed. Once again he put on his best, "Aw shucks, it's nothing really" look.

"Oh, he's a real scholar," Jaz said. "His tastes are so **eclectic** and his research so **scrupulous** that he knows all the gut courses on campus. Don't you, Simon?" She gave him a **scathing** look. "But, if you're interested in what the really stimulating courses are," she continued, "maybe my other friends and I can give you some help."

"I'd really appreciate that," the girl said.

"Hey," Jaz said. "I have an idea. Why don't you come over to our place?"

"That sounds great," the girl said. "You know, I'm an art major. Do you guys know much about that stuff?"

"Between us we know a prodigious amount of stuff," Jazz said. "If I don't know about it, I can find someone who does. And, anyway, Axel knows just about everything."

"Axel?"

"Oh, he's our roommate. He's a science major, but basically he's an all-round genius. Even professors come over to get his **assessment** of their ideas."

"Yeah," Simon said, "he's our little **Renaissance** dude."

"Wow, that's amazing" the girl said. "I can't wait to meet him. I've got this paper on Chagall due at the end of next week and I've been doing all this research, but I've kind of reached a dead end. I really need someone with a different **perspective**. I can't wait to meet this guy! He sounds like a real **savant**."

Jaz and Simon looked at each other.

"Axel is really brilliant, but he's a pretty **reclusive** guy," said Simon.

"Oh, Simon," Jaz said. "I'm sure you can lure him out to help this young damsel."

She looked at the girl. "By the way, I'm Jaz," she said. "You've met Simon. I didn't catch your name."

"Christine," the girl said.

"OK, great," Simon said. "Christine, why don't you come over—let's see—today's Saturday. Maybe you could come over on Monday night."

"Sounds good. Yeah, I can make it on Monday."

"And make sure you bring what you've done on your paper so far—and all your research notes. That kind of stuff always helps to **pique** Axel's interest."

"OK, I will, Simon," Christine said. "See you guys."

"Bye bye," Jaz said, and turned to leave.

Christine looked at Simon and said, "Bye bye, Simon." She started to leave. After a few steps, she stopped, turned around, looked at Simon—and *winked.*

Simon sighed as he watched her walk away.

Definitions

1. **ebullient** ADJ. over-flowing with enthusiasm
2. **acerbic** ADJ. sharp tempered
3. **volatile** ADJ. tending to vary frequently
4. **bellicose** ADJ. aggressive
5. **mollify** V. to soothe
6. **ravine** N. deep, narrow gorge
7. **alacrity** N. speed (also: cheerful willingness)
8. **query** N. question
9. **impassive** ADJ. showing no emotion
10. **appease** V. to calm; pacify
11. **pedagogical** ADJ. related to teaching
12. **eclectic** ADJ. selecting from various sources
13. **scrupulous** ADJ. very thorough
14. **scathing** ADJ. very severe or harsh
15. **assessment** N. appraisal
16. **Renaissance** N. the humanistic revival of classical art and learning that occurred in 14–16th century Europe (also—renaissance: rebirth; revival; note: a "Renaissance man" is a man with diverse interests)
17. **perspective** N. point of view

18. **savant** N. learned person
19. **reclusive** ADJ. seeking seclusion
20. **pique** V. to arouse

Simply Simon

Think you know the words? Then prove it! Choose the *best* word to fill in the blank in each of the sentences below.

Renaissance   assessment   mollified   queries

ebullient   scathing   reclusive   ravine

scrupulous   perspectives

1. When I first came to this college I had a lot of _____ about things, but now I've settled into life here.

2. I have learned to be _____ when doing research for my papers: I make sure I check all my sources thoroughly.

3. In my freshman year our team lost every game up until the final game of the season; Coach Wilson said winning that game was the beginning of our long climb out of a/an _____.

4. College education has helped me gain many new _____ on the world.

5. During the _____ much of the knowledge of ancient Greece and Rome was rediscovered.

6. The cheerleaders were _____ after we won the Big Bowl last year.

7. At a forum on globalization at our college a visiting scholar delivered a/an _____ criticism of its effects on the world that was the harshest speech I've ever heard.

8. My _____ of a work of art is pretty limited because I've had little training in that area.

9. As a certified party animal who seeks out people by instinct, I could not accurately be described as _____.

10. During the years that our team was not winning many games, Coach Wilson_____ the alumni by saying he had a rebuilding program in place and success would come soon.

Making Sense

Indicate whether or not each of the words in **bold** makes sense in the sentence. If it makes sense, put Y (Yes); if it doesn't make sense, put N (No).

1. Once when I was having trouble coming up with an idea for a political science paper Axel suggested that I pretend I was some great **savant** and write down what that great scholar in the field would say. ____

2. Our college library has an **eclectic** collection of books to meet the needs of students and scholars in practically every area of learning. ____

3. Often in presidential campaigns the vice-presidential candidate is more aggressive and **acerbic** than the presidential candidate, who remains somewhat above the struggle. ____

4. Nothing **piques** my interest in a subject like a really dull lecture. ____

5. Professor Chandler says that there is some evidence that democratic countries are less inclined to become **bellicose** and attack their neighbors than are countries with nondemocratic systems of government. ____

6. **Appeasing** an angry person is certain to just make them angrier. ____

7. You can tell a lot about how a girl feels about you if her expression is **impassive**. ____

8. When Coach Wilson tells you to move, it is advisable to do so—and with **alacrity**. ____

9. It's important that a country's leaders have **volatile** natures so that they will not be likely to continually change their policies. ____

10. Professors here divide their time pretty evenly between their **pedagogical** duties and their research. ____

Match It

Match each of the following words to its meaning.

1. volatile	a. very thorough
2. bellicose	b. learned person
3. mollify	c. appraisal
4. impassive	d. varying frequently
5. acerbic	e. point of view
6. savant	f. aggressive
7. eclectic	g. selecting from various sources
8. scrupulous	h. showing no emotion
9. assessment	i. soothe
10. perspective	j. sharp tempered

Axel Speaks

Greetings! I believe that you are now ready for something more intellectual. Choose the *best* word to fill in the blank in each sentence.

1. Technology has become so diverse and complex that no one person—even a highly trained engineer with _____ interests—is able to fully understand it.

(A) legitimate

(B) discerning

(C) scrupulous

(D) eclectic

(E) impassive

2. Since the end of World War II many commentators have been predicting the death of the great American cities; however, in recent times there have been signs that many of these cities are enjoying a/an _____ , reinvigorated and transformed by a new wave of immigrants from Asia and other areas.

(A) reinforcement

(B) renaissance

(C) prerogative

(D) advance

(E) magnification

3. A number of economists are concerned that the ability investors now have to quickly move capital from one market to another has created a situation that could lead to _____ prices and destabilize the world economy.

(A) alluring

(B) prosperous

(C) volatile

(D) exotic

(E) sporadic

4. The astronomer Tycho Brahe's _____ observations of a comet in 1577 established that, based on its motion, it was an astronomical body rather than an occurrence originating in the earth's atmosphere.

(A) pedagogical

(B) furtive

(C) impassive

(D) pedantic

(E) scrupulous

5. Some observers believe that a high level of social mobility (that is, frequent changes in status) makes people uncertain about their position in society, causing them to continually make _____ of their situation in relation to that of their neighbors; some of these observers feel that this tends to breed mistrust and anxiety in society.

(A) queries

(B) assessments

(C) speculations

(D) restrictions

(E) conjectures

Answers on page 445.

And now, on with the story.

A Little Digression

I promised to introduce you to my friends, didn't I? Well, it looks like Jaz introduced herself. I was just getting around to telling you about her. She's a great friend. A *really* great friend, in fact. It might be a kind of outdated expression, but the best word I know of to describe her is "girlfriend." I know "partner" is the trendy word now, but I've got this thing about not wanting to think of my girlfriend as a bridge partner or tennis partner—or even a business partner. In sociological **jargon** I know they say "significant other," but that's kind of impersonal for me. I'm sort of **obstinate** about these things. I prefer to call her my girlfriend—not **subtle**, but not **ambiguous** either. Simple and direct. She's a girl and she's my friend—"girl friend." Except she's the person who's **paramount** in my affections—*numero uno*.

So, it looks like we've just made another friend. Christine seems like a great person to know. She's so **cordial**.

Now, where did we leave off before Christine appeared? Right, I was talking about the library (way back in Episode 2). Of course, I'm really lucky because my best buddy is virtually a walking library. Sometimes I wonder how he fits all those books in his head. There isn't much Axel doesn't know. He gives new meaning to the term "brainiac." I've told you a little about him already and about how he's helped me so much with the academic side of things. I certainly wouldn't be where I am today without Axel. When I have a paper due we have a little **colloquy** on it and he puts me on the right track. And before a test he crams information into me until I can

48

replicate it **verbatim**. He tirelessly **reiterates** concepts that I'm too **obtuse** to understand. He **rebukes** me when my attention wanders. He even **revivifies** me when I find the discussion **soporific** and I become **somnolent** and take a little **sojourn** in slumberland. He just keeps going, **undaunted** by anything.

Anyway, that's Axel. Are you a little curious about his name? It's kind of unusual, isn't it? Actually, his full name is Axelrod. His name situation is a little **convoluted**, but I'll try to unravel it for you. You see, he has a number of **appellations** (tags, to use the **vernacular**). To some people, he's Axel. Other people call him Rod. That's OK with Axel. But a lot of his friends just call him Ax. He's pretty **amenable** to any of them.

I know I was going to tell you about the library, but I got talking about Ax. In fact, all of this talk about Ax reminds me of something I learned in English class a few days ago. Have you heard the **idiom** "has an ax to grind"? Yeah, it means that the reason someone is doing something is selfishness. Have you ever wondered where it came from? According to Dr. Miller, it's from a story by a man named Charles Miner, a nineteenth-century American journalist. The story tells how a man was able to use flattery to get a boy to turn a grindstone for him. After that, people started using it more and more. Interesting, huh? It's amazing what you learn in college.

Well, I see that once again my attempt to stay on one topic has been **abortive.** In fact, I've forgotten what the main thread of this little **narrative** was. It's become a regular **mélange**. But hey, that's me. Love me or leave me.

1. **jargon** N. specialized language
2. **obstinate** ADJ. stubborn
3. **subtle** ADJ. not immediately obvious
4. **ambiguous** ADJ. unclear in meaning
5. **paramount** ADJ. foremost; primary
6. **cordial** ADJ. warm and sincere
7. **colloquy** N. conversation (especially a formal one)
8. **replicate** V. to duplicate; repeat
9. **verbatim** ADV. in exactly the same words
10. **reiterate** V. to repeat
11. **obtuse** ADJ. stupid; dull
12. **rebuke** V. to scold; reprimand
13. **revivify** V. to give new energy
14. **soporific** ADJ. sleep producing
15. **somnolent** ADJ. sleepy
16. **sojourn** N. visit
17. **undaunted** ADJ. not discouraged
18. **convoluted** ADJ. complicated
19. **appellation** N. name
20. **vernacular** N. everyday language used by ordinary people
21. **amenable** ADJ. agreeable
22. **idiom** N. expression whose meaning differs from the meaning of its individual words
23. **abortive** ADJ. interrupted while incomplete
24. **narrative** N. story
25. **mélange** N. mixture

Simply Simon

Think you know the words? Then prove it! Choose the *best* word to fill in the blank in each of the sentences below.

idioms **appellation** **soporific** **replicate**

revivify **mélange** **paramount** **sojourn**

undaunted **verbatim**

1. _____ frequently don't seem very logical; the expression "it's raining cats and dogs" is a good example of this.

2. Last summer I convinced Axel to take a/an _____ with me to Florida.

3. "Yahweh" is the Hebrew _____ for God.

4. I can still recite _____ Lincoln's Gettysburg Address, which I learned in eighth grade.

5. For me there is nothing quite so _____ as a mathematics class on a late Friday afternoon.

6. I failed my first three mathematics tests in freshman year, but I was _____; I persevered and eventually passed.

7. In science, other researchers must be able to _____ your experiment for its results to be accepted.

8. America is the _____ economic and military power in the world.

9. Jaz uses a remarkable _____ of ingredients in her cooking.

10. A pep rally can really _____ a team's spirit after a tough loss.

Making Sense

Indicate whether or not each of the words in **bold** makes sense in the sentence. If it makes sense, put Y (Yes); if it doesn't make sense, put N (No).

1. Professor Jones keeps telling us in literature class that we should make our interpretations of the texts we analyze as **ambiguous** as we can so that our meaning will be perfectly clear. ____

2. I'm so **obtuse** that I can understand Albert Einstein's most difficult ideas quite easily. ____

3. Christine was **amenable** to Jaz's invitation to come to our house to meet Axel. ____

4. In psychology class something I had suspected might be true was confirmed: praise is generally more effective than **rebuke** in changing a person's behavior. ____

5. Recently, Axel had some professors over to the house for a **colloquy** on new developments in physics. ____

6. Ordinary speech is so full of weird **jargon** that everyone can understand it with no problem. ____

7. My high school English teacher never tired of **reiterating** his belief that clear thinking leads to clear writing, and vice versa. ____

8. Professor Jones tells jokes that are so **subtle** that most of the class misses them. ____

9. A good referee is **obstinate** and willing to change his call with the least bit of persuasion. ____

10. It always amazes me how an English teacher is able to take a student's disorganized, vague, **convoluted** writing and suggest improvements that make it clear. ____

Match It
Match each of the following words to its meaning.

1. cordial   a. interrupted while incomplete

2. somnolent   b. scold

3. vernacular   c. sleepy

4. abortive   d. story

5. narrative   e. unclear in meaning

6. subtle   f. warm and sincere

7. amenable   g. complicated

8. rebuke   h. everyday language

9. ambiguous   i. agreeable

10. convoluted   j. not immediately obvious

Axel Speaks
Greetings! I believe that you are now ready for something more intellectual. Choose the *best* word to fill in the blank in each sentence.

1. Modern research has led experts to conclude that although human beings use a number of different ways to communicate with one another, language is the _____ means by which information is exchanged.

(A) paramount

(B) novel

(C) spontaneous

(D) circumspect

(E) articulate

2. According to the Big Bang theory of creation, the universe in its initial state was extremely hot and consisted of a/an _____ of elementary particles such as electrons and quarks.

(A) magnification

(B) mélange

(C) appellation

(D) reinforcement

(E) saga

3. It is sometimes difficult to assess the status of individuals who claim asylum in another country on the basis of political persecution, because the definition of "political refugee" is

_____ .

(A) bizarre

(B) eclectic

(C) reclusive

(D) conclusive

(E) ambiguous

4. The term "feedback"—_____ from the field of electronics—has come to be used in ordinary conversation: "I want to get *feedback* from our customers on ways we can improve our products."

(A) appellations

(B) jargon

(C) denotation

(D) lexicon

(E) erudition

5. In recent years many cities in the United States have been _____ by a new wave of immigrants who are eager to work hard to improve their position in society.

(A) piqued

(B) inspired

(C) revivified

(D) perused

(E) overcome

Answers on page 446.

And now, on with the story.

55

Episode 7

IQ and EQ

Did I tell you that Jaz is a psychology major? Yeah, she loves analyzing people. Maybe that's why she likes me; I'm so **voluble** and **uninhibited** that my mind is quite open to her investigation. She says that I'm one of those people who processes information verbally. Apparently, this makes my mental functioning easy to study.

So, what's my inner mind, my subconscious, like? Well, it's a little embarrassing, but Jaz says she hasn't actually been able to find any scientific evidence for it. It seems that all her tests come up empty. Take dreams, for example. They're supposed to tell about your subconscious mind, right? Not with me they don't. I mean, I dream, but my dreams are pretty straightforward. Football, girls ... , girls, football ... football, girls .... . No complex symbolism there from my subconscious mind. Jaz says I have to have a subconscious, at least according to the **tenets** of Freudian psychology (Freud's ideas are considered **obsolete** in many universities, but the old geezer is still **predominant** in our psych department.)

Anyway, Jaz says she'll keep **plumbing** the depths of my mind looking for it. She says it's got to be in there somewhere. She keeps waiting for me to make a **cryptic** remark so she can look for some **profound** meaning in it, but I never do. It would be an **anomaly** for me to say anything ambiguous or enigmatic. In fact, on a personality test that Jaz used to assess me, I scored 100 percent on the extroversion scale. The head of the psych department, Dr. Brown, says this is **unprecedented** in the annals of psychological research.

Yeah, 100 percent pure unadulterated extrovert—one gargantuan party animal, in other words. I just love people.

In fact, I scored almost as high on my EQ test. EQ means emotional quotient. That means your **affective** abilities as opposed to your cognitive abilities, things like how well you **empathize** with people. Ninety-eight percent—not as high as Jaz's 99 percent, but pretty high. Professor Goldman came up with EQ in the 1990s, and it's still in fashion. That's pretty cool for guys like me.

So, how's this guy's IQ? you might be wondering. IQ is the one area where perhaps I **dissemble** just a little. I've always been kind of touchy about having my intelligence measured. But every few months Jaz talks me into taking an IQ test. Taking tests is definitely not one of my favorite pastimes, but I do it to help Jaz out with her psych project on intelligence testing. She says my results give her a baseline. Anyway, common sense would tell you that since you're learning all this stuff in college, your brainpower should be increasing. Well, it doesn't seem to work that way, at least with me. The result is always the same—let's just say it's above average and leave it at that. Jaz says I should take some comfort in two things. Number one: At least my score isn't declining, which proves that my intellect isn't **atrophying**. Number two: It confirms the **validity** of the test and its **methodology**. Great. I've contributed to the advancement of the science of psychology. But where does it leave me? My IQ is still—well, not **minuscule**, but not exactly genius level, either. I am definitely no threat to Axel's title of Super Brain.

OK, so I may not be up with the really heavy-duty intellectuals like Jaz and Axel. But I can hold my own with practically everyone else. So, it annoys me when people portray me as a dumb jock. It's so **facile**. It **conjures** up an image of a pedestrian intellect in the body of an athlete. However, I do admit that although the caricature of me as a fun-loving jock is not entirely consistent with reality, it does contain an element of truth. It's not **chimerical**. But there's a lot more to me than that. You'll see.

1. **voluble** ADJ. talking a great deal with ease; fluent
2. **uninhibited** ADJ. unrepressed
3. **tenet** N. belief; doctrine
4. **obsolete** ADJ. outmoded; old-fashioned
5. **predominant** ADJ. having greatest importance or authority
6. **plumb** V. to examine deeply (also: determine the depth)
7. **cryptic** ADJ. having an ambiguous or hidden meaning
8. **profound** ADJ. deep; not superficial
9. **anomaly** N. deviation from the norm
10. **unprecedented** ADJ. never occurring before; novel
11. **affective** ADJ. relating to the emotions
12. **empathize** V. to put oneself in another's place
13. **dissemble** V. to disguise; conceal
14. **atrophy** V. to waste away
15. **validity** N. the state of being well grounded and sound
16. **methodology** N. set of procedures and principles applied in a specific branch of knowledge
17. **miniscule** ADJ. very small
18. **facile** ADJ. superficial (also: done with little effort; easy)
19. **conjure** V. to bring to mind (also: call forth a spirit)
20. **chimerical** ADJ. imaginary; unreal

Simply Simon

Think you know the words? Then prove it! Choose the *best* word to fill in the blank in each of the sentences below.

miniscule   **empathize**   **uninhibited**   **cryptic**

unprecedented   **atrophy**   **validity**   **chimerical**

tenet   **predominant**

1. A/an _____ of capitalism is that the free market will set the correct price of goods and services.

2. Westerners are generally more _____ in their dress than Asians.

3. My dream of winning the Nobel Prize in physics is _____ , since I could barely pass high school physics and I'm terrible at mathematical calculations.

4. I think it is important to _____ with people in the world who live in poverty.

5. After I finally passed my first mathematics test everyone in the class rose to his or her feet and applauded this _____ occurrence.

6. The automobile is the _____ method of travel in the United States.

7. Dr. Williams, an economics professor here, is famous for his _____ comments to journalists about the economy that leave them wondering what he means.

8. Mr. Savage, my high school algebra teacher, always used to tell us, " The brain is like a muscle. You have to use it regularly or it will _____ ."

9. Jaz eats such a/an _____ amount of food everyday, I sometimes wonder how she survives.

10. The _____ of the Theory of Evolution has been well established by biologists.

Making Sense

Indicate whether or not each of the words in **bold** makes sense in the sentence. If it makes sense, put Y (Yes); if it doesn't make sense, put N (No).

1. Scientists must precisely describe the **methodology** they employ in an experiment so that other scientists can reproduce it. ____

2. A competent novelist can **conjure** up an imaginary world that seems quite real. ____

3. Fresh water is a **voluble** resource that we must try to conserve as much as possible. ____

4. A psychologist should have the ability to **plumb** with patients. ____

5. Dr. Jones praised me for my **facile** interpretation of Melville's *Moby Dick*. ____

6. An engineer likes to see an **anomaly** when he's testing equipment so that he can be sure that it's working OK. ____

7. I buy the most **obsolete** computer I can afford so that I keep up with the latest technology. ____

8. A person who **dissembles** regularly is sure to be believed whenever he talks. ____

9. Philosophy deals with **profound** questions such as the nature of reality and the meaning of life. ____

10. To understand the characters in a work of literature we must use **affective** as well as cognitive skills. ____

Match It

Match each of the following words to its meaning.

1. tenet   a. deviation from the norm

2. obsolete   b. never occurring before

3. predominant   c. outmoded; old-fashioned

4. profound   d. superficial

5. anomaly   e. put oneself in another's place

6. unprecedented   f. imaginary; unreal

7. empathize   g. the state of being well grounded

8. validity   h. belief

9. facile   i. deep; not superficial

10. chimerical   j. having greatest importance

Axel Speaks

Greetings! I believe that you are now ready for something more intellectual. Choose the *best* word to fill in the blank in each sentence.

1. The denotation of many words changes over time; for example, the word *nice* used to mean "wanton" or "coy," but that meaning has become _____ , and the word is now commonly used to mean "pleasing" or "enjoyable."

(A) cryptic

(B) convoluted

(C) facile

(D) doubtful

(E) obsolete

2. Technology played a major role in the mass migration of people from Europe to the United States in the nineteenth and early twentieth century because developments in transport (such as steamships) gave people _____ mobility.

(A) peripatetic

(B) imaginative

(C) amenable

(D) profound

(E) unprecedented

3. Distinguished twentieth-century novelists such as James Joyce, Marcel Proust, and William Faulkner moved away from portraying social reality toward representing inner thought processes and _____ states.

(A) aesthetic

(B) innocent

(C) reclusive

(D) garrulous

(E) affective

4. Science has its roots both in wonder before the mysteries of nature and in systematic doubt about _____ answers to important questions.

(A) astute

(B) facile

(C) necessary

(D) voluble

(E) profound

5. In his book *The Case for Mars,* in which he argues for a manned mission to Mars, Robert Zubrin advances the argument that new frontiers, such as space, provide a healthy stimulus for society that helps to prevent it from _____ by providing a worthwhile collective enterprise.

(A) empathizing

(B) expanding

(C) prospering

(D) atrophying

(E) dissembling

Answers on pages 446–447.

And now, on with the story.

Episode 8

TERM PAPER TIME

I guess I've been talking too much about myself. Let me tell you more about Jaz. One thing about Jaz is that she's one of the few people whose intellect has ever really impressed Axel. That means she's one sharp woman. And, as I told you before, her EQ is so high it's practically off the scale. Come to think of it, she's sort of a **synthesis** of Axel and me, who are the **antithesis** of each other. Jaz has my affective skills ("people smarts," in other words) and Axel's "cognitive smarts". You should see Jaz talk to children with emotional problems. She gets them to open up to her so that she can understand their problems and help them to understand themselves better.

Have I made Jaz sound like a **paragon**? Well, maybe she's not perfect, but she comes pretty close. Not only is she incredibly intelligent and superb at relating to people, she's also a naturally kind and caring person. With all of these **attributes**, Jaz is going to end up being a great psychologist some day. She meets all of the **criteria** for it.

Sometimes I ask myself why I'm so lucky to have Jaz as my girlfriend, but as I said, I'm a real people guy. I'm naturally **amiable**. So, I would **surmise** that Jaz likes my friendly, open personality. And I guess I do have a sort of animal magnetism that she likes. That probably helps, too. I'm no match for Jaz's **pulchritude**, but girls do seem to find me kind of cute.

OK, so now you're a lot better clued in about Jaz so I'd better tell you a little more about Axel to balance things out.

I don't want you to get a **skewed** view of the scene here. As I said, Ax is at the **acme** in the brains department. He's a **titan** even among the erudite crowd. You'll see how true this is later on when my tale wanders into some more **obscure** areas.

The scene is pretty neat, really. (Every time I say "neat," Ax tells me "neat" is out-of-date slang, but I like it. So I use it. I don't believe that my vocabulary has to **conform** completely to the way people are talking now. I think those cats in the fifties were pretty hip.)

Anyway, the scene is so neat because a typical **scenario** runs like this: I've got a political science term paper due in a week. Unfortunately, I'm not exactly up on the latest developments in that particular area. I've been a little bit **negligent** in keeping up with Professor Chandler's **discourses** on the emergence of a new political **consensus** in America because I find them, in all honesty, to be . . . . Well, let's just say they tend to be—for me, anyway—a little bit soporific.

In this class we're allowed to get ideas for our papers from anywhere we want to, as long as we acknowledge them. So, I get on the cell to one of my acquaintances on the political science faculty who's an expert in that area, and, after a little chitchat, I drop a few hints that Axel has been really flipped out recently on discussing the emergence of the new political consensus in America. Sometimes I even juice it up with a little exaggeration: "Man, he's so **immersed** in this subject, it's all he's been talking about. He's driving us crazy. All day it's, 'What do you guys think about the emergence of a new political consensus in America?'"

Now, when the faculty type hears that Axel has gone totally loopy on this topic, he generally kind of freaks. Why is this, you ask? It's because these guys know that Axel's so smart that in one *hour* he can give them enough to **ponder** for the rest of the *year*.

Anyway, this professor comes over and chews the fat with Axel for a few hours, making good use of his vast knowledge and remarkable **acumen**. Meanwhile, I kick back and watch a ballgame with not a care in the world. Good old Ax is on the job.

Definitions

1. **synthesis** N. combination
2. **antithesis** N. the opposite of
3. **paragon** N. model of perfection
4. **attributes** N. qualities
5. **criteria** N. standards used in judging (*sing.* criterion)
6. **amiable** ADJ. friendly; likable
7. **surmise** V. to make an educated guess
8. **pulchritude** N. beauty
9. **skewed** ADJ. distorted in meaning
10. **acme** N. highest point
11. **titan** N. person of great stature or achievement
12. **obscure** ADJ. not easily understood (also: dark; indistinct; not well known)
13. **conform** V. to be in accord (agreement)
14. **scenario** N. possible situation or chain of events (also: outline of the plot of a literary work)
15. **negligent** ADJ. careless; inattentive
16. **discourse** N. formal, lengthy discussion (also: conversation; verbal expression)
17. **consensus** N. general agreement
18. **immersed** ADJ. deeply involved; absorbed
19. **ponder** V. to think deeply
20. **acumen** N. keenness of insight

Simply Simon

Think you know the words? Then prove it! Choose the *best* word to fill in the blank in each of the sentences below.

synthesis   acme   criterion   immersed

discourses   ponder   acumen   amiable

conform   pulchritude

1. Coach Wilson is a gentle, _____ man, except during practice, when he runs the tightest ship you'll ever see.

2. The main _____ I use in assessing a book is whether it's interesting.

3. Sociologists believe that people generally _____ to the expectations of their society.

4. Yesterday I got so _____ in the game on TV that I forgot to take my TV dinner out of the oven.

5. Axel has tapes of some of the _____ of the famous physicist, Richard Feynman.

6. My history teacher believes that America represents the _____ of human civilization, but I'm not so sure.

7. Jaz's cooking is a/an _____ of Asian and Western styles.

8. Professor Jones says that to develop our literary _____ we should read critically and think deeply about every text we read.

9. Some religions object to displays of female _____ that are common in the Western media.

10. My English teacher says that sometimes it's better to just start writing an essay than to _____ what you want to say.

Making Sense

Indicate whether or not each of the words in **bold** makes sense in the sentence. If it makes sense, put Y (Yes); if it doesn't make sense, put N (No).

1. In literature class we learned that the short story is the **antithesis** of the novel because the two forms share many of the same characteristics. ___

2. Two of the **attributes** of a good teacher are knowledge of the subject and ability to understand the student's point of view. ___

3. A dedicated coach is **negligent** of all those little details that separate a mediocre team from a good team. ___

4. If there is a solid **consensus** on an issue in support of his position, a president will have serious problems taking action on it. ___

5. I like **obscure**, down-to-earth subjects that are easy to understand. ___

6. English teachers sometimes hold up famous essays as **paragons** students should imitate. ___

7. Axel says physicists first **surmised** the existence of black holes from theory and observation of their effects on the surrounding areas of space. ___

8. Axel keeps photographs of some of the **titans** of modern science—Edwin Hubble, Albert Einstein, Max Planck, and guys like that—on his desk for inspiration. ___

9. A judge should take a **skewed** view of a case so that she can reach a fair decision. ___

10. Coach Wilson and his staff take us through different **scenarios** before a game so we are prepared for any situation. ___

Match It

Match each of the following words to its meaning.

1. synthesis		a. friendly; likeable
2. antithesis		b. not easily understood
3. paragon		c. combination
4. amiable		d. think deeply
5. surmise		e. be in agreement with
6. obscure		f. model of perfection
7. conform		g. general agreement
8. negligent		h. opposite
9. consensus		i. make an educated guess
10. ponder		j. careless

Axel Speaks

Greetings! I believe that you are now ready for something more intellectual. Choose the *best* word to fill in the blank in each sentence.

1. Most people in ancient Greece thought of Zeus as living in a house on Mount Olympus, from where he watched over mankind, punished evil and rewarded good and, occasionally, was smitten by the _____ of a human female.

(A) pulchritude

(B) discourse

(C) acumen

(D) generosity

(E) background

2. Some of the commonly used _____ for determining whether a country is developed are an affluent populace, a complex economy, widespread use of technology, an educated population, little poverty, and a stable and respected government.

(A) scenarios

(B) interpretations

(C) paragons

(D) illusions

(E) criteria

3. Although the _____ of scientists is that the recent rise in the earth's temperature was caused by the greenhouse effect, a minority of scientists are persuaded that it was due instead to an increased output of energy from the Sun.

(A) verdict

(B) methodology

(C) perspective

(D) assessment

(E) consensus

4. Since the Great Depression of the late 1920s and 1930s, the policy of the American government has been _____ heavily toward avoiding depression, even at the risk of tolerating some inflation.

(A) digressing

(B) obscured

(C) skewed

(D) animated

(E) conformed

5. The case of scientists who have _____ that life once may have existed on Mars is supported by strong evidence of dried riverbeds and other features that can be formed only as a result of hydrological processes (such as large amounts of flowing water), indicating that Mars at one time probably possessed a hydrosphere.

(A) conjured

(B) expounded

(C) pondered

(D) inscribed

(E) surmised

Answers on pages 447–448.

And now, on with the story.

Perfect Camaraderie

As I was saying, Axel's little colloquy goes on for quite a while. After a few hours the professor leaves and Ax tells me all about the ideas that these mega brains batted around.

What usually happens next is that I have trouble comprehending what Ax is talking about. The **impediment** to my understanding the ideas is that Ax uses a lexicon so **confounding** that I have to ask Jaz to explain what he said in normal English. I mean, you wouldn't find most of these words even in a very good dictionary. Many of them aren't even in the gigantic dictionary I told you about before—the one we keep on the kitchen table. But, as always, Jaz is really great: she **succinctly** expresses what I need to know in words I can understand. Ideas that were **opaque** to me gradually become clear.

Now, all this brainwork leaves me feeling kind of **lethargic**, so I head for my favorite sofa to cop some Zs. This gives the organ of cognition up there time to process all this new information without blowing a fuse. I sleep like a log, letting my brain idle over, doing its job without disturbing my sleep. In the morning I'm ready to take care of business— the actual writing.

Generally, things go pretty smoothly. The points I need are basically all there, so I just have to kind of let the words flow. And I'm pretty good at that, as you've seen. If I need some extra points to **buttress** my argument or **rebut** counterarguments to my **thesis**, I ask Ax to give me some ideas. Then Jaz peruses my paper and gives me her **critique** of it. I make a few minor modifications and I'm ready to roll. All I have left to do is hit the Print button once more, staple the pages together, and head down to the place where the political science savants hang out and hand in my masterpiece.

So, as you can see, the three of us have a real **camaraderie**. We get along really great. And don't get me wrong—we all help each other. It's not just those two helping me. You'll see this later. So now you've got the data on my best two buddies. Everything is excellent. Well, maybe except for one thing that's kind of been bothering me. As you've heard already, Ax is cool, but he's too reclusive. I mean, his social skills are **negligible.**

Remember I told you the score I got on the personality test for extroversion? Perfecto. 100 percent. Jaz says these things are on a continuum. A total party animal can get 99.9 percent or a complete hermit can get 0.01 percent, but nobody can get 100 or 0 percent according to their **paradigm**. Well, when I came along, they had to go back and revise their paradigm—totally retool it in fact. In **retrospect**, it was kind of amusing. The academic types were shaken up, big time.

So can you surmise what Axel's score was? One percent! When he told me his score I said to him—and I'm not really the sarcastic type—"pretty good, dude." I thought he might be a little **perturbed**, but like I've said, Ax is cool. All he said was, "This lends **empirical** confirmation to my theory concerning the nature of my personality as **evinced** in its interaction with other members of the species *Homo sapiens.*"

"Huh?" I said.

"It means I like to keep to myself."

I thought, "Man, he is cool. He's cooler than I thought. He even looks at *himself* from a totally **unbiased** perspective."

I said, "Yeah, Axel, it's real cool. But do you think there just might be some things in life that you're maybe just a tiny bit negligent about?" Although I had just used **circumlocution** to break the truth gently to my friend, I decided that from this moment I would **eschew** it. Axel needed to hear the truth. He needed to be **chided** and shown reality.

Definitions

1. **impediment** N. obstacle
2. **confounding** ADJ. confusing; puzzling
3. **succinctly** ADV. briefly; concisely
4. **opaque** ADJ. obscure; unintelligible
5. **buttress** V. to support
6. **rebut** V. to present opposing evidence or arguments; refute (N. rebuttal)
7. **thesis** N. proposition put forward for consideration
8. **critique** N. critical commentary
9. **camaraderie** N. good will and rapport among friends
10. **negligible** ADJ. not significant enough to be worth considering.
11. **paradigm** N. model
12. **lethargic** ADJ. sluggish; dull
13. **retrospect** N. looking back at the past
14. **perturbed** ADJ. greatly disturbed
15. **empirical** ADJ. derived from observation or experiment
16. **evince** V. to show clearly
17. **unbiased** ADJ. impartial
18. **circumlocution** N. indirect way of saying something
19. **eschew** V. to avoid
20. **chide** V. to scold

Simply Simon

Think you know the words? Then prove it! Choose the *best* word to fill in the blank in each of the sentences below.

succinctly   retrospect   eschew   empirical

impediments   chides   perturbed   lethargic

unbiased   confounding

1. One of the biggest _____ faced by developing countries is a lack of an educated work force.

2. Newspaper headlines describe events _____ because there is little room for a long description.

3. I found the language of the great writer Henry James _____ until my English teacher explained it.

4. In _____, I wish I had studied harder in high school so that I'd now have a more solid academic foundation.

5. Jaz _____ me when I eat pizza, but I think it's OK to eat it in moderation.

6. If he wants to win, a coach must be _____ in selecting the players for his team so that he can choose the best available players.

7. I'm pretty _____ after I eat all day on Thanksgiving.

8. One of my assignments in political science was to find if there is any _____ evidence to support the idea that democratic countries are less warlike than other types of countries.

9. Jaz gets a little _____ whenever I chat with another girl.

10. A serious athlete like me should _____ unhealthy food.

Making Sense

Indicate whether or not each of the words in **bold** makes sense in the sentence. If it makes sense, put Y (Yes); if it doesn't make sense, put N (No).

1. Most places have laws that prevent landlords from **evincing** tenants for no reason. _____

2. Jaz is such an effective debater that she **buttresses** all of her opponent's positions. _____

3. Some political scientists support the **thesis** that the democratic-capitalist system of the United States and other Western countries has reached a state of near perfection. _____

4. An essay should have plenty of **circumlocution** so the reader can easily follow its argument without a lot of extra words to confuse him. _____

5. Miss Bridget, my creative writing teacher, is so dedicated that she writes a long **critique** of each of our assignments explaining what is good and bad about it and how it can be improved. _____

6. My friend on the lacrosse team says there's so much **camaraderie** on the team that many players are thinking of quitting. _____

7. Axel's knowledge is so **negligible** that he is constantly being asked to help solve problems in physics, mathematics, and other complex areas of study. _____

8. Dr. Miller says that there is no single **paradigm** to be followed in writing an essay, but that we should read the essays of excellent practitioners of the art such as Lewis Thomas, Bertrand Russell, and Freeman Dyson to get an idea of how it can be approached. _____

9. Religion and philosophy help to explain what people find **confounding** about life. _____

10. A good debater continually **rebuts** her own positions on the central issues under discussion. ____

Match It

Match each of the following words to its meaning.

1. impediment   a. good will and rapport among friends

2. succinctly   b. indirect way of saying something

3. opaque   c. obstacle

4. thesis   d. model

5. critique   e. scold

6. camaraderie   f. briefly; concisely

7. paradigm   g. sluggish; dull

8. lethargic   h. proposition put forward for
                        consideration

9. circumlocution   i. obscure; unintelligible

10. chide   j. critical commentary

Axel Speaks

Greetings! I believe that you are now ready for something more intellectual. Choose the *best* word to fill in the blank in each sentence.

1. Latin had a profound direct influence on the English language, as _____ by, for example, the words *amorous, amity, amiable,* and *amicable,* all of which are derived from the Latin *amor* (love).

(A) evinced

(B) buttressed

(C) reiterated

(D) justified

(E) surmised

2. Middle-aged Americans sometimes say that there has been a/an _____ improvement in their standard of living over the last two decades; however, when we consider that many goods formerly regarded as luxuries are now viewed as necessities, this view appears to be erroneous.

(A) tenuous

(B) prodigious

(C) unprecedented

(D) invisible

(E) negligible

3. The theory of star formation is not based on guesses about ancient events: it is well supported by _____ evidence—observations of stars forming in areas of high hydrogen density.

(A) opaque

(B) negligible

(C) empirical

(D) chimerical

(E) inexplicable

4. A/an _____ to the argument that the Internet is bad for the world because it is increasing the gap in wealth between rich countries and poor countries is that it allows developing countries to "leapfrog" a stage of economic growth and enter the knowledge-based electronic economy, "piggybacking" on the development of other countries.

(A) impediment

(B) rebuttal

(C) critique

(D) thesis

(E) antithesis

5. Perhaps the most successful attempt to write realistic novels was in France in the nineteenth century, when writers such as Balzac, Flaubert, and Stendhal wrote powerful books that _____ the use of extravagant devices, had believable plots and characters, and presented an almost sociological view of life.

(A) eschewed

(B) rebutted

(C) evinced

(D) replicated

(E) rebuked

Answers on page 448.

And now, on with the story.

Episode 10

The Chiding

"Axelrod, how old are you?" Simon asked.

Axel looked up. Simon called him Axelrod only when something really important was up. Axel rarely looked his **interlocutor** directly in the eye. Now he gazed steadily at Simon with a puzzled expression.

"You know how old I am, my good man," he replied.

"This is not the time for humor, Axel." Simon looked at him **reproachfully**.

Axel had never seen Simon so serious.

"Look. *You're* twenty-one. *I'm* twenty-one."

Axel continued to look at his friend. He nodded.

"And how many girls have I kissed in my life, do you think?"

Axel didn't answer.

"Just a wild surmise. You can **extrapolate** based on data, say, from the past month."

Axel smiled slightly at Simon's **jocularity**. This was the Simon he knew and loved. "**Myriads**," Axel said. "An **incalculably** large number. Truly gargantuan."

"Yeah."

Axel could see it coming. The truth was painful.

"And you?"

"Ummm ..."

"Ten?"

Axel looked down. He didn't answer.

"Five maybe?"

Axel shook his head slightly.

81

"One?"

Axel looked up. His countenance was almost completely blank.

"You mean you didn't even really kiss Sheila after the high school graduation party? We all thought ..."

Axel shook his head. The movement was so slight that probably only Simon could have perceived it.

Simon was silent.

Axel grew uneasy. When Simon was silent it meant he was thinking. And since Simon thought only when it was absolutely necessary, Axel knew he must have been really **musing** about his friend's situation.

Finally, Simon said, "Listen. We've been best friends our whole lives, right?"

"Yes."

"Have I ever steered you wrong about anything?"

"No."

"You say you value the truth above all else, don't you?"

"Yes."

"You quote Plato: 'The search for truth is more desirable than any woman,' etc."

"Yeah."

"OK, then. What do you perceive to be the truth about your—ummm—social life?"

There was silence. Simon looked hard at his friend and waited.

Finally, a small voice said, "Weak?"

"Weak? *Very* weak. How about *nonexistent*? Goose egg. Big round O. Nil. Nada. Zero. Zilch. Zip. Beyond **infinitesimal**. Man, an **ascetic** is more **gregarious** than you are."

"I know a few girls," Axel piped up.

"Yeah. And I know a few mathematicians. That doesn't mean I'm going to solve Fermat's last **theorem** or whatever it is anytime soon, does it?"

"Actually, Simon, Andrew Wiles at the Institute for Advanced Study in Princeton has published a rigorous proof of that mathematical **conundrum**. And not only did he prove Fermat's theorem—something that mathematicians had sought for centuries—in the course of his proof he also established the validity of an idea called the Taniyama-Shimura conjecture, another incredibly difficult and fascinating ... ."

Simon looked hard at Axel, who fell silent. Simon sat, looking thoughtful.

Axel **rallied**. "So, my friend, I **deduce** that what you have been trying to **intimate** is that I need to make the acquaintance of a young female and, perhaps, if we are **compatible**, and each of us has analyzed the relationship and all of its **innumerable** and **multifarious** intricacies from all of the appropriate perspectives, and it appears likely that it may be mutually **advantageous** for us to continue the relationship ... ." He stopped. Simon looked like he was ready to explode.

"No dude," said Simon, **enunciating** each word. "You *need* a *girl* friend!" he practically shouted.

1. **interlocutor** N. someone taking part in a dialogue
2. **reproachfully** ADV. in a way that expresses blame
3. **extrapolate** V. to estimate by projecting known information
4. **jocularity** N. jest; joke
5. **myriad** N. large number; innumerable
6. **incalculably** ADV. incapable of being calculated
7. **muse** V. to consider something at length; ponder
8. **infinitesimal** ADJ. extremely tiny
9. **ascetic** N. person who renounces the comforts of society to lead a life of self-discipline
10. **gregarious** ADJ. sociable
11. **theorem** N. idea that is demonstrably true or assumed to be so
12. **conundrum** N. difficult problem (also: riddle; problem with no satisfactory solution)
13. **rally** V. to recover (also: assemble; recuperate)
14. **deduce** V. to draw a conclusion by reasoning
15. **intimate** V. to communicate indirectly; imply
16. **compatible** ADJ. capable of getting along with another harmoniously
17. **innumerable** ADJ. too many to be counted
18. **multifarious** ADJ. diverse
19. **advantageous** ADJ. having benefit; useful
20. **enunciate** V. to pronounce clearly

Simply Simon

Think you know the words? Then prove it! Choose the *best* word to fill in the blank in each of the sentences below.

multifarious   advantageous   theorem

interlocutor   gregarious   innumerable

reproachfully   rallied   incalculably   enunciate

1. Sociologists believe that human beings are basically _____ creatures who hate to live alone.

2. It is _____ for us to play big football games at home because of the great support we get.

3. In my first essay in Freshman English the teacher said my errors were practically _____ , so she stopped circling them after the first page.

4. Jaz looks at me _____ when I'm too friendly to another girl.

5. Usually, I _____ more clearly when I'm talking to my teachers than I do when I'm talking to my friends.

6. Scientists dealing with _____ large numbers use exponents to make their computations easier.

7. In biology I learned how evolution explains the _____ forms that nature takes.

8. I believe it is a/an _____ of plane geometry that two parallel lines, if extended infinitely, will never meet.

9. When I was flirting with Christine things looked pretty bad, but I _____ and so everything was cool again.

10. In sociology class we learned how the distance between you and your _____ in a conversation is determined by a number of factors, such as how well you and the other person know each other and the cultural background each of you comes from.

Making Sense

Indicate whether or not each of the words in **bold** makes sense in the sentence. If it makes sense, put Y (Yes); if it doesn't make sense, put N (No).

1. A number of distinguished scientists such as Freeman Dyson and Sir Fred Hoyle have been so struck with how **compatible** the laws of the universe are with the needs of life that they see evidence that it was consciously designed. ____

2. Several astronomers have tried to estimate the number of intelligent civilizations in our galaxy by **extrapolating** from information such as the number of stars, the number of planets, the probability of life arising, and the probability of intelligent life destroying itself. ____

3. One of Jaz's favorite films is *Contact*, which is based on a novel by Carl Sagan; she sometimes quotes a **jocularity** of one of its main characters about the possibility of life elsewhere in the universe: "If there isn't life anywhere else, it would be an awful waste of space." ____

4. Axel says that with **myriads** of solar systems in the universe, it seems reasonable to suppose that life originated in some in addition to ours. ____

5. It **muses** me to think that a far superior civilization might be observing us as we observe ants. ____

6. The famous scientist Sir Fred Hoyle has said that the chance of the carbon atom that is central to life occurring through natural forces alone is so **infinitesimal** as to be almost impossible. ____

7. Being an **ascetic** would be pretty cool because you could do a lot of partying. ____

8. Sometimes it's better to come right out and just **intimate** openly what you feel. ____

9. Jaz asked me what I thought could be **deduced** from the fact that nearly all mathematicians are eldest sons. ____

10. Axel once tried to explain to me the **conundrum** created for mathematicians by Goedel's Theorem proving that there exist mathematical statements that are meaningful but that are not provable or disprovable. ____

Match It

Match each of the following words to its meaning.

1. reproachfully	a. sociable
2. extrapolate	b. consider something at length
3. muse	c. capable of getting along with another harmoniously
4. ascetic	d. diverse
5. gregarious	e. in a way that expresses blame
6. conundrum	f. large number
7. deduce	g. draw a conclusion by reasoning
8. compatible	h. person who renounces the comforts of society to lead a life of self-discipline
9. multifarious	i. estimate by projecting known information
10. myriad	j. difficult problem

Axel Speaks

Greetings! I believe that you are now ready for something more intellectual. Choose the *best* word to fill in the blank in each sentence.

1. Modern American society is composed of a/an _____ of subcultures, each of which is unified by factors such as shared social class, age, sex, vocation, religion, and race.

(A) myriad

(B) consensus

(C) association

(D) anomaly

(E) conundrum

2. Georges Buffon said, "The style is the man himself," _____ that the way a writer expresses himself is a part of his nature.

(A) reflecting

(B) deducing

(C) enunciating

(D) intimating

(E) sensing

3. Astronomers _____ the existence of neutron stars from radio waves that are of high frequency and regularity, indicating that they are being emitted by a rapidly rotating body, such as an extinguished star.

(A) defended

(B) invented

(C) speculated

(D) mollified

(E) deduced

4. Epidemiologists, _____ from present trends, predict that 90 percent of the adult population of the United States will be obese by the year 2030.

(A) musing

(B) dissembling

(C) extrapolating

(D) embellishing

(E) evincing

5. The ways in which a person can be exposed to carcinogens are _____: for example, one can inhale tobacco smoke, ingest nitrates, absorb pesticides through the skin, or expose oneself to X-ray or ultraviolet radiation.

(A) infinitesimal

(B) convoluted

(C) innumerable

(D) comprehensive

(E) advantageous

Answers on page 449.

And now, on with the story.

All You Need Is Love

Axel was startled by the force of his friend's **expostulation**. It was not in Simon's nature to become angry. He must be really ticked off, Axel thought.

"But I've gone out with some girls," he said.

"Where?"

"To the library."

"Yeah. And who always introduces you to these girls and **coerces** you to date them?"

"You and Jaz."

"And what exactly do you *do* on these dates?"

"Talk."

"Talk about *what*?"

"Ideas ... philosophy ... the mind in all its glorious **manifestations**."

Simon sighed. He looked almost sad. He spoke deliberately. "And do you truly think that there are many 19-year-old girls who really like that on a date? I mean *only* that?"

Axel shook his head. "Perhaps my perception of my social life has not been entirely **congruent** with reality."

"Axel, your perception is entirely *inconsistent* with reality. In fact, it's completely chimerical. It has no basis in fact .... no ...." Simon trailed off. He was at a loss for words. He drew a deep breath.

"Let me tell you something that Jaz told me last night," Simon continued. "She said that a lot of those girls think you're pretty cool."

Axel brightened a little.

"Some even think you're kind of cute, but after a while ..... ." Simon shrugged his shoulders. "You know, girls just don't want to be in a classroom on a date. You can't treat a woman like a mathematical theorem."

Axel looked hurt.

"Hey, buddy. That's the bad news," Simon said.

Axel hated these **trite** "Good news, bad news" **formulations**. But Simon never seemed to tire of them. Axel waited for what must, he **presumed**, be the good news.

"The good news is that Jaz and I want to help you become more sociable. Help you get a life."

"You mean a project? I'm to be your *project*?" Axel said. He had suddenly become more animated. He was almost indignant. "How very **droll**. Upon what paradigm am I to be modeled? Exactly whom am I to **emulate**?"

"Hey, Ax, chill, man. You're our best buddy. The three of us share a unique camaraderie. We're chums. One for all and all for one and all that."

"So, may I inquire as to what the **ramifications** of your plans are for my immediate future?"

Simon smiled broadly. "The bottom line?"

Axel winced. Another **cliché.** But he simply replied, "Yes, the bottom line, as you so **aptly** put it."

"A double date. On Monday night. We'll go see a movie."

Axel let out a long sigh. The idea of some **interminable** motion picture with an **implausible** plot, **insipid** acting, and ridiculous special effects that lacked all **verisimilitude**, horrified him. Also, the thought of the effort it would take to make himself socially presentable and the willpower it would require to endure two hours of listening to the sound of other patrons munching, **incessantly**, on apparently bottomless buckets of popcorn and gigantic bags of candy, depressed him. And, to top off the evening, he would no doubt be expected to engage in **trivial** small talk about the **inane** motion picture.

"Can we see a documentary?" Axel asked. "There's a great feature on **ornithology** at the West End."

Simon groaned.

1. **expostulation** N. scolding; reproof
2. **coerce** V. to force
3. **manifestation** N. one of the forms in which something is revealed
4. **congruent** ADJ. corresponding
5. **trite** ADJ. unoriginal
6. **formulation** N. something prepared in a specified way
7. **presume** V. to assume to be true
8. **droll** ADJ. amusing in an odd, wry way
9. **emulate** V. to imitate
10. **ramification** N. consequence; implication
11. **cliché** N. overused expression
12. **aptly** ADV. expressed in a precisely suitable manner
13. **interminable** ADJ. endless
14. **implausible** ADJ. difficult to believe
15. **insipid** ADJ. dull
16. **verisimilitude** N. quality of appearing real
17. **incessantly** ADV. continuously
18. **trivial** ADJ. unimportant
19. **inane** ADJ. senseless
20. **ornithology** N. the scientific study of birds

Simply Simon

Think you know the words? Then prove it! Choose the *best* word to fill in the blank in each of the sentences below.

coerces   emulate   ornithology   ramifications

expostulation   insipid   droll   formulation

incessantly   interminable

1. Jaz greeted me with a/an _____ after her best bud told her she had seen me chatting with a cheerleader after football practice.

2. Jaz sometimes _____ me to go with her to see classical musical performances.

3. The saying "Buds before duds" is a modern _____ of the idea that your friends are more important than dates.

4. Jaz sometimes likes to spice up a dish she finds _____.

5. Psychologists believe that boys tend to _____ their fathers.

6. The _____ of a win over Big State next week will be major; we'll really be in the hunt for the national title.

7. _____ was one of the topics we covered in biology; I learned that birds are descended from dinosaurs.

8. The hours before a big game seem _____ to me; I can't wait to get on the field and start the game.

9. Coach Wilson_____ stresses the need for us to improve our play in every game.

10. I sometimes don't appreciate my English professor's _____ remarks until I think about them after class.

Making Sense

Indicate whether or not each of the words in **bold** makes sense in the sentence. If it makes sense, put Y (Yes); if it doesn't make sense, put N (No).

1. Fresh, original writing is full of **clichés** that spark off new ways of thinking in the reader's mind. ____

2. In English class we read some of the novels of the American social realists such as Theodore Dreiser who attempted to achieve **verisimilitude** in their work. ____

3. Axel says it's amazing how the non-Euclidean geometry devised by the mind of the great nineteenth-century mathematician Georg Riemann turned out to be **congruent** with reality as described by Einstein's space time. ____

4. Jaz believes it is **implausible** that the structure of the universe would be hospitable to life and consciousness merely as the result of the blind workings of nature. ____

5. **Trivial** questions such as whether or not there is a God have been discussed for ages by philosophers. ____

6. Jaz's philosophy is complex, but she definitely believes that life is the **manifestation** of a spiritual power working in nature. ____

7. The great philosophers such as Plato, Kant, and Spinoza are full of **inane** comments. ____

8. My ninth-grade English teacher was **aptly** named Mr. English. ___

9. I don't think it's fair that Jaz tends to **presume** I'm guilty of flirting with other girls. ___

10. **Trite** ideas such as evolution, the subconsciousness, and relativity have shaped modern thought. ____

Match It

Match each of the following words to its meaning.

1. coerce   a. dull

2. congruent   b. endless

3. trite   c. unoriginal

4. ramification   d. consequence

5. cliché   e. difficult to believe

6. interminable   f. corresponding

7. implausible   g. overused expression

8. insipid   h. force

9. verisimilitude   i. senseless

10. inane   j. quality of appearing real

Axel Speaks

Greetings! I believe that you are now ready for something more intellectual. Choose the *best* word to fill in the blank in each sentence.

1. The belief that fiction should be realistic, accurately and thoroughly portraying both the good and bad in society and human nature, was _____ expressed by the French novelist Emile Zola: "We novelists are the examining magistrates of men and their passions."

(A) aptly

(B) spontaneously

(C) implausibly

(D) comprehensively

(E) ambiguously

2. All cultures studied by anthropologists contain certain cultural "universals," such as religion, structure, and economic organization; the _____ that these universals take depend on the peculiarities of each particular culture.

(A) ramifications

(B) distortions

(C) manifestations

(D) rituals

(E) appellations

3. A competent sociologist can determine a person's class quite accurately from such seemingly _____ facts as the hobbies she pursues and the books she reads.

(A) droll

(B) miniscule

(C) trivial

(D) subtle

(E) obsolete

4. Capitalists remind us _____ that too much social welfare is detrimental to the free market because it destroys the incentive to work to improve oneself, which is at the heart of the capitalist system.

(A) anxiously

(B) ambiguously

(C) aptly

(D) hopefully

(E) incessantly

5. Researchers in the area of artificial intelligence have found the human brain's ability to recognize patterns less easy to _____ than its problem-solving ability.

(A) revivify

(B) deduce

(C) intimate

(D) emulate

(E) enunciate

Answers on pages 449–450.

And now, on with the story.

Reality Check

Simon and Jaz were sitting in the kitchen, enjoying their usual late night **repast**.

"You know, Jaz," Simon said, "I have a good feeling about that girl we met at the library on Saturday."

"I bet you do," Jaz said.

"Hey, I am simply thinking about the welfare of my best buddy. I'm hurt that you could **impute** unfaithful thoughts to me, of all people." Simon said. He put on a hurt, pouting look.

Jaz laughed. "But seriously," she said, "do you really think that girl—what was her name?"

"Christine." Simon said. He grinned. "I never forget a name," he said.

"Yeah, Christine," Jaz said. "Anyway, do you really think she's a possibility for Axel?"

Simon looked puzzled. To him, *any* girl was a possibility for Axel.

"I don't follow you," he said. "Christine is charming and **vivacious**, studious, and interested in meeting Axel. What more could you want? Am *I* missing something, here?" He studied Jaz's face. "Oh, *I* get it!' he said. "You think she's *too* pretty. That *I* might **succumb** to her charms. Right?"

Jaz shrugged. "You certainly seemed pretty chummy with her in the library," she said.

Simon laughed. "Hey, you know me. I'm everybody's buddy."

"Yeah, I know," Jaz said. "But make sure it's *just* buddies."

"Hey, you know you're my only really best bud and always will be," Simon said. "I know I have my little **foibles** ...."

"Foibles," Jaz said.

Simon looked confused. "What?" he said. Then he smiled.

"Gotcha!" Jaz said.

"Wow! Beautiful and a language expert too. Correction. I have my *foibles*—which are small by definition, so *little* is redundant." Simon paused. "Now, where was I," he said, "before you started **quibbling** about my language?"

"You were saying how much you love me and only me. That you never even *look* at other girls."

Simon laughed. He got up from his chair and walked around the table to Jaz. He kissed her on the cheek.

"So, anyway, what makes you feel so **optimistic** about Christine?" Jaz asked.

"I don't know. As I said, I just have a feeling about her."

"You think Axel and Christine will get along just famously, right?"

"Yep."

"May I ask what inspires such a **sanguine** outlook?"

"I don't know. I guess it's because she seems really intelligent and studious. And she seemed so enthusiastic about meeting Axel."

"*If* she gets to meet him. Boy, you are an **inveterate** optimist, aren't you?"

"Over the last few months we've tried really hard to get a girlfriend for Axel, haven't we?"

"Yes. We've worked **indefatigably** at it."

"I mean, how many times have we found suitable candidates, lured them over here, made all the arrangements for where they'd go with Axel?"

Simon thought about it. "Many times," he said.

"Yes, many times," Jaz said. "Like maybe 50 times?"

"Yeah, that sounds about right."

"Simon, you know how much I want Axel to meet the right girl, but we also have to face reality. Maybe we should do a little reality check, to use psychological jargon. Out of those, let's say 50 times, how many did Axel even come downstairs to *meet* the young woman we had so cleverly lured here to go out with what we so **enticingly** described as 'our fascinating, **convivial**, adorable, total *hunk* of a roommate'?"

Simon looked at his girlfriend admiringly. It was amazing how she could say remarkably long sentences without pausing for breath. But that one word, *hunk*. Simon couldn't remember ever hearing Jaz use that word. In fact, she never used language that had the slightest possibility of being regarded as sexist in its **connotations** or in any way degrading to other people. Even when she was describing all of Axel's wonderful qualities to a girl she wanted him to meet, she was always careful to confine her description to his nonphysical attributes and avoided saying anything that might be seen as a generalization based on gender. What, he wondered, was up?

"I've never heard you use the word *hunk* before," Simon said.

"Just testing," Jaz said.

"It's interesting," Simon said. "We tend to think of sexism as directed at women, but men can also be its target."

"That's my point, I guess," Jaz said.

"But do you think calling a guy a *hunk* is so bad?"

Jaz laughed. "What do you think?" she asked.

"I guess it's not so bad. If a girl called me a *hunk* I wouldn't mind."

"But you *are* one, Simon," Jaz said, laughing.

"Thank you," Simon said. He paused. "I guess," he added. "But," Simon continued, "what if a girl calls a guy a *hunk* who isn't one? Or what if she calls a guy a *hunk* who is a hunk but who doesn't like being considered a hunk? Or what if .... ." Simon stopped talking. He looked at Jaz, who was peering at him with a serious look on her face.

"And *what*," Jaz said, "if you're trying to **embroil** me in **peripheral** issues so you don't have to face reality?"

101

"Me?" Simon laughed. "You're the one who said *hunk*," he said.

"Yeah. But you're the one who would appear to be using any excuse you can find to talk about anything except the subject we're trying to deal with here. Could it be, Simon, that you don't want to face an unpleasant truth about your best friend?"

Simon was silent. He was looking down at the floor.

"Maybe," Jaz said, "you're having trouble coming to terms with Axel's ......" She paused. How, she wondered, can I put this diplomatically? Simon hated **euphemisms**, but stating the truth directly would be cruel. She needed a phrase that would be true but sort of **dispassionate** and scientific-sounding. There must, she thought, be some politically correct sort of phrase. She took a deep breath. "Maybe," she said, "you're having trouble coming to terms with Axel's *female-specific social disability*."

Simon looked at Jaz and shook his head. "Enough, enough," he said. "You don't have to soften the truth with circumlocution. I can take it like a man. What you're saying is my best friend has a major problem."

"Yeah, Simon. A *major* problem. Like he's girl *impaired*. He won't go *near* a female under 70 years old."

Simon was silent.

"Simon," Jaz said. She spoke softly but there was **resolve** in her voice. "I want you to tell me on how many of these occasions in the last year Axel has come down to *meet* the young woman we've asked over to meet him. Occasions, I don't have to remind you, that he refers to as 'my **onerous** social obligations.'"

Simon thought for a moment, and then let out a long sigh. "Twice," he said. He thought some more. "Well, actually three times," he added.

"Three? Oh, yes, you're right. Three. I had forgotten the last time. We had to practically drag him down the stairs. That girl, ..."

"Laura."

"Right, Laura. She must have thought we were having some kind of **fracas**, with all that yelling and screaming. What amazes me is that she didn't take the chance to make a quick getaway then. We finally get Axel down to the living room. He looks at the girl like she's a Martian or something. And when we introduce him to her, he *shakes her hand.*"

"Hey, at least he made contact. That was a big step for the guy."

"Sure, I appreciate that," Jaz said. "But the *way* he shook her hand. It was *so* **suave**. I mean it was like, "Welcome to Earth, Miss Martian Ambassador.""

"You have to admit, the look on Laura's face was really funny. He just kept shaking her hand—up and down. He wouldn't let go. It was like he was in a trance. He didn't say a word. He just kept shaking."

Jaz smiled slightly. "Simon, I do not consider Axel's social situation a subject for **mirth**," she said. She looked very serious now. "In fact, I consider it tragic. And so should you."

"I do, I do," Simon said. "You know, that Laura was a real knockout. All that pulchritude at one time can be a little tough on a fellow, especially for a **neophyte** like Axel who's had a rather **circumscribed** experience of the fair sex."

Jaz said, "There's one thing I wonder about."

"What?"

"If Axel is so afraid of girls, how can he bear to spend so much time with *moi?*"

"I thought you modern liberated women didn't go fishing for compliments."

"Yeah, but so how do you explain it, Sherlock?"

"Well, we're different. The three of us are buddies," Simon said.

Great, Jaz thought. Now I'm one of the guys.

"I mean," Simon said, "he doesn't think of you as a *girl.*"

Jaz gazed steadily at Simon.

"I mean," he said, "you are a girl, of course. It's just that he doesn't *think* of you as one."

Jaz continued to look at Simon. There was a completely impassive expression on her face. "So, what do *you* think he thinks of me as?"

"A friend."

"That's very nice. And how do you think of me?"

"Jaz, cut me some slack. All this verbal jousting is tough on a guy."

"Yeah, but it's fun watching you try to wriggle out of tight corners."

"So, what's the verdict? Am I out yet?"

Jaz looked at Simon and laughed. "Yeah," she said. "Barely."

Definitions

1. **repast** N. meal
2. **impute** V. to attribute; ascribe
3. **vivacious** ADJ. lively; spirited
4. **succumb** V. to yield; give in
5. **foibles** N. minor weaknesses
6. **quibbling** V. finding fault for petty reasons
7. **optimistic** ADJ. looking on the positive side
8. **sanguine** ADJ. cheerfully optimistic
9. **inveterate** ADJ. deeply rooted; confirmed
10. **indefatigably** ADV. tirelessly
11. **enticingly** ADV. temptingly; attractively
12. **convivial** ADJ. sociable
13. **connotations** N. secondary meanings suggested by a word
14. **embroil** V. to involve in
15. **peripheral** ADJ. of minor importance; not central
16. **euphemisms** N. inoffensive language used in place of unpleasant language

17. **dispassionate** ADJ. impartial
18. **impaired** ADJ. diminished in strength
19. **resolve** N. firmness of purpose; determination
20. **onerous** ADJ. burdensome; troublesome
21. **fracas** N. loud dispute
22. **suave** ADJ. smoothly gracious or polite
23. **mirth** N. merriment; laughter
24. **neophyte** N. beginner
25. **circumscribed** ADJ. limited

Simply Simon

Think you know the words? Then prove it! Choose the *best* word to fill in the blank in each of the sentences below.

succumb   embroiled   dispassionate   onerous

resolve   fracas   connotations   peripheral

repasts   suave

1. An athlete must have regular _____ in order to have enough energy to compete successfully.

2. Jaz's _____ to find a girlfriend for Axel is undiminished.

3. Last week one of our offensive linemen got involved in a/an _____ with a player on the opposing side.

4. During my freshman year when we were getting clobbered by such scores as 61–0 my teammates and I didn't _____ to the temptation of blaming each other; we just kept working together to improve our performance in every game.

5. To write a well-argued essay I have to focus on the central issues and try to ignore the _____ ones.

6. A skillful writer is aware of the many _____ words have.

7. Some guys seem naturally _____ , whereas others seem to be born "nerds" who never seem to know how to act cool.

8. Jaz thinks it's unfair that in most countries only males are required to perform the _____ duty of military service.

9. After political science class yesterday I got so _____ in a debate about the effects of Western culture on the world I completely forgot about my mathematics class.

10. Social scientists should try to be _____ in evaluating public policies.

Making Sense

Indicate whether or not each of the words in **bold** makes sense in the sentence. If it makes sense, put Y (Yes); if it doesn't make sense, put N (No).

1. Jaz believes a life based on reason and science alone is far too **circumscribed** because such a life doesn't leave room for a spiritual dimension. ___

2. Axel is a pretty intense and serious guy, but he's full of **mirth** when he listens to Professor James' stories about the peculiar habits of some of the physicists he has known. ___

3. One of the people Jaz admires greatly is the distinguished Indian astrophysicist Subramanyan Chandrasekhar, a man who worked **indefatigably** into his seventies to solve some of the most complex problems in physics. ___

4. **Quibbling** over unimportant points is an efficient way to get something done. ___

5. **Euphemisms** help a writer express his or her ideas honestly and directly. ___

6. Professor Jones believes that a reader of a fictional story should be careful in **imputing** ideas expressed by characters to the author. ___

7. Axel says one of the wonderful things about science is the way in which many different types of people—with all their human **foibles**—work together to uncover nature's secrets. ___

8. Jaz and Axel are **inveterate** stargazers; many evenings after a late-night poker game with my buddies I'll see those two out on the balcony with their five-inch reflector telescope. ___

9. Axel says he would be far more **sanguine** about humanity's future if so many countries didn't possess nuclear weapons. ___

10. If you want a job done right the best thing to do is to ask an experienced **neophyte**. ___

Match It
Match each of the following words to its meaning.

1. convivial	a. lively; spirited
2. optimistic	b. sociable
3. enticingly	c. yield; give in
4. impaired	d. beginner
5. vivacious	e. involve in
6. succumb	f. temptingly; attractively
7. peripheral	g. looking on the positive side
8. neophyte	h. limited
9. circumscribed	i. of minor importance
10. embroil	j. diminished in strength

Axel Speaks

Greetings! I believe that you are now ready for something more intellectual. Choose the *best* word to fill in the blank in each sentence.

1. In his Barsetshire novels, the English writer Anthony Trollope portrayed life in early Victorian England with a unique blend of affectionate wit and irony, at once sympathizing with his characters and showing up their _____ .

(A) mirth

(B) impediments

(C) foibles

(D) similarities

(E) connotations

2. Rather than seeing the youth movement of the 1960s as an indication of social decline, some observers have interpreted it _____ as a reaction against excessive materialism, individualism, and violence in American society.

(A) comprehensively

(B) historically

(C) benignly

(D) disdainfully

(E) optimistically

3. During World War II, the United States government imprisoned many Americans of Japanese ancestry in what were known by the _____ "relocation centers."

(A) foible

(B) denotation

(C) euphemism

(D) exaggeration

(E) caricature

4. *The Double Helix,* the book by James Watson that tells the story of his part in the discovery of DNA, portrays the process of scientific discovery more as a race for glory than a/an _____ quest to unravel the secrets of nature.

(A) pretentious

(B) dispassionate

(C) optimistic

(D) circumscribed

(E) convoluted

5. From the viewpoint of evolutionary theory, the only purpose of life is to survive in order to reproduce; all other activities are, therefore, _____ .

(A) enigmatic

(B) sanguine

(C) onerous

(D) peripheral

(E) inveterate

Answers on pages 450–451.

And now, on with the story.

Episode 13

MEMORIES

"Anyway," Simon said to Jaz, "let's **reminisce** a little more. I remember the first time we lured a girl over. The only reason Axel came down to meet her was because we tricked him. We told him that you and I weren't coming home until about eight o'clock. So he decides to slip away around 7:30. He comes down the stairs, and *surprise!* The three of us are sitting quietly on the living room floor. Cindy ... ."

Jaz looked sharply at Simon. Simon looked perplexed. "Cindy. That was her name, right?" he said.

"I was just thinking how her name tripped so easily off your tongue, that's all," Jaz said. She smiled sweetly.

Simon didn't know if you could describe a smile as "**facetious**," but if you could this would be it. Another word that came into his mind was "**saccharine**."

"So, as I was trying to say, Cindy did look pretty bewildered," Simon continued.

"I kept wondering what she was thinking when we kept hushing her," Jaz said. "I mean, why should we want to be so quiet in our own house? She must have thought we were totally out to lunch."

"Yeah. And then Axel comes waltzing down the stairs, thinking nobody's around." He laughed at the recollection.

Jaz did not laugh. She could derive some slight humor from the situations Axel got into, perhaps. But she found nothing at all amusing in the memory of another abortive attempt to hook Axel up with a girl. For Jaz, getting a girl-friend for Axel was a matter of the utmost importance. An

111

image came into her mind. Generation after generation of women—women just like her, really—fixing up young couples. She was a *matchmaker*. You could call it what you wanted to, but that's what it was. And, she reflected, she did it instinctively and with her whole soul. *Why?* she wondered. I'm supposed to be a modern woman and all. I should let Axel find his own girlfriend. An image of Axel trying to call a girl for a date came into her mind. She shuddered. No, it was too horrible to contemplate. Talk about social **ineptitude**. He was off the scale. No, it was just not an option to leave Axel on his own. Her family's long **lineage** of matchmakers would not end with her.

"Axel is in a league of his own," Simon said. "He gets halfway down those stairs, takes one look at Cindy and ..... ," Simon said. He was laughing so hard he couldn't continue.

"And he *tumbles down the stairs*," Jaz said. The **unmitigated** horror of it, she thought. What a **fiasco**.

Simon was still laughing. "Hey, at least he made one *spectacular* entrance."

Jaz did not look at all amused. "Yeah," she said. "Some entrance. I couldn't *even* introduce him to Cindy."

"Yeah, because he was flat on his back, unconscious. That didn't stop you from trying though."

"Well, it wasn't funny. He could have been seriously hurt."

"Hey, who rushed him to the hospital?" Simon said.

"Right. And you stayed there with him for two days to make sure he was OK," Jaz said. "That was very **humane**."

Simon glowed.

"So, Simon," Jaz said, "how good is your recollection of the second time we tried to lure a suitable girl over here for our beloved amigo?"

"Unfortunately, pretty good. We put a lot of work into that one," Simon said.

"Yes, our preparation was **impeccable**," Jaz said. "Your assignment was to find a girl who met a very **stringent** set of criteria so that Axel would be enticed but not scared off by

112

her feminine charms: highly intelligent, graduate student in astrophysics, superb chess player, amiable but just a little **aloof**, vivacious but not a total bundle of energy; and, of course, she had to be **susceptible** to your powers of persuasion—but not *too* susceptible."

Simon laughed. "Yeah, you were sure the **vaunted** computer in your psych lab would find this unique person, weren't you?" he asked.

"Sometimes it needs the human touch," she said.

"Yeah. Well, I got the job done. And the plan was brilliant. Tell Axel there's this girl who's totally into the latest findings from the Hubble Space Telescope on black matter or whatever—that she just wants to meet him to talk about this. Nothing else. Oh, and maybe a little *superb* chess on the side."

"And it worked so well. He was really eager to meet her—at least 'in principle,' as he put it."

"Ax is the only guy in the universe who would agree to a date 'in principle,'" Simon said.

"OK. But at least he agreed."

"We had everything planned down to the smallest detail. I had Ax really chilling, playing a decent game of chess and listening to that weird music he likes."

Jaz laughed. "Yeah, that music is pretty bizarre. It sounds like a **cacophony** to me. Nothing is in time. At least to anything on this planet."

"It has the weirdest **syncopation**," Simon said.

"Yeah. He was *gone*. He was in **nirvana.** There was this look of absolute bliss on his face."

"You have to admit, I did OK with the chess."

"Full marks, Simon," Jaz said. "You know, I was flabbergasted when I saw somebody other than a chess master actually giving Axel a decent game of chess."

Simon stood and took three bows. "Thank you, thank you," he said.

"By the way, how did you manage that?" Jaz said. "Nobody's been able to give Axel a serious game since that

Russian grandmaster was here to play some exhibition matches, and they played to a draw. He's like the number five player in the world or something."

"That was pretty cool. That guy threw everything he had at Axel, but old Ax was **intrepid**. He just calmly absorbed it and then launched a really vicious counterattack. I kind of felt sorry for the Russian guy. It looked like he was just trying to hang on in the end. I don't think he would have ever recovered if he had lost that game."

"He certainly looked pretty happy after he squeezed out that **perpetual** check of Axel's Queen," Jaz said. "I've never seen a person *sweat* so much. I mean he was **saturated**."

Jaz paused. "You know, Simon, one thing's always puzzled me about that game. I'm no chess expert, but I checked with some pretty heavy-duty players, like the president of the chess club. It's pretty clear that if Axel had played King takes Rook instead of King takes Bishop, there would have been no draw."

Simon was silent.

Jaz looked at Simon. "Axel *let* the guy have that draw, didn't he?"

Simon nodded.

"He didn't want to humiliate him, did he?" Jaz said.

"Yeah. I'm not supposed to tell anybody. Axel knew which was the winning combination and which was the drawing one. He chose the latter."

"So, anyway, how *did* you manage to give Axel such a good game?"

"Well, there were some **machinations** involved. You see, I persuaded a visiting mathematics professor I know who also happens to be the reigning Russian national female chess champion ... "

Jaz's eyebrows went up.

"Female? A female chess champion," she muttered. Of course, she thought; a female *had* to be involved somewhere. This, after all, was Simon.

1. **reminisce** v. to recollect and tell of past experiences
2. **facetious** ADJ. playfully humorous
3. **saccharine** ADJ. excessively sweet or sentimental
4. **ineptitude** N. incompetence; awkwardness
5. **lineage** N. ancestry
6. **unmitigated** ADJ. not lessened or moderated in intensity
7. **fiasco** N. disaster
8. **humane** ADJ. merciful; kind
9. **impeccable** ADJ. flawless
10. **stringent** ADJ. imposing rigorous standards; severe
11. **aloof** ADJ. detached
12. **susceptible** ADJ. easily influenced; vulnerable
13. **vaunted** ADJ. boasted about
14. **cacophony** N. jarring, unpleasant noise
15. **syncopation** N. temporary irregularity in musical rhythm
16. **nirvana** N. ideal condition of rest, harmony, or joy (also: state of absolute blessedness)
17. **intrepid** ADJ. fearless and bold
18. **perpetual** ADJ. endless
19. **saturated** ADJ. soaked
20. **machinations** N. crafty plots

Simply Simon

Think you know the words? Then prove it! Choose the *best* word to fill in the blank in each of the sentences below.

lineage   syncopation   nirvana   humane

saturated   perpetual   susceptible   intrepid

fiasco   unmitigated

1. Our normal practice field had been _____ by three days of rain, so we had our last practice in the field house.

2. Sometimes I think _____ is achieved more easily by people who don't look for it than by those who do.

3. When he was ten years old Axel won first prize in the state science fair for a _____ motion machine that one judge said came remarkably close to actually working.

4. Everyone said our last party was a/an _____ success.

5. A person's _____ is generally considered to be more important in Europe than in the United States.

6. I think it's possible that human drummers are better than electronic drum machines because of their _____.

7. The one party we convinced Axel to have was a/an _____ because he insisted that the only music he would play was by J. S. Bach.

8. The _____ treatment of animals has become a significant political issue in some parts of the world.

9. Jaz believes that it's normal for a person to have fears, but that we should be _____ in facing them.

10. A major problem in many poor countries is that officials are _____ to bribes.

Making Sense

Indicate whether or not each of the words in **bold** makes sense in the sentence. If it makes sense, put Y (Yes); if it doesn't make sense, put N (No).

1. It's fun to **reminisce**, thinking about what I'll be doing when I'm 40 years old. ____

2. I was kind of immature in tenth grade; looking back, I regret making so many **facetious** comments in class. ____

3. Jaz says that Axel acts **aloof** because he's shy, not because he feels superior to others. ____

4. I have a friend doing mechanical engineering who has such **ineptitude** with machinery that he designed and built his own car at the age of 18. ____

5. In high school I always used to try to get out of taking physics tests; of all my **machinations**, the one that's still talked about is when I tried to convince Mr. Joule that if a physicist with the reputation of Albert Einstein had hated taking exams, I certainly shouldn't be expected to take them. ____

6. I love nothing better than to kick back and listen to the **cacophony** of a really mellow group like the Beach Boys. __

7. Jaz believes that science, for all its **vaunted** knowledge, cannot tell us what is morally right and wrong. ____

8. My preparation for the barbecue last week was **impeccable**—I forgot to buy the steaks and we ran out of hot dogs. ____

9. A person must meet **stringent** standards as both a student and an athlete to be selected for the Academic All-American Team. ____

10. I was a little embarrassed when Jaz showed me my love letters to her from two years ago; I thought they were pretty **saccharine**. ____

Match It

Match each of the following words to its meaning.

1. reminisce   a. imposing rigorous standards

2. facetious   b. endless

3. ineptitude   c. recollect and tell of past
                         experiences

4. unmitigated   d. easily influenced

5. impeccable   e. incompetence; awkwardness

6. stringent   f. crafty plot

7. aloof   g. not lessened or moderated in
                         intensity

8. susceptible   h. playfully humorous

9. perpetual   i. flawless

10. machination   j. detached

Axel Speaks

Greetings! I believe that you are now ready for something more intellectual. Choose the *best* word to fill in the blank in each sentence.

1. The great French artist Georges Seurat believed that a painter should portray light scientifically, using primary colors as though the light had passed through a prism, and he produced _____ works, such as *A Sunday Afternoon on the Island of La Grande Jatte,* which are painted in the pointillist technique—using tiny dots of color—that he created.

(A) stringent

(B) impeccable

(C) uninhibited

(D) identical

(E) implausible

2. In rich countries, people come to expect a comfortable and increasing income, while in poor countries people come to expect continuing poverty; this acceptance of poverty acts, in the view of some economists, to make poverty _____ in these countries.

(A) perpetual

(B) intrepid

(C) susceptible

(D) troublesome

(E) peripheral

3. The prevalence of guns in America makes it difficult for bans on them to be effective because black markets arise in states with lax gun control laws and people in states with _____ laws travel to the former type of states to buy guns.

(A) inept

(B) humane

(C) stringent

(D) impeccable

(E) vaunted

4. Judging from the widespread poverty in Russia today, that country's movement in the late twentieth and early twenty-first century from a communist economic system to a capitalist one has not been a/an _____ success.

(A) saccharine

(B) facetious

(C) unmitigated

(D) didactic

(E) undaunted

5. According to scholars, the view that _____ essentially means the destruction of the individual "self" was clearly rejected by Gautama Buddha.

(A) renaissance

(B) nirvana

(C) ornithology

(D) cacophony

(E) syncopation

Answers on page 451.

And now, on with the story.

Chess Games

"Anyway," Simon said, "I **cajoled** this woman into showing me this really obscure opening gambit. She was saving it for when she plays the world champion in an exhibition match next month, but she said as a very special favor I could use it. It's not in any of the chess literature. And I checked to make sure it's not in Axel's computer."

"Impressive. A very thorough job."

"Yeah. So, this woman taught me the opening. But I wanted to make sure I had all the variations down cold. It took us *days* working closely together." Simon stopped. Perhaps, he thought, I am sailing into some dangerous waters. His **hypothesis** was confirmed by the look on Jaz's face.

"I'm curious," she said. "What does this mathematics professor—chess champion look like?"

"Look like?"

"Yeah, *look like*. As in, *what is her physical appearance*?"

Simon nodded but was silent.

"I mean, she must be pretty old to be a professor ... ."

"Full professor."

"OK, *full* professor. To be a full professor *and* the Russian national female chess champion would take a person years and years of work. Wouldn't it?"

"Not necessarily," Simon said.

"Well, you'd have to be at least, say, 40 ... ." Jaz looked at Simon. He was impassive.

"Thirty?"

Simon shook his head up and down and from side to side simultaneously, and pursed his lips. They were the same gestures her father had made when she was a little girl in Bangalore and she asked him questions like, "What existed *before* the Big Bang?" (She still couldn't really understand his answer—"It's not allowed." What kind of answer was that? How could a question not be *allowed*?) With Simon, she knew, these gestures meant something like, "You're on the right track, but perhaps this is an area that would be better not to explore in any great detail." Jaz knew she was getting warmer but still had a ways to go.

"Well, she *couldn't* be 21. Even Axel isn't a professor." Simon smiled and nodded his head slowly up and down.

"Twenty-five?" No response.

"Twenty-*two*?" Bingo! Simon's face lit up in a broad smile.

"OK," Jaz said. "She must be one clever woman, huh?" Simon nodded.

An image of a frumpy, heavy-set Eastern European intellectual came into Jaz's mind. The vision was completely **lucid**, like the most intense dream she had ever had. The woman was carrying a huge sack on her back. Jaz could see the opening at the top of the bag: books were spilling out onto the sidewalk as she walked, but she was **oblivious** to the laughter of the people around her. She trudged on **stolidly** through the icy, snow-covered street. She wore a bulky gray coat as she shuffled along, a **dour** expression on her face. The vision changed. Now the woman was squinting **myopically** through the thick lenses of her wire-rim glasses at a complex mathematical formula that completely covered an ancient, **dilapidated** blackboard in a **squalid** classroom. Jaz could see her face. She looked like she was nearly 50 years old. The **vicissitudes** of Russian life since the fall of the Soviet Union had obviously taken their toll. Poor, poor woman, thought Jaz. To look like a *babushka*, a grandmother, at 22.

Jaz shook her head. How can such *stereotypes* be a part of my mind? she thought. Really! You're the one always

123

telling people stereotypes are **demeaning** to the unique individual dignity of each person. Anyway, Jaz reasoned, this person couldn't *possibly* be attractive.

"Hey, I have the young woman's photo here," Simon said. "She wanted me to keep it to remind me of all the games we played together. You know what she said?"

"No. What did she say?"

"That I gave her some really interesting games. A real mental workout. Here's her picture."

Jaz examined the photograph. The image of the heavy-set Eastern European intellectual would have to be replaced, she saw. The photograph showed a beautiful girl, smiling radiantly. She was dressed—well, sort of dressed—in a one-piece bathing suit that highlighted a very feminine figure. There was a number—38, Jaz read—pinned to her suit. In her hands she held an enormous trophy.

Jaz let out a long breath and looked at Simon. *This* was the professor Simon had been with for two days playing chess? She knew the competition was fierce, but this was ridiculous. This was a **patent** violation of the laws of probability, of the very structure of the universe, in fact. No one *that* smart had a right to look *that* good.

"The professor certainly is some woman," she said.

"Yeah. I think she was Miss Russia or something last year."

"So, you not only charmed this woman into giving you your own private chess lessons, but also this exotic opening she'd probably been guarding with her life. All so you could give Axel a good game of chess. Bravo!"

"Thank you. Yeah, old Ax was pretty surprised by this variation of the Scottish opening. The look on his face when I took his king's pawn! He probably thought it was just one of the blunders I sporadically make."

"Sporadically?"

"Yeah. As in *very occasionally*. I mean I'm a pretty decent player, you know. Anyway, I could see just the slightest doubt in his mind when I took that pawn. He must have

124

been thinking, *what if this is some brilliant, **unorthodox** variation I've never seen?* You could almost see that powerful brain analyzing the combinations. He gave me the strangest look. It was a look that kind of said, 'Pretty cool, dude. I don't know where that came from, but it sure is one very interesting chess move.'"

"You must have felt pretty good," Jaz said.

"Yep. I had his King side under pretty good pressure for a while because of the initial advantage I had gotten from the opening. Of course, he gradually recovered and beat me, but he had to resort to a lot of pretty extreme **stratagems**. I mean, he sacrificed three Queens. After the game, he said, 'Thank you, Simon, for an interesting game.' I was really proud."

"Simon, you never cease to amaze me," Jaz said. "So, Axel was really cool by the time that girl ..., uh ..."

"Diane," Simon said.

"So," Jaz said, "by the time ... " She paused and looked at Simon. "By the time *Diane* arrived, Ax was really chilling, huh?"

"He was as cool as a cucumber. So the doorbell rings. I get it, Diane comes in. Everything's good. Axel's sitting there, just chilling."

"Then I came in and introduced them," Jaz said. "Axel actually shook her hand. Like a human being."

Simon recalled the scene. It had been the nearest thing to a moment of triumph Jaz and he had experienced in the whole saga of Axel's social life. Of course, it had just been one brief, **transitory** moment, but he cherished it nevertheless.

"Yep, that was certainly the highpoint of the evening," he said. "I mean, how was I to know that Diane would be practically as **taciturn** as Axel?"

Jaz looked at Simon. *He looks **rueful**,* she thought. *He's probably blaming himself for another **debacle**.* She felt sorry for him. All of his effort had, once again, come to nothing. Their scheme had **foundered** on one little factor that they had, **inadvertently**, overlooked.

"Hey," she said, "don't feel so bad, Simon. They talked for almost a whole hour before she left."

"Talked? Oh yeah, an hour of the most romantic dialogue. It was so **intimate** I started to get embarrassed being there with them." Simon spoke now in a falsetto, mimicking the conversation —

"'So, which do you prefer as an alternative to the traditional Einsteinian view of spacetime, the Lagrangian formulation of general relativity or the Hamiltonian one?' she asks **coyly**."

"'Now, that's a very interesting question,' Axel replies. 'I have recently adopted a neo-Einsteinian view that harkens back to Minkowki's model of spacetime. In some situations, of course, I follow Lorentz and his group of disciples, but in view of my recent Riemann tensor analysis and considering the Bianchi identity, and in light of the many advantages of adopting an orthonormal basis in tensor calculations, alternative approaches now seem unfruitful at best,' Axel replies in his usual knock'em dead approach to women. Yeah, it was real hot stuff."

Jaz tried to **stifle** a laugh. Despite the **gravity** of the situation, she had to admit, Simon could be pretty amusing.

"So," he continued, "other than that little burst when they were going at it hot and heavy for a few minutes, discussing the nature of spacetime in light of recent theories about the singularities at the heart of black holes, neither of them hardly spoke a word."

"Well, at least Axel demonstrated that he can talk to a woman in a social situation," Jaz said.

"Yeah, it was a real **coup**, wasn't it? I mean, what a combination! Two almost completely **laconic** people."

"Hey, you got everything right except one little thing. That's pretty good."

"Yeah, next time I'll have to check out the candidate's **loquaciousness** index."

"Yes, we just have to keep trying. We have to find the one unique girl who's right for Axel. I know she's out there somewhere."

"Yeah, but where? If she exists, I don't think we'll find her—at least on this planet."

"Simon," Jaz said. "You said before you had a really good feeling about Christine, didn't you?"

"Jaz, I *always* have a good feeling about the girls we meet. I always think, '*This* is the perfect girl for Axel.' And it's *always* a disaster. Maybe I'm just jinxed or something."

"Come on, Simon. It isn't you. You're not a miracle worker. Nobody could have done any better than you've done. In fact, I think you've done amazingly well, considering the nature of the problem."

Simon smiled. "You know what's funny?" he said.

"What?"

"A little while ago, I was the optimist. I was thinking, 'Man, this Christine is really the one for Ax.' And you were the skeptic, saying how many times we've tried and failed. Now we've reversed. I'm the **pessimist** and you're the optimist."

"Weird, huh? I'll have to bring that up in my social dynamics class. But listen, really, we've got to go with the world famous Simon **Intuition**, right?" She smiled her most endearing smile.

"I guess so," he said.

"OK. So, Axel has agreed to a double date on Monday night, right?"

"Yeah. But, of course, with his record I don't rate the chances of him being around for it very high."

"But you told me you really let him have it with both barrels when you chided him about his circumscribed social life. I think he'll at least show up. I don't think he'd want to let you down after he saw how strongly you felt about it."

"Yeah, I guess."

"And, anyway, I've worked out a little plan."

"I love plans. What is it?"

Jaz smiled. "Let's just say, I can handle Christine if you can handle Axel. I'm planning a little surprise for Axel. But our timing has to be perfect. I'll fill you in on the details later."

"Sounds like fun."

"Oh, it will be," Jaz said. "So, did you get Christine's phone number?"

"Yeah," Simon said, taking his personal digital assistant out of his shirt pocket. "I got her dorm number, her parent's home number, three e-mail addresses, her fax, cell phone, ICQ number, and, of course, her web site."

"That should be sufficient," Jaz said.

Simon was still looking at the screen of the digital assistant. "Oh yeah," he said. "And I got the extension where she works part time at the art museum."

"OK," Jaz said. "Here's the plan."

Definitions

1. **cajole** v. to persuade
2. **hypothesis** N. provisional explanation of facts (*pl.* hypotheses)
3. **lucid** ADJ. clear
4. **oblivious** ADJ. not aware
5. **stolidly** ADV. showing little emotion
6. **dour** ADJ. sullen and gloomy
7. **myopically** ADV. in a near-sighted manner
8. **dilapidated** ADJ. ruined because of neglect
9. **squalid** ADJ. dirty
10. **vicissitude** N. sudden change in life
11. **stereotype** N. oversimplified idea
12. **demeaning** ADJ. degrading
13. **patent** ADJ. obvious; unconcealed
14. **unorthodox** ADJ. breaking with convention or tradition
15. **stratagem** N. trick designed to deceive an opponent
16. **transitory** ADJ. existing only briefly
17. **taciturn** ADJ. not inclined to speak much
18. **rueful** ADJ. regretful; sorrowful
19. **debacle** N. total failure
20. **founder** v. to fail; collapse
21. **inadvertently** ADV. carelessly
22. **intimate** ADJ. very personal; private
23. **coyly** ADV. in a shy and flirtatious manner
24. **stifle** v. to suppress
25. **gravity** N. seriousness
26. **coup** N. brilliantly executed plan
27. **laconic** ADJ. using few words
28. **loquaciousness** N. talkativeness
29. **pessimist** N. person who tends to take the gloomiest possible view of a situation
30. **intuition** N. power of knowing without reasoning

Simply Simon

Think you know the words? Then prove it! Choose the *best* word to fill in the blank in each of the sentences below.

dour   intimate   hypotheses   cajole   debacle

stolidly   gravity   oblivious   vicissitudes

myopically

1. Usually on the weekend I _____ Jaz into cooking one of her delicious meals.

2. Scientists must be creative in thinking of _____ to explain their observations.

3. Only in the most extreme cases should the _____ of a situation prevent a person from partying.

4. An effective leader must sometimes act like she is _____ to criticism so that she can do what she thinks must be done.

5. During games Coach Wilson stands _____ on the sidelines, hardly saying a word.

6. Axel is not _____; he's just a quiet guy.

7. During last week's game my tight end lost his contact lenses; when I saw him open over the middle he was squinting back at me _____.

8. Jaz and I sometimes go to Pete's Place if we want to have a/an _____ dinner.

9. My attempt to cook Jaz's favorite dish, seafood saffron risotto, was a _____ ; the rice was dry and the fish was tasteless.

10. It is important to retain a sense of humor through life's _____.

Making Sense

Indicate whether or not each of the words in **bold** makes sense in the sentence. If it makes sense, put Y (Yes); if it doesn't make sense, put N (No).

1. Coach Wilson addressed the team in **rueful** tones after we won the Gigantic Bowl last year. ____

2. Dictators often resort to brutal means to **stifle** opposition to their rule. ____

3. The most **lucid** speaker does not always win a debate; factors besides clarity and logic determine how persuasive a speaker is. ____

4. Through a process of **intuition** astronomers can measure the precise distance between the moon and the earth. ____

5. My father always says that the good thing about being **laconic** is that you're less likely to say something stupid than you are if you're a chatterbox. ____

6. The salesperson at the audio store talked about **stereotypes** for so long I got lost in all of his technical talk. ____

7. Christine seems to be suffering from a **patent** case of "freshman girl has crush on charming football star." ____

8. **Loquaciousness** seems to come naturally to some people—like me. ____

9. Professor Chandler believes that all civilizations are **transitory**; they arise, flourish, decline, and finally, disappear.

____

10. The "color" member of a sportscasting team should be the **taciturn** type, always ready to tell a little story to add human interest to the account of the game. ____

Match It

Match each of the following words to its meaning.

1. coyly	a. degrading
2. dilapidated	b. trick designed to deceive an opponent
3. squalid	c. person who takes a gloomy view
4. inadvertently	d. ruined because of neglect
5. demeaning	e. carelessly
6. unorthodox	f. fail; collapse
7. stratagem	g. in a shy and flirtatious manner
8. founder	h. brilliantly executed plan
9. pessimist	i. dirty
10. coup	j. breaking with convention or tradition

Axel Speaks

Greetings! I believe that you are now ready for something more intellectual. Choose the *best* word to fill in the blank in each sentence.

1. Genetically modified foods are seen by some scientists as a long-term solution to the problem of the shortage of food; however, many consumers are concerned that unknown and harmful mutations might _____ be created by this technology.

(A) inadvertently

(B) succinctly

(C) accurately

(D) furtively

(E) fortunately

2. The failure of centrally planned economies to achieve productivity levels on a par with those of capitalist countries should not make one _____ to the fact that government planning was central to the remarkable success of the economies of such countries as Japan, South Korea, and Singapore, in which crucial industries were identified and built up through the cooperation of the public and private sectors.

(A) peripheral

(B) myopic

(C) oblivious

(D) enigmatic

(E) impassive

3. The chess match between world champion Gary Kasparov and IBM's computer "Deep Blue" was intriguing because it illustrated a human's ability to think _____ , in contrast to the computer's reliance on calculating tens of thousands of possible outcomes.

(A) cognitively

(B) intuitively

(C) stolidly

(D) myopically

(E) furtively

4. If the _____ that the earth and distant astronomical objects are moving apart is correct, according to the Doppler effect there should be an increase in the wavelength of light, making it appear redder; observation shows that this is indeed what is happening.

(A) hypothesis

(B) predilection

(C) stereotype

(D) diagnosis

(E) stratagem

5. The Romans regarded the phoenix as an appropriate symbol of their eternal empire, which they believed would undergo _____, but would always reemerge, enduring forever.

(A) vicissitudes

(B) gravity

(C) stratagems

(D) revisions

(E) pessimism

Answers on page 452.

And now, on with the story.

Episode 15

LOVE AND WAR

Christine was looking forward to going to Simon's and meeting Axel. A double date was pretty lame, but it was *so* retro it was sort of cool. Like the kids in those old movies from the 1950s. Obviously, she thought, they were trying to get her together with this guy. That was OK with her. Jaz and Simon seemed really cool, so maybe their friend was too. Anyway, it sounded like she'd at least get some ideas for her paper on Chagall from this Axel. It would also be interesting to see if he was really as **perspicacious** as they said he was.

And then, of course, there was *Simon*. Obviously, he liked her. That really is flattering, she thought. But there was one teensy little problem. No, she thought, actually there were two teensy little problems. One, she had been completely blown away by Simon. At first she had flirted with him because it was fun. A little game. He was obviously a **consummate** flirt, so she thought she'd try out a little **coquette** routine herself. Except it had gotten out of hand. At some time during the flirtation she had fallen for the guy: big time. Now he was all she could think about. In short, it seemed like a classic case of love-at-first sight. She had always ridiculed this when it happened in movies or books. *Really*. It was *so* uncool. So un-new woman. Except it had just happened to *her*.

Yes, Simon was all she wanted to think about. She was **obsessed**. All she thought about was being near him. She remembered holding his arm. She must have seemed like such a smooth operator to him—but inside she was going *crazy*. And then, when she knew for sure how much he dug *her*... .

And then there was the *wink*. O my *God*! she thought. I *winked* at the guy! With his girlfriend a few feet away! That certainly shows **pluck**, girl. See something you want, no problemo. You just go ahead and try to take it. Wonderful. Maybe he thinks you're crazy. You're not supposed to *wink* at a guy you've just met. Even in the new **millennium** guys were, at least **nominally**, supposed to be the aggressors. The girl, of course, had to maintain at least an appearance of **decorum**. She could not show her interest **overtly**.

What was she supposed to do, call him up and say, "Oh, about, that wink, Simon. That was an accident. You see, I have this uncontrollable tic, this aberration that makes me wink at guys. I've been to all sorts of specialists, but they say it's **congenital**, that I'll have to learn to live with it." Or, how about, "Now, about what you *thought* was a wink. It never happened. It was just a figment of your imagination, a chimera. What girl in her right mind would wink at a guy in front of his *girl*? You must be seriously **delusional** or *something*. Give me a *break*."

So, what was the second teensy little problem? Ah, yes. The matter of this girl, Jaz. Simon had already been spoken for. And it looked like they were a lovely couple. No, she'd just have to put thoughts of Simon out of her mind. Vanish! Be gone! And out they went. *Adios*, thoughts of Simon. *Arrivederci. Au revoir. Auf Wiedersehen. Sayonara.* Yes, completely gone from her mind without a trace. Until, that is, they came back stronger than ever, revivified. Simon throwing a touchdown pass, Simon talking intimately with her, like she was the only girl in the world. Simon smiling. Simon walking, her by his side, holding on to that powerful arm that could rifle a football 60 yards downfield with perfect accuracy—or pull her near to him. Simon having dinner with her. Simon, Simon, Simon. Simon was **ubiquitous**.

And then a thought crossed the mind of a girl who had never had a naughty thought in her life (or, at least, one of any consequence). If, she thought, she met Axel and *acted* like she liked him, hung out with him, she would get to be around Simon. OK, it wouldn't be like being his main squeeze, but **propinquity** did have some pretty heavy-duty virtues. She would be right there in the center of the action. If, by some terrible misfortune, the relationship of the beautiful couple should ever founder, she would be there for Simon. It was, she was well aware, not the noblest thought that had ever crossed her mind, but, she reflected, at least I'm not a **hypocrite**; I mean, at least I'm not trying to *deny* I'm a **conniver**.

Anyway, what was that **maxim** she was always sticking into her English essays on those nineteenth-century novels? Ah, yes—"All's fair in love and war." Dr. Paunch, her English instructor, kept crossing it out in her essays and writing, DO NOT USE THIS. *EVER!* IT IS A **PLATITUDE**. IT IS TOTALLY **HACKNEYED**. But she kept writing it anyway. And he kept crossing it out. It was kind of their little game. What she didn't get was what was wrong with using a **truism** if it was *true*, and expressed what you wanted to say *perfectly*. Like in this case. How *else* could you say it? "You can play dirty in love just as they do in war because both provoke uncontrollable feelings, so it's like kind of excusable"? Right. *That* sounds *great*. Really **pithy**.

Yes, Christine thought, this was love. And, maybe, war.

Definitions

1. **perspicacious** ADJ. able to understand keenly
2. **consummate** ADJ. supremely accomplished
3. **coquette** N. woman who flirts
4. **obsessed** ADJ. preoccupied with excessively
5. **pluck** N. courage; spirit
6. **millennium** N. thousand-year period
7. **nominally** ADV. in name only
8. **decorum** N. proper behavior

9. **overtly** ADV. openly
10. **congenital** ADJ. existing since birth
11. **delusional** ADJ. having a false belief
12. **ubiquitous** ADJ. being or seeming to be everywhere simultaneously
13. **propinquity** N. nearness
14. **hypocrite** N. person who claims to have virtues he or she doesn't have
15. **conniver** N. person who schemes (v. to connive)
16. **maxim** N. concise statement of a fundamental principle
17. **platitude** N. stale, overused expression
18. **hackneyed** ADJ. worn out by overuse
19. **truism** N. a self-evident or obvious truth
20. **pithy** ADJ. precisely meaningful; cogent and terse

Simply Simon

Think you know the words? Then prove it! Choose the *best* word to fill in the blank in each of the sentences below.

connivers   congenital   millennium   ubiquitous

propinquity   delusional   coquette   pluck

overtly   pithy

1. It's exciting to be living at the time of both a new century and a new _____.

2. The _____ is a common type of female character in literature.

3. Professor James, the famous physics professor here, seems to be _____—you turn on the TV and there he is.

4. There are several students I admire greatly for the way they have overcome their _____ disabilities.

5. There's a reserve wide receiver on our team who can't weigh 150 pounds dripping wet; I admire the _____ he shows going up against the giants who play defense in our conference.

6. Guys can be _____ just as much as girls can; sometimes they're just crafty in different ways.

7. Coach Wilson is well known for his _____ comments to the press after games.

8. The _____ of a college to your home is often a big factor in deciding where you want to apply.

9. On the football field—unlike in everyday life—aggression can be displayed _____.

10. When I was in high school and I told my friends I wanted to be president some day they said I was _____.

Making Sense

Indicate whether or not each of the words in **bold** makes sense in the sentence. If it makes sense, put Y (Yes); if it doesn't make sense, put N (No).

1. In many traditional societies a man is **nominally** the head of the family; however, in many cases it's the women who have more real power. ____

2. Ideas of **decorum** vary over time with changes in values and customs. ____

3. Jaz is so **obsessed** with football that I have to beg her to go to games with me.____

4. Axel says that perhaps the least **perspicacious** experimental physicist of all time was Sir Ernest Rutherford, who did more than any other scientist to unravel the mysteries of the atom. ____

5. Whatever their political views, most commentators would agree that Bill Clinton and Ronald Reagan were **consummate** politicians. ____

6. When I asked him to explain Einstein's theory of gravitation, Axel quoted a **maxim** in a lecture by the distinguished physicist J. A. Wheeler: "Space tells matter how to move and matter tells space how to curve." ____

7. Football coaches tend to use quite a few **hackneyed** phrases such as "swing in momentum" and "critical situation." ____

8. The ultimate goal of philosophy is to find a **platitude** that summarizes the underlying nature of reality. ____

9. A common **truism** used in sports broadcasts is, "It ain't over till it's over." ____

10. Unless the president of the college is a **hypocrite**, academic honesty and freedom will not flourish in a college. ____

Match It

Match each of the following words to its meaning.

1. perspicacious   a. openly

2. obsessed   b. person claiming virtues he or she doesn't have

3. decorum   c. stale, overused expression

4. overtly   d. able to understand keenly

5. ubiquitous   e. concise statement of a fundamental principle

6. propinquity   f. worn out by overuse

7. hypocrite   g. nearness

8. maxim   h. proper behavior

9. platitude   i. being everywhere simultaneously

10. hackneyed   j. preoccupied with excessively

Axel Speaks

Greetings! I believe that you are now ready for something more intellectual. Choose the *best* word to fill in the blank in each sentence.

1. Many Third World leaders argue that, although colonialism has disappeared, it has continued to flourish in the more _____ form of neocolonialism—cultural and economic domination.

(A) hackneyed

(B) covert

(C) congenital

(D) ubiquitous

(E) identical

2. The antitrust suit filed by the American federal government and a number of state governments against the computer software company Microsoft accused that company of _____ to weaken the positions of its competitors in the market.

(A) coercing

(B) extrapolating

(C) cajoling

(D) meddling

(E) conniving

3. Some modern critics believe that works of literature should embody moral values but should not teach them _____, so that the reader can make his or her own judgments.

(A) nominally

(B) insipidly

(C) comprehensively

(D) overtly

(E) inadvertently

4. Mass production has helped to make products incorporating sophisticated technology, such as computers, _____.

(A) congenital

(B) consummate

(C) ubiquitous

(D) perspicacious

(E) limitless

5. The case of the sedative drug thalidomide is often cited by proponents of strict testing of new drugs; in that case governments allowed the drug to be released and, tragically, it caused severe _____ defects in thousands of children.

(A) delusional

(B) pithy

(C) congenital

(D) perspicacious

(E) moderate

Answers on pages 452–453.

And now, on with the story.

Episode 16

Girls Just Want to Have Fun

Christine walked up the steps of Simon's house and rang the doorbell. While she waited she looked around. This looks like a cool place to live, she thought. It was a big two-story house with a good-sized yard. Though it was dark, she could see a ring that Simon used to practice passing. She could see him—taking the snap from center, dropping back ... looking, looking ... *whoosh*! the perfect pass, like a bullet, right through the middle of the ring.

Jaz opened the door, breaking in on Christine's **reverie**. "Hi! Come on in," she said. "It's great you could make it. Axel is really looking forward to meeting you."

"Hi," Christine said.

Jaz said, "Simon and Axel just left for the art museum."

"Art museum?"

"Yeah. Axel got this overwhelming urge to see the Chagall paintings over there."

"Wow! That's amazing! I'm doing a big paper on Chagall right now. I think I told you, right?"

"Yeah. Well, it looks like this is your lucky night because Axel is really into Chagall right now. And when Axel is into something, watch out! I mean, he'll be a world authority on Chagall in a few months at this rate."

"That is unbelievably great. You know, I'm kind of stuck, and I could really use someone to bat some ideas around with."

"Well, it looks like you just found your man!"

Christine laughed. This Jaz is really cool, she thought. A twinge of guilt crept into her mind. She was violating this girl's trust to get near her *boyfriend*. How **loathsome**. What had happened to the sisterhood of women thing and all that? She felt like an **anachronism**—a throwback to a time when women were **wily**, scheming creatures, using every **ploy** in the book, stopping at nothing to get the man they wanted. **Coveting** another woman's boyfriend. Really! It was something from a soap opera.

She was filled with shame. The thought of throwing herself at Jaz and telling her how she felt about Simon came into her mind—how she had plotted to be near him, how she would do anything to be near him, how she was so ashamed of planning to violate the trust of another woman, how she would leave and never see either of them again. For several painful moments these thoughts **exercised** her conscience. She felt trapped. It was a conundrum: abandon all hope of seeing Simon or admit that she was no angel. The choice was clear. *I'm no angel*, Christine thought.

"Hey, I've got an idea!" Jaz said. "You could use some inspiration for your Chagall research, right? Would it help you to see some original Chagall paintings? I mean, it might be kind of cool to see the real stuff instead of just those plates in a book."

"Would it help? It would be *great*! There's nothing better than seeing the actual art when you're trying to get ideas about it."

"So, why don't you and I go to the museum and join the guys? You can see the Chagalls. And maybe, if you're really lucky, Axel will give you one of his incredible lectures. If he does, I guarantee you'll learn more in 30 minutes than you would in a month in class. We can go to the movie after the museum."

"Sounds like fun."

"Hey, I just got another idea. Why don't we sneak into the museum, hide in a room, and surprise the guys when they come in. It'll be a scream. Are you up for it?"

145

This was really strange, Christine thought. These people must be *crazy*. She'd hardly met them and already she was involved in one of their **escapades**. "Yeah," she said. "Why not? Sounds like it should be a real hoot."

"Great. Here's what we'll do. We'll **surreptitiously** break into one of the small exhibition rooms at the back of the museum. We can get in through the back door so Simon and Axel won't see us."

"Break in?" Christine said. "I don't know; that's going a little far, isn't it? I mean, it's like illegal. Anyway, how could we manage that?"

Jaz looked a little sheepish. "I was sort of hoping that since you work there part time you might have a key to the back door."

Christine smiled. So Jaz had *planned* on her having the keys. But that was strange. She never carried them around unless she was going to work, and yet she had put them into her bag before coming over here. She looked closely at Jaz. *Was this woman telepathic or something?* she wondered.

Christine reached into her bag and pulled out a set of keys. "This should do the trick," she said. She frowned. "But we really could get into trouble."

"Don't worry, nobody will know. We'll be **discreet**. We'll lock the door after us and it will be like nobody was *ever* there."

"OK. I guess it's cool. So, what happens next?"

Jaz smiled. "Well, at this hour there'll hardly be anyone left in the museum."

"That's true," Christine said. "Monday nights are always dead over there." She thought for a moment. Then she looked at her watch. "Hey," she said, "on Mondays it closes at 7:00. It's already 7:30."

Jaz laughed. "Don't worry. That's been taken care of."

Christine gave Jaz a quizzical look.

"You see, Axel suddenly really wanted to go, so Simon called a pal of his who happens to be the **curator** over there."

146

"Wow, those guys must be *really* good friends."

"Oh, Simon can be pretty persuasive. It isn't very easy to say 'No' to him."

Christine tried to imagine saying "No" to Simon. She really tried. But nothing came to mind. She just couldn't come up with a scenario that was **credible**. Finally, she came up with one that seemed **plausible**: "No, Simon. We really *must* be separated while we take our final exams. You could get in trouble if they found you hiding here in the exam hall so you can be with me while I'm taking my art exam. But we'll be together again soon. Yes, I know two hours is an eternity for you to be away from me, but somehow you'll have to endure it."

"I *work* for Miss Beaufort," Christine said. "I can't imagine her doing *anything* nice for *anyone*. Especially keeping the museum open late for a couple of students."

"*Miss* Beaufort? The curator is a *woman*?"

"Oh, yes. She's been there a year now. This is her first job. Ph.D. University of Paris. It's great fun working for her—she's a real slave driver—a regular **martinet**."

"Sounds like loads of fun," Jaz said.

"I mean, I spent my first week there cleaning every piece of glass in sight," Christine said. "Dr. Beaufort says she wants to be able to see a perfect reflection of herself when she looks in any mirror in the building. And she looks at herself in mirrors pretty regularly."

Jaz laughed.

"In fact," Christine said, "she looks at herself in mirrors *really* regularly."

"It sounds to me like the woman has some seriously **narcissistic** tendencies," Jaz said.

"She's always stopping in front of a mirror to just stand and gaze at herself," Christine said. "And, she's really **condescending**. She seems to regard herself as French culture's gift to us poor **provincial** Americans. But I do have to admit, she's certainly gotten that place into shape in a hurry. She's improved every **facet** of the museum. They say it's on the way to being one of the better college art museums in the country. And, even though I don't exactly like that woman, I do have to admit, she certainly does fit right into an art museum."

"What do you mean?"

Christine laughed. "Well, let's just say that with Miss Colette Beaufort around the place, all of the beauty is not on the walls of the museum."

Jaz thought back to when she had given Simon his assignment to get the museum to stay open a little longer. He had **acquiesced** almost instantly. What had he said? Oh, yes. "No, problemo. I have a good buddy over there. I'll just have a little chat."

The job had seemed really tough, even for Simon. Christine was right. Why would they keep the museum open for a few undergrads? It defied reason. And not only had the curator agreed to keep the museum open. He—no *she*—had said she'd mount a special Chagall exhibition just for him and his friends. The museum had half a dozen of the artist's paintings from different periods of his life that she could show. She wanted Simon and his friends to have a reasonably comprehensive view of the artist's work. No, she had said, it would be no trouble at all to spend her one free afternoon unpacking valuable paintings, lugging them up from the basement, and putting them on display just so a couple of undergraduates could look at them for an hour or so. She had also said they could have the place to themselves for a while. She would work in her office and then close up after they left. Yes, Jaz had thought, Simon has really outdone himself this time.

"It really is amazing," Christine continued. "How Simon ever **inveigled** that woman into *this*, I can't imagine."

The two young women looked at each other. Maybe I *can* imagine, Christine thought. From the look on Jaz's face, Christine could see an alarm going off in her brain too. It looked to Christine that Jaz was thinking something along the lines of, *I'd better get over to that museum, pronto.*

148

Simon is there and this gorgeous creature is there, no doubt giving him her special tour of the museum. Sure, Axel was there too. But Axel was way out in space. He was hardly chaperone material.

"I guess," Christine said, "that Simon and Dr. Beaufort must be really great friends."

Definitions

1. **reverie** N. daydream
2. **loathsome** ADJ. abhorrent; disgusting
3. **anachronism** N. something out of its proper time
4. **wily** ADJ. sly; deceiving
5. **ploy** N. trick to obtain an advantage
6. **covet** V. desire something belonging to another
7. **exercise** V. to absorb the attention.
8. **escapade** N. prank; adventurous action violating conventional conduct
9. **surreptitiously** ADV. secretly; stealthily
10. **discreet** ADJ. prudent
11. **curator** N. director of a museum or other similar institution
12. **credible** ADJ. believable; plausible
13. **plausible** ADJ. apparently likely (also: having a show of truth but open to doubt)
14. **martinet** N. strict disciplinarian
15. **narcissistic** ADJ. excessively admiring oneself
16. **condescending** ADJ. bestowing courtesy with a superior air; patronizing
17. **provincial** ADJ. limited in outlook; unsophisticated
18. **facet** N. aspect (also: side)
19. **acquiesce** V. to agree without protesting
20. **inveigle** V. to win over by persuasion; cajole

Simply Simon

Think you know the words? Then prove it! Choose the *best* word to fill in the blank in each of the sentences below.

ploy   curator   anachronisms   provincial

escapades   inveigle   exercised   discreet

wily   loathsome

1. Jaz says I'll make a good politician because I can _____ people into doing just about anything.

2. There is nothing more _____ than cheating on an exam.

3. _____ defensive coaches have tried a lot of schemes to slow down our high-powered offense, but none have worked so far.

4. One _____ I occasionally use is to call a play at the line after I've checked out the defense's alignment.

5. Dr. Larsen, the head librarian, also serves as the _____ of the library's special collection of works in Sanskrit, the ancient language of India.

6. Coach Wilson's vivid description of what the atmosphere would be on campus if we lost the bowl game last year _____ my mind for days.

7. It's fun to try to spot _____ in low-budget movies; one time I saw a man wearing a wristwatch in a movie set in ancient Rome.

8. I've got a buddy who lives in a fraternity house famous for the _____ of its members.

9. Growing up in a small town, I had a pretty _____ outlook on life until I came to college.

10. Experience has taught me that it's advisable to be _____ in describing other women to Jaz.

Making Sense

Indicate whether or not each of the words in **bold** makes sense in the sentence. If it makes sense, put Y (Yes); if it doesn't make sense, put N (No).

1. My grandfather sometimes goes into a bit of a **reverie** when I talk to him about his past and he recalls fond memories from his childhood. ____

2. A well-rounded education should develop every **facet** of a person. ____

3. Although Axel is basically not an envious person, he did confess to me that the one thing he **covets** is access to the super computer at Fermi Lab so that he can complete his physics research with Professor James. ____

4. Cheerleaders do their energetic routines **surreptitiously** in front of the crowd at every game. ____

5. It's important that young children develop a healthy, **narcissistic** liking for themselves. ____

6. A good scientist ignores **credible** explanations of the data from her experiments so that she can concentrate on more believable explanations. ____

7. When Miss Bridget, my creative writing teacher, tells a person in her class to rewrite an assignment, he or she **acquiesces** immediately since they know the alternatives are not exactly pleasant. ____

8. Coach Wilson isn't a coach who tries to be "one of the guys," but he's certainly not a **martinet** either. ____

9. People who feel inferior to other people should try to be less fearful, shy, and **condescending**. ____

10. Axel says scientists have pieced together a **plausible** picture of the origin and evolution of the universe. ____

Match It

Match each of the following words to its meaning.

1. reverie   a. strict disciplinarian

2. surreptitiously   b. prudent

3. discreet   c. daydream

4. covet   d. limited in outlook

5. plausible   e. aspect

6. martinet   f. desire something belonging to another

7. narcissistic   g. win over by persuasion

8. provincial   h. apparently likely

9. facet   i. excessively admiring oneself

10. inveigle   j. secretly; stealthily

Axel Speaks

Greetings! I believe that you are now ready for something more intellectual. Choose the *best* word to fill in the blank in each sentence.

1. Compared to mythology, folklore tends to be less serious, less concerned with the supernatural, and less concerned with providing a/an _____ explanation for events such as the creation of the world.

(A) volatile

(B) forlorn

(C) sensitive

(D) ancient

(E) credible

2. An argument against the jury system is that it favors defendants who can afford to hire _____ and persuasive lawyers with the ability to deceive people serving on juries who are, in general, not trained in law.

(A) wily

(B) narcissistic

(C) discreet

(D) condescending

(E) pedantic

3. By the late nineteenth century, European powers could only _____ in the extension of the Monroe Doctrine by the United States to include its dominance of the entire American continent.

(A) acquiesce

(B) connive

(C) inveigle

(D) reminisce

(E) mollify

4. A/An _____ theory of the origin of myths is that they began as "vegetation stories" that sought to explain the cycle of birth and death in nature.

(A) didactic

(B) compatible

(C) provincial

(D) plausible

(E) revealing

5. A/An _____ sometimes used by debaters is to portray an opponent's argument as more simplistic than it is, and then proceed to show how their own argument is, by contrast, much more sophisticated.

(A) reverie

(B) ploy

(C) scenario

(D) escapade

(E) martinet

Answers on pages 453–454.

And now, on with the story.

Episode 17

THE KNOCKOUT

Jaz and Christine parked a block from the library and walked toward the museum. It was dark, and both women were quiet. Christine was thinking, *so this is what the junior and senior girls do for kicks.* Sneak into museums at night and scare the wits out of their boyfriends. Great fun. She felt like a glamorous spy on some **clandestine** operation. A Bond girl. She remembered Professor McCleod in her media studies class telling them how the media is so powerful and **pervasive** in American society that it shapes our images of ourselves, our desires, even our fantasies. She had thought, "Hellooo. Ms. Professor. Like that is *so* out of date. You must be living in the last *millennium!* Today, a girl can do what she wants. The media is just a joke, something you just use for kicks. You don't take it *seriously* or anything. Give me a *break!*"

They tiptoed up the back steps of the museum. "I have to deactivate the motion sensor," Christine said.

Jaz gave Christine a look that said, "You're really *into* this, aren't you?" Christine climbed on the railing and reached up. She grabbed hold of a beam and hoisted herself up. Jaz watched as she **clambered** onto the roof. *Who does she think she is, Superwoman or something?* she thought.

Christine looked down at Jaz from the roof. "I feel like I'm in *Mission Impossible,* or that I'm one of those three girls in *Charlie's Angels,*" she whispered. "This is fun. I'll just kill the detector."

Jaz waited a minute. Then Christine was lowering herself down off the roof.

Jaz wondered if her hair would still be perfect after her exertions like it always was in the movies. Christine stood in front of her, smiling. "That was easy," she said. "Somebody must have changed the access code, but I **circumvented** the photodiode and rerouted the circuit by plugging in a parallel port transponder. It's cool now."

Jaz looked at Christine, who shook her head to get her mane of blond hair out of her face. Perfect, Jaz noted. Not one hair was out of place. She looked just like a character in the movie.

"Let's get inside. The security people might see us," Christine said.

Jaz led Christine down a darkened hallway. They went into a large room, which was illuminated only by security lights.

"This is the sculpture room," Christine whispered.

"Yes, I know," Jaz said.

The room was filled with life-sized statues of characters from Greek mythology. They had been done by a **contemporary** Greek sculptor who seemed determined to portray every god and goddess in the Greek **pantheon**, as well as the famous human beings. Christine examined one of the figures near her. It was Artemis, standing proudly.

"She's *beautiful*," she whispered to Jaz.

"Yeah," Jaz agreed.

"And here is Athena," Christine said. She shook her head in wonder. "Look how noble and pure she seems."

"Check out Helen of Troy," Jaz said. "That is one awesome lady."

"I've seen this room before, of course," Christine whispered to Jaz. "But not at night. It seems so *real* now. The sculptures are so **imposing**. This is really exciting."

She turned to examine another statue. Apollo.

"Impressive," she said, pointing to the statue.

Jaz laughed quietly. She handed Christine a small cardboard box. "Here, take this."

"What's this?"

"You'll see." She held another box in her hand. "We can change in the ladies' room."

Christine shrugged. "Change?" she asked. But she followed Jaz.

Jaz and Christine emerged after several minutes, dressed in shimmering gowns. Christine recognized the style. Classical Greek gowns. They both wore heavy makeup. They looked very much like the statues in the room.

The two girls stood admiring each other. "You look gorgeous, Christine. A work of art. Truly **beguiling**. A complete knockout."

"You look fantastic too, Jaz. Like a goddess. So now what happens?"

"So, now," Jaz said, "we wait." She looked at her watch. "In precisely five minutes," she announced, "Simon will lead Ax through *that* door." She pointed to a door at the far side of the room. That was fun, Jaz thought. Two could play at being the glamorous spy.

"You see," Jaz said, "Axel loves Greek sculpture almost as much as he does Chagall."

She took a marker and a piece of paper from her handbag and wrote the word "Nausikaa" on it. She put it in front of a recessed area that did not have a statue in it. Then Jaz walked to another area and stood. Suddenly, she struck a pose like Athena's.

"Hey, pretty good," Christine said. Jaz really does look like a goddess, she thought. Her face and hair were illuminated softly by the security lights. She remained motionless.

"Living sculpture," Christine said.

Jaz nodded slightly. "It's in **vogue** now," she said.

Christine, realizing that she was to be Nausikaa, stood in the **niche** behind the sign that Jaz had made. She also struck a pose. Jaz looked at her. Christine is so beautiful, she thought. A real knockout. She stood so gracefully. And she looked so **sensual**. Then a doubt **assailed** her. Maybe Christine was *too* sensual. At least for Axel. But she wasn't going to turn back now. Anyway, what a sensational way to introduce him to Christine—their own little **tableau**. And there would be no place that Axel could flee to. They'd have a quiet little party right here and Axel would get to know Christine. Everything would work out great.

They waited. In a minute they heard Simon's booming voice. Whew, we cut that pretty close, Jaz thought. She glanced at Christine again. She looks exactly like a statue of some beautiful Greek goddess, she thought. Yes, Axel certainly would be surprised.

"Yeah, the Egyptian stuff is great," Simon was saying. "But personally I find it a little spooky—kind of **macabre**. I mean, all those mummies. Don't they belong in a tomb or something?" The Egyptian mummy exhibit always reminded Simon of the one—and only—time he had let himself be convinced to watch a horror flick. It had been *The Return of the Mummy*. It had taken him months to recover. He had imagined that mummies were everywhere. In fact, he had never fully recovered. Even now he got a little jumpy around mummies.

"Hey! I've got an idea," Simon said. "Why don't we take a look at the Greek sculpture? It's right through there. I know I said we'd look at the special Chagall display, but I also know how you *love* Greek sculpture. Like I always say, you can't beat the Greeks for sculpture—they were masters at **rendering** the human form. We'll just take a quick look in here and then move on to the Chagalls."

Jaz and Christine listened to footsteps coming into the sculpture room.

"Let's leave the lights dim. It's more dramatic that way," they heard Simon say.

Simon and Axel walked slowly around the room, examining the life-sized sculptures in the round. They had separated, each apparently preferring to enjoy the exhibit on his own. Jaz watched as Axel peered closely at the statues. Several pieces in particular he **scrutinized** for several minutes. Jaz felt she could almost hear the thoughts going through Axel's mind. *This is stunning*, Axel seemed to be thinking. *Here is brave Odysseus. And faithful Penelope. There is Helen of Troy. The most beautiful woman in history—a mortal goddess. And Athena, that most noble and* **benevolent** *of goddesses.* He knew each piece intimately. *They are all my friends*, he thought.

He reached out and softly touched Athena's arm. A few tears came to Jaz's eyes as she watched. It was so **poignant**. There was an expression of something like love on Axel's face. He reached up and gently touched the face of the statue. Several more tears flowed down Jaz's cheeks. *Deep inside, Axel is really sensitive*, she thought. She had always known he was; he just **repressed** it, buried it deep inside himself, under all those ideas.

Simon approached Jaz. He saw her eyes move as she glanced at him. He looked closely at her face and saw that her cheeks were wet and her makeup was smudged. He looked puzzled. Then he followed Jaz's gaze. He turned and saw Axel looking at Athena. Now he understood why Jaz was weeping.

Axel left Athena and moved on to the next exhibit. "Nausikaa," a crudely lettered sign read. *That must be new*, Axel thought. *The museum must have just acquired it. Funny, I don't remember this artist having done Nausikaa. Maybe, he had just recently completed it and the museum has just put it out on display*, he thought.

He looked at the sculpture. *So beautiful. And so lifelike. Whoever the artist was, he or she was a* **virtuoso**.

Axel gazed at the girl. *Yes, Nausikaa*, he thought. *It reminds me of Odysseus in the* Odyssey *meeting the beautiful nymph Nausikaa by the river,* **entreating** *her to help him, after he emerged naked and encrusted with ocean spray from his* **arduous** *ocean voyage. The glorious girl Homer described as "the nearest likeness to Artemis/ the daughter of great Zeus, for beauty, figure, and stature."*

Jaz looked at the scene. Somehow, Axel seemed taller—no, *larger*—as he stood looking at the statue. There was in his bearing a nobility and grandeur she had never seen before in him. He could almost *be* Odysseus, she thought.

"I have never with these eyes seen anything like you,/neither man nor woman," Axel was saying softly to the statue. As it had to Odysseus so many years ago, the thought of grasping the girl's knees to **importune** her came into Axel's mind. And, like Odysseus, he wondered: Is this a mortal or a goddess?

Axel gazed tenderly at the face. So lovely. So kind. The one girl of the group doing laundry by the river that hadn't fled in horror when Odysseus had emerged looking like a monster from the river. She had pitied him, given him a cloth to cover himself, and welcomed the wandering hero to her land.

The tender expression. So gentle and feminine. So lifelike. Remarkable verisimilitude. And the lines of the face. Amazing. Had any other artist so perfectly portrayed feminine tenderness? And what was that *sound*? In the nearly perfect quiet you could almost hear someone breathing—breathing very, very softly. Remarkable. The immediacy, the **potency**, of great art! It so stimulated the imagination that you fancied you could hear this wonderful creature *respiring*. She was, essentially, *alive*, though of course she had been dead for over 2,000 years. Why, he wondered, had this piece not been discussed in the literature? Even if it had just been found, surely there should have been some mention of something so lovely having been created.

Axel knelt down in front of the statue. Slowly, he reached out both of his arms and grasped Nausikaa's knees. So lifelike, he thought. It actually felt warm, not like bronze would normally feel. You could almost feel life flowing in this statue. As Jaz watched the scene, tears streamed down her face. Yes, she thought, it truly is Odysseus. He is alive and here with Nausikaa, whom he always must have loved. What, she wondered, was he imploring from sweet, beautiful Nausikaa? Jaz nearly cried out; she watched, fascinated, at once horrified and moved by the scene unfolding before her.

"Gentle Nausikaa, kindest and most beautiful of girls," Axel said very softly, gazing up into the face of the statue. "Sweet, kind Nausikaa."

Christine's eyes opened. They looked down at Axel. Axel looked up.

"Hi," Christine said. "Welcome, O brave Odysseus. Welcome to my land."

Axel crumpled soundlessly to the floor.

******

"He's out cold," Jaz said.

"He'll be OK," Simon said.

"I don't know. He's completely limp," Jaz said.

Christine looked worried. "I didn't think he'd do *that!*' she said, pointing to Axel, motionless on the floor.

"Don't worry." Simon said. "He'll be fine. But we'd better get him back to the house." He looked at Christine and laughed. "You certainly gave him an art lesson he won't forget anytime soon!"

Definitions

1. **clandestine** ADJ. secret
2. **pervasive** ADJ. spread throughout every part
3. **clamber** v. to climb by crawling
4. **circumvent** v. to avoid by going around
5. **contemporary** ADJ. present-day
6. **pantheon** N. all the gods of a people; a group of famous persons
7. **imposing** ADJ. awesome
8. **beguiling** ADJ. charming
9. **vogue** N. prevailing fashion or practice
10. **niche** N. recess in a wall
11. **sensual** ADJ. suggesting sexuality; voluptuous
12. **assail** v. to attack

13. **tableau** N. scene presented by costumed actors who remain silent and motionless (also: a striking scene)
14. **macabre** ADJ. suggesting death and decay
15. **render** V. to represent; portray (also: provide)
16. **scrutinize** V. to examine closely
17. **benevolent** ADJ. kindly
18. **poignant** ADJ. emotionally moving
19. **repress** V. to hold in; restrain (ADJ. repressed)
20. **virtuoso** N. someone with masterly skills
21. **entreat** V. to plead
22. **arduous** ADJ. extremely difficult
23. **importune** V. to beg earnestly
24. **potency** N. power
25. **respire** V. to breathe

Simply Simon

Think you know the words? Then prove it! Choose the *best* word to fill in the blank in each of the sentences below.

potency   tableau   sensual   poignant

benevolent   render   entreating   macabre

pervasive   clamber

1. My writing is improving, but I don't think I will ever be able to _____ human character as well as such masters as Jane Austen and Charles Dickens.

2. There is a/an _____ moment near the end of the movie *Castaway* in which the character played by Tom Hanks must decide whether to begin a new life and relationship.

3. When I was little I used to _____ onto the top of my family's station wagon to watch the fireworks on the Fourth of July.

4. Jaz and I went to a play that closed with a/an _____ that made me think about what the future held for the characters I had come to know so well.

5. My art teacher says a simple test of the _____ of a work of art is whether it makes your jaw drop in wonder.

6. Edgar Allan Poe is famous for his _____ stories about death and horror, but he also wrote excellent analytical criticism and detective stories.

7. Miss Bridget, my creative writer teacher, is constantly _____ us to try to write what we really think and feel.

8. Jaz looked _____ in her evening gown when we went to the formal dance last month.

9. I believe that it is important to try to perform at least one _____ act every day.

10. There is a/an _____ feeling on campus that the college should become more involved in the community.

Making Sense

Indicate whether or not each of the words in **bold** makes sense in the sentence. If it makes sense, put Y (Yes); if it doesn't make sense, put N (No).

1. Professor Chandler has done quite a bit of consulting work for government agencies such as the Central Intelligence Agency and National Defense Agency analyzing data gathered through **clandestine** means. ____

2. Modern media allows a president to **circumvent** an uncooperative Congress and speak directly to the people. ____

3. I am such a **virtuoso** that I volunteer five hours a week to help in the shelter for homeless people. ____

4. After the last game of the season I like to take off to spend an **arduous** weekend on the beach, just chilling and enjoying the scenery. ____

5. I once asked Professor Chandler to list the three people in the **pantheon** of American presidents he considered the greatest. "George Washington, Abraham Lincoln, and Franklin Roosevelt," he said. ____

6. I hate to take a course in a really in **vogue** subject because there probably won't be many other students in the class. ____

7. A person who **represses** her true feelings tends to tell other people what she honestly thinks about everything. ____

8. Free trade has been **assailed** as one of the crucial ingredients needed to ensure economic prosperity. ____

9. I **scrutinized** Axel's 100-page paper on number theory and found one error—he had written *it's* when he had meant *its.* ____

10. I once tried **importuning** a mathematics professor I know to try to make her field less complex so that ordinary people like me would have a better crack at understanding the stuff they put in college books; she just laughed. ____

Match It

Match each of the following words to its meaning.

1. clandestine	a. emotionally moving
2. circumvent	b. awesome
3. contemporary	c. breathe
4. imposing	d. charming
5. beguiling	e. secret
6. niche	f. avoid by going around
7. benevolent	g. kindly
8. poignant	h. extremely difficult
9. arduous	i. recess in a wall
10. respire	j. present-day

Axel Speaks

Greetings! I believe that you are now ready for something more intellectual. Choose the *best* word to fill in the blank in each sentence.

1. In Greek mythology's _____ vision of the afterlife, Hades is guarded by Cerberus, a many-headed dog with a mane and a tail of snakes; newly dead arrivals must be ferried from the world of the living across the river Styx by Charon to their new home.

(A) macabre

(B) historical

(C) beguiling

(D) imposing

(E) glorified

2. The crew of the space shuttle *Challenger*, which exploded shortly after launch on January 28, 1986, has become part of the _____ of astronauts who gave their lives in the endeavor to advance space exploration.

(A) tableau

(B) pantheon

(C) lineage

(D) colloquy

(E) camaraderie

3. Sigmund Freud believed that the Oedipus myth (the Greek myth in which Oedipus accidentally kills his father and unknowingly marries his mother) reflects a/an _____ universal desire in children to marry the parent of the opposite sex and kill the rival for that parent's affection.

(A) repressed

(B) facetious

(C) contemporary

(D) benevolent

(E) occasional

4. A by-product of photosynthesis is oxygen, which is vital to life because it allows both plants and animals to _____.

(A) founder

(B) entreat

(C) respire

(D) emulate

(E) digress

5. The influence of psychoanalytic theory has been _____ in modern thought; it has influenced literary criticism, history, anthropology, and a number of other fields.

(A) redundant

(B) transitory

(C) pervasive

(D) impeccable

(E) clandestine

Answers on page 454.

And now, on with the story.

The Advent of Xela

Jaz scrutinized the girl sitting across from Simon. Being Simon's devoted girlfriend sometimes **entailed** somewhat undignified activities, such as surreptitious observation of his extracurricular activities. From her position in the restaurant in a booth not far from theirs, Jaz could **covertly** observe Simon and the girl without their noticing her. She certainly is attractive, Jaz had to admit—albeit somewhat reluctantly. Her long hair was black. She wore a kind of close-fitting out-fit of a type that Jaz had never seen before, but that was very becoming on her. Whoever this girl is, Jaz thought, she's cer-tainly something special. Clearly, it would be wise to observe the couple closely.

Jaz saw that Simon was engaged (no, *entranced*) in deep conversation with the girl. As usual with Simon, she had to be discreet—let him flirt with other girls because this behavior seemed to be **innate** in him and thus practically **inevitable**. But be ready to move in to break things up if it became necessary.

Simon was, Jaz reflected, an **incorrigible** flirt. She put up with it because ... exactly why *did* she put up with it? she wondered. Ah, yes, because she knew very well that Simon was, in his own **inimitable** words, "irresistibly attractive to girls, couldn't help himself, and swore to have only **platonic** relationships with other young women."

This pledge was fine in principle, Jaz thought. And thus far, it seemed to have worked perfectly. Absolutely no evidence of infidelity had come to her attention. Simon's flirtations were completely innocent. He was, bless him, just a natural: Girls were drawn to him like bees to honey (or was it pollen? She always got confused about that image.) Women simply found Simon incredibly **virile** and exciting. And so did Jaz. *That's* why she put up with his flirtations.

She sighed: Yes, that was her Simon. And the thing was, his very openness—his **naiveté** almost—made him all the more endearing. He had a childlike quality that women loved. And he had this remarkable ability to establish a **rapport** with anyone. Once she had seen him **regale** a group of nuns with his stories. They had been **enthralled** by his tales, laughing like schoolgirls. Even the **staid** "Mom nun" (as Simon called her) had been beside herself with laughter.

Yes, Simon had an **uncanny** knack for making people feel happy.

*****

Right now, Simon's female companion certainly seemed happy enough. In fact, she seemed to be having such a great time that an internal alarm had started to sound somewhere deep in Jaz's mind. Maybe the girl was *too* happy. She seems almost **elated**, Jaz thought. As she continued her surveillance, sipping a frapuccino, Jaz became increasingly concerned. She slipped into a booth closer to the couple's. Simon was so involved in his conversation that he wouldn't notice anything outside his gaze, directed, laserlike, on the girl.

"So, what's your name?" Simon was saying.

"Xela." (*Xela*? thought Jaz.)

"Pretty name" said Simon. "Pretty exotic, too. What is it, **ethnic** or something?"

"Sort of," she replied. "So, do you have any roommates, Simon?" Xela asked.

Simon hesitated. Jaz waited to see what his response would be. Suddenly, the house band began playing a loud rock song. They were into their nightly gig. Jaz could no longer hear the conversation and realized that she wouldn't be able to hear any more for the rest of the evening. She saw that Simon must still be thinking about his response to the girl's question about who his roommate was, however, because he hadn't opened his mouth to reply.

Simon was, if truth be told, considering answering with something less than the entire truth. *This is tricky*, he was thinking. *I can't lie about Jaz, but then again, I don't have to be completely **veracious** either*. As Simon thought, he gazed into Xela's eyes. He felt that he was looking into the girl's soul, plumbing endless depths. A beautiful, **unsullied** soul. Who *is* this girl, Simon asked himself. He searched for a word to describe her; "**seraphic**" was the word he finally decided on. The statue of Artemis he had seen in the art museum came into his mind—noble and **sublime**, yet infinitely alluring—the **exemplar** of the feminine.

Xela's eyes narrowed so slightly that it was barely perceptible. But it was enough to jar Simon from his reverie. "Oh, sorry. I ... ."

The girl looked a little puzzled as she patiently waited for his reply. Simon gazed at Xela. Truly like an angel, Simon thought. He couldn't even tell this girl a fib, he decided.

"I live with some friends. A guy and a ... a girl."

Xela's expression showed a trace of amusement. "A girl?"

"Yeah, we're sort of ... ."

"Friends?"

"Yeah." Simon didn't really want to **elaborate,** but somehow he felt he should. He didn't feel at all coerced, just that any dissembling on his part would be perceived by this girl and somehow, gently but firmly, disapproved of.

"Yeah, well, this guy Axel is my close friend. And this girl Jasmine is ... uh ... my ... ."

It went against Simon's nature to tell a sublimely, angelically, **transcendentally** gorgeous girl who had shown even a **modicum** of interest in him that he had a steady girlfriend. But one more look into those eyes and the truth was out.

"She's my girlfriend."

1. **advent** N. arrival or coming
2. **entailed** V. caused or involved by necessity
3. **covertly** ADV. secretly; hidden
4. **innate** ADJ. inborn
5. **inevitable** ADJ. unavoidable
6. **incorrigible** ADJ. incapable of being corrected
7. **inimitable** ADJ. not able to be imitated
8. **platonic** ADJ. beyond physical desire (for example, spiritual)
9. **virile** ADJ. manly
10. **naiveté** N. the quality of being unsophisticated and simple like a child
11. **rapport** N. a harmonious emotional relationship
12. **regale** V. to entertain and delight
13. **enthralled** V. enchanted
14. **staid** ADJ. self-restrained
15. **uncanny** ADJ. mysterious; strange
16. **elated** ADJ. very happy; jubilant; in high spirits
17. **ethnic** ADJ. relating to cultures or races
18. **veracious** ADJ. truthful
19. **unsullied** ADJ. untarnished
20. **seraphic** ADJ. like an angel
21. **sublime** ADJ. exalted; uplifting
22. **exemplar** N. model to be imitated
23. **elaborate** V. to add details
24. **transcendentally** ADV. in a way beyond the ordinary; surpassingly
25. **modicum** N. limited quality

Simply Simon

Think you know the words? Then prove it! Choose the *best* word to fill in the blank in each of the sentences below.

covertly   inimitable   uncanny   ethnic

incorrigible   inevitable   unsullied   innate

elaborating   entails

1. Friendly governments must sometimes communicate with one another _____ to prevent enemies from learning classified information.

2. Leading a football team _____ a lot of hard work, but you know your effort is worth it when you hear the fans cheer.

3. I'm a/an _____ party animal; for me, a day isn't complete if I haven't met my buds and chilled out a little.

4. I asked my religion professor what her definition of a saint was; she said it's a person who is able to live in the world and remain _____ by it.

5. It is _____ that Jaz will find out if I flirt with another girl.

6. All of us should do all we can to promote understanding among the different _____ groups in our society.

7. Some athletes have a/an _____ style that works for them but can't be copied successfully by others.

8. Having _____ ability isn't much use unless you do something with it.

9. Dr. Chandler asked me to rewrite my last essay, _____ on my argument that globalization does far more good than bad.

10. Jaz has a/an _____ ability to tell whether I'm not telling the truth.

Making Sense

Indicate whether or not each of the words in **bold** makes sense in the sentence. If it makes sense, put Y (Yes); if it doesn't make sense, put N (No).

1. Astronomers believe that the **advent** of the universe will be the "big crunch," a process in which everything will contract into a tiny point. ___

2. These lines from *Hamlet* stress the importance of being **veracious**:

This above all: to thine own self be true

And it must follow, as the night the day,

Thou canst not then be false to any man. ___

3. Most people believe that marriage should be a purely **platonic** relationship between a man and a woman. ___

4. Professor Jones is an old-fashioned guy, but he's kind of cool; for example, I like how he frequently remarks, "If everyone behaved with just a **modicum** of decency toward his or her fellow human beings, the world would be such a better place." ___

5. Axel said he read that the one regret of the great Indian physicist Subramanyan Chandrasekher in later life was that his scientific work kept him so busy that he never had time to fulfill his dream of reading all of the **sublime** works of William Shakespeare. ___

6. The one time a scientist is likely to become really **elated** is when the theory that she has been working on for the last five years is disproved. ___

7. Our last pep rally was such a **staid** affair that the dean of students had to pass the word that we were way beyond what is allowed by the city ordinance on noise pollution. ___

8. The **virile** young woman was considered a model of femininity. ____

9. A standard character in soap operas is the crafty, scheming older woman who is full of **naiveté**. ____

10. I'm not the greatest singer in the world, but I can play some licks on the electric guitar; so, sometimes at a party some of my friends and I **regale** people with a few tunes. ____

Match It
Match each of the following words to its meaning.

1. rapport	a. enchanted
2. enthralled	b. model to be imitated
3. seraphic	c. arrival or coming
4. exemplar	d. truthful
5. transcendentally	e. harmonious emotional relationship
6. advent	f. unable to be imitated
7. elated	g. like an angel
8. veracious	h. in a way beyond the ordinary
9. inimitable	i. exalted; uplifting
10. sublime	j. very happy

Axel Speaks

Greetings! I believe that you are now ready for something more intellectual. Choose the *best* word to fill in the blank in each sentence.

1. Researchers are trying to determine whether aggression is a/an _____ or a learned behavior.

(A) incorrigible

(B) innate

(C) inevitable

(D) inadvertent

(E) unorthodox

2. Cupid is depicted in a variety of ways in Roman mythology— sometimes as a handsome, _____ young man, and at other times as the infant son of Venus.

(A) ethnic

(B) susceptible

(C) virile

(D) negligent

(E) insipid

3. A number of studies conducted by established researchers at major universities have reported good evidence for precognition, a phenomenon in which a person exhibits a/an _____ ability to predict the future.

(A) sublime

(B) uncanny

(C) platonic

(D) veracious

(E) macabre

4. Realizing that in working with complex equipment it is nearly _____ that some problems will arise, a sensible engineer always keeps Murphy's Law—"If something can go wrong, it will"—in the back of her mind.

(A) plausible

(B) inevitable

(C) inimitable

(D) interminable

(E) advantageous

5. Many theologians believe that, although logical arguments based on purpose and design* in the world can bolster a person's belief in God, such logical proofs are, ultimately, insufficient since God is _____, existing beyond human reason.

(A) multifarious

(B) prescient

(C) discreet

(D) transcendent

(E) seraphic

Answers on page 455.

And now, on with the story.

*Note: The argument from design says that God must exist because the universe exists.

Episode 19

An Inkling of Another Realm

Xela smiled, in the process **metamorphosing** from an angel into something like a goddess. Simon recalled how in art history class Professor Walters had been so enthusiastic in describing Renoir's **depiction** of girls and women. He thought he must have just been getting carried away, until Professor Walters had showed the class slides of Renoir's paintings. Simon had been stunned. Professor Walters said he believed that Renoir had portrayed the **quintessence** of femininity and of female beauty better than any other artist. Simon could only agree. And now, looking at Xela, all of those images flooded into his mind. Xela's beauty was all of them combined. Simon gazed at her. This girl combined the innocence of Renoir's girls and the knowing charm of his women. And yet Xela's beauty transcended even that; it was, as he had felt before, **untainted**—pure, noble, and sublime. Yes, she *must* be an angel, he thought, or even a goddess.

Simon sat in awe, **transfixed** by the **celestial** being before him. He felt that she was almost **luminous**. But, oddly, he felt no regret at a lost opportunity. In fact, he felt that somehow, inexplicably, the girl had known that he was already in love with someone else.

"So, you guys must be pretty good friends, I guess," Xela said.

"Yeah. We're pretty close. We do practically everything together. It's like each of us brings out the best in the others."

Xela was silent. Simon knew she wanted him to continue.

"You can probably tell," Simon said, "I'm not exactly the reclusive or ascetic type."

Xela smiled.

"I mean, I like to enjoy, to live; I'm not into **vicarious** experience. So, sometimes I'm a little **cavalier** about the, uhh ... academic side of things. **Serendipitously**..."

"Nice word," she said.

Simon continued. "Yeah. Well, Axel and Jasmine are, **fortuitously**, both eggheads. They're both always after knowledge."

"What kind of knowledge?"

"Anything. They love it all. And you know what I respect about them?"

"What?" Xela asked.

"They don't just want **inert** facts. They want the truth. They really want to find out."

"Find out what?"

"Well, why things are like they are. Why we're here, for example," Simon said. "I mean, why we exist."

Xela smiled. "Some pretty profound topics."

"Yeah, they're always discussing physics, **cosmology**, evolution, the place of consciousness in the universe. Stuff like that."

"Pretty **esoteric** areas. And what about you?"

"Well, I'm not really the enquiring, intellectual type. I don't go around looking for the truth all the time."

She looked at him. "Maybe, you do too, Simon, but in a different kind of way."

Simon looked back at Xela. It was the first time she had used his name. And the way she had said it made it sound to him that she had known him for **eons**.

"Maybe you're looking for a different *kind* of truth," she said.

Simon was silent. It was a rare occasion on which he did not have a humorous **riposte** ready.

179

"Maybe, Simon, your truth is special. Maybe, it's in here." As she said this, Xela reached her hand toward him and placed it on his chest, over his heart. Simon felt a thrill go through his body that he had never before experienced. He felt a purity that made him forget all **turbulence** in his soul. His world was, for one **ephemeral** moment, **transmogrified**. In that instant he glimpsed another realm of being.

Definitions

1. **inkling** N. hint
2. **metamorphose** V. to change; transform
3. **depiction** N. portrayal
4. **quintessence** N. purest and most concentrated essence of something; defining, essential quality of something (ADJ. quintessential)
5. **untainted** ADJ. not contaminated
6. **transfix** V. to make motionless by awe
7. **celestial** ADJ. heavenly; sublime
8. **luminous** ADJ. glowing; full of light
9. **vicarious** ADJ. enjoyed through imagined participation in another's experience
10. **cavalier** ADJ. showing offhand disregard
11. **serendipitously** ADV. occurring accidentally and bringing fortunate results
12. **fortuitously** ADV. occurring by chance
13. **inert** ADJ. unable to affect anything
14. **cosmology** N. theory of the origin and structure of the universe
15. **esoteric** ADJ. hard to understand; known only to a few
16. **eon** N. indefinitely long period of time
17. **riposte** N. quick reply; retort
18. **turbulence** N. unrest; agitation
19. **ephemeral** ADJ. short lived
20. **transmogrify** V. to change into a different form

Simply Simon

Think you know the words? Then prove it! Choose the *best* word to fill in the blank in each of the sentences below.

luminous   **turbulence**   **inkling**   **eons**

transfixed   **serendipity**   **metamorphose**

depictions   **untainted**   **cavalier**

1. Christopher Columbus probably had no _____ that the land he had discovered for Spain would, several hundred years later, become a great nation.

2. I don't think it's likely that Axel will _____ into a party animal any time soon.

3. In history class we compared various _____ of the same event to see how people's interpretations of events vary.

4. Because of modern communications, anthropologists are finding it increasingly difficult to find groups of people _____ by contact with other cultures.

5. The first time I saw Jaz I was _____ by her beauty.

6. Professors in this college do not accept a/an _____ attitude to learning on the part of students.

7. Several very important scientific discoveries, such as penicillin and X rays, were made as a result of _____.

8. The introductory geology course I took helped me to appreciate the _____ of time over which the earth underwent vast changes.

9. Jaz believes that meditation can lessen the _____ in a person's mind.

10. Axel says that astronomers determine how _____ a star is to help establish its distance from Earth.

Making Sense

Indicate whether or not each of the words in **bold** makes sense in the sentence. If it makes sense, put Y (Yes); if it doesn't make sense, put N (No).

1. Novelists often try to portray the **quintessence** of humanity in their works. ____

2. Even poets and philosophers must sometimes concern themselves with the ordinary **celestial** matters of everyday life. ____

3. Jaz and I were startled last week to see Dr. Larsen, the librarian, in a club dancing with a woman; apparently, he had been **transmogrified** into a party animal. ____

4. Adventurers are people who seem to need to live a **vicarious** life, always experiencing things as directly and immediately as possible. ____

5. Jaz is always ready with a clever **riposte** when I make a wisecrack. ____

6. Axel says that some subatomic particles are so **ephemeral** that they're only around for a tiny fraction of a second. ____

7. **Fortuitously**, the earth orbits the Sun in a fairly regular orbit in a temperature zone well suited to life. ____

8. To me it's a mystery how an organism that is **inert** becomes lifeless. ____

9. Historians believe that women as long ago as Cleopatra used **cosmology** to make themselves more attractive. ____

10. Professor Jones says that modern literary criticism is so **esoteric** that a graduate student in literature could easily spend more time trying to understand theories of literature than actual works of literature. ____

Match It

Match each of the following words to its meaning.

1. metamorphose
2. depiction
3. transfix
4. celestial
5. cavalier
6. fortuitously
7. inert
8. cosmology
9. esoteric
10. ephemeral

a. make motionless by awe
b. showing offhand disregard
c. theory of the origin and structure of the universe
d. transform
e. hard to understand
f. heavenly; sublime
g. short lived
h. portrayal
i. occurring by chance
j. unable to affect anything

Axel Speaks

Greetings! I believe that you are now ready for something more intellectual. Choose the *best* word to fill in the blank in each sentence.

1. Astronomers believe that quasars exist toward the fringes of the universe, as much as twelve billion light-years away; astoundingly, although they appear faint from Earth, they are as _____ as 1,000 galaxies.

(A) celestial

(B) exotic

(C) plentiful

(D) ephemeral

(E) luminous

2. The Greek philosopher Aristotle believed that in _____ experiencing the difficulties of another person, spectators at a play are purged of their own "pity and fear."

(A) vicariously

(B) serendipitously

(C) fortuitously

(D) sporadically

(E) obediently

3. Fruit flies are often used to study evolution in the laboratory because they reproduce very rapidly and because from the human point of view they are _____, being born and dying in a matter of days, allowing scientists to study many generations.

(A) untainted

(B) ephemeral

(C) esoteric

(D) inert

(E) uncertain

4. Robin Hood can be considered the _____ English folk hero, embodying the qualities of the resourceful member of the lower class in bringing justice to the oppressed and regularly frustrating the authorities.

(A) quintessential

(B) cavalier

(C) insipid

(D) vaunted

(E) aloof

5. In the United States, the internal combustion engine _____ the landscape, as roads were built for cars and people thus became free to live farther from their places of work, creating vast suburbs.

(A) transfixed

(B) assailed

(C) emulated

(D) transmogrified

(E) saturated

Answers on pages 455–456.

And now, on with the story.

Telepathy and UFOs

All of this **transpired** so quickly that Simon was hardly **cognizant** of it. The conversation in the outside world continued, though deep inside Simon something **fundamental** had changed.

"I think, Simon," Xela said, "that you make people happy, don't you? And I think you know more than you like people to know that you know."

He shrugged, but looked like a person whose deepest secrets had just been revealed—and didn't care one **iota.**

"So, what's Jaz like?" Xela asked.

"Oh, she's great. It's like she's **clairvoyant**. She seems to practically read my thoughts, my feelings. "

"You love her, don't you?" Xela said.

Simon looked surprised. "Yeah. I guess I do," he said.

"What does she study?" Xela asked. "Here," she added, gesturing to indicate the college.

"Oh, psych is her major, but as I said before, she's into *everything*—philosophy, religion, science, literature, mythology. Right now, she's helping out in Dr. Robinson's laboratory doing research on extrasensory perception. Now they're studying telepathy."

"Interesting. So has anything exciting turned up in their research?"

"Well, it's kind of **abstract**," Simon said. "There's all this statistical, mathematical stuff. Dr. Robinson says they have very interesting data, but they need more **corroborating** evidence before they can publish their conclusions. If there's any

spurious data, he wants to know about it. The subject is so **controversial**, he wants to be really careful. He doesn't want to be labeled a charlatan and lose his funding."

"Sometimes it takes courage for the truth to be revealed," Xela said.

"The truth? Do you think it's true? I mean, telepathy?"

Xela looked very serious.

"I mean the truth about anything, Simon. If there weren't people **altruistic** enough to sacrifice their personal interests for the **objective** truth, a species ... I mean, *the* species, couldn't advance."

"Like Galileo in the seventeenth century," Simon said. "He published his findings that confirmed the Copernican theory of the solar system—the theory that the planets revolve around the Sun—even though it **contravened** the **dogma** of the Church. His theory was condemned by the authorities and he was warned not to pursue the theory further, but he did anyway. I mean, he was quite aware of the fact that he would probably be tried by the Inquisition and **censured**. And he was."

"Yes, Galileo is an excellent example," Xela said. "Without the establishment of the Copernican theory, modern astronomy and space travel could not have developed."

"Yeah," Simon replied. "I guess it would be pretty hard to calculate the path of a probe to Mars if you thought Mars was revolving around the earth."

Xela laughed. "Yes, exactly," she said. "So, what does Jaz think about it? I mean about telepathy."

"She thinks the evidence for it is **irrefutable**. Right now, she's trying to build a case for her thesis that ESP is a **vestigial** ability that for some reason fell into disuse as mankind evolved. She thinks that maybe for language to evolve this method of communication had to be **suppressed**."

"So people—at least some people—could have ESP abilities that are **dormant**?" Xela asked.

"Yes. But Jaz says that there are some subjects that demonstrate consistent ESP ability," Simon answered.

"So it's possible that some people are still using it?"

"Yeah, I guess so."

"I was just wondering," Xela said. "Why do you think Jasmine is so interested in ESP **phenomena**?"

"Well, as I said, her interests are so eclectic," Simon said. "But maybe there is some sort of a **motif** to what she studies. I can't put my finger on it, but it seems like she's looking for something—a common denominator, I guess—in myths, religions, dreams, science ... many things. Even UFOs."

Definitions

1. **transpire** v. to occur
2. **cognizant** ADJ. aware
3. **fundamental** ADJ. forming an essential part of something; basic; central
4. **iota** N. very tiny amount
5. **clairvoyant** ADJ. able to perceive things outside the natural range of senses; psychic
6. **abstract** ADJ. complex
7. **corroborating** ADJ. confirming
8. **spurious** ADJ. false
9. **controversial** ADJ. causing considerable dispute
10. **altruistic** ADJ. unselfishly generous (N. altruism)
11. **objective** ADJ. unbiased
12. **contravene** v. to violate; contradict
13. **dogma** N. belief asserted on authority
14. **censure** v. to officially reprimand
15. **irrefutable** ADJ. impossible to disprove
16. **vestigial** ADJ. remaining as a remnant of something that previously existed
17. **suppress** v. to restrain
18. **dormant** ADJ. inactive
19. **phenomena** N. observable occurrences
20. **motif** N. dominant theme

Simply Simon

Think you know the words? Then prove it! Choose the *best* word to fill in the blank in each of the sentences below.

motif   irrefutable   objective   cognizant

vestigial   suppress   contravened   spurious

corroborated   dogma

1. I believe we should be _____ that there are many ways of looking at the world other than our own.

2. Jaz is waiting for the results of some psychology experiments she did with Professor Robinson to be _____ by a lab in Britain.

3. As a scientist gains experience, she becomes better at recognizing data that is _____ and therefore should not be considered in reaching a conclusion.

4. My literature teacher, Professor Jones, asked me what I thought the main _____ was in *The Great Gatsby*.

5. Scientists must be as _____ as they can in their analysis of data, but they can still be passionate in their interest in their subject.

6. When I came home with a speeding ticket Axel asked me if this meant that I had _____ the regulations governing the operation of motorized vehicles in our locality.

7. Jaz thinks that _____ arises mainly to meet a human need for certainty.

8. Scientists aim to find _____ evidence for their hypotheses; however, nature is often not so cooperative.

9. Many biologists believe that the pineal gland in primates is a/an _____ organ that used to be a functional *eye*.

10. Toward the end of a long lecture I sometimes have to _____ a yawn.

Making Sense

Indicate whether or not each of the words in **bold** makes sense in the sentence. If it makes sense, put Y (Yes); if it doesn't make sense, put N (No).

1. Physicists in the late nineteenth century thought that they had discovered the **fundamental** laws of nature; little did they know that even more basic laws could be formulated based on discoveries that were to be made in the early twentieth century such as General Relativity and Quantum Mechanics. ____

2. One of the greatest honors a lawyer can achieve is to be **censured** by the bar association in his or her state. ____

3. On a trip to Western Australia I learned that several species of flies are **dormant** in the summer but become inactive in the winter. ____

4. Jaz is doing some psychology research on the motivation for **altruistic** behavior, such as a person sacrificing his or her life for someone else. ____

5. Physicists attempt to summarize the complex **phenomena** of nature in a series of precise and elegant equations. ____

6. Since not one **iota** of evidence exists to prove the existence of UFOs, it's almost impossible to argue that they aren't real. ____

7. Sometimes Jaz gets hunches that turn out to be so accurate she seems almost **clairvoyant**. ____

8. I prefer difficult to grasp subjects to **abstract** ones such as philosophy and mathematics. ____

9. Some of the professors at our college are involved in **controversial** military research for the government. ___

10. After an organism **transpires** nothing is left of it except a pile of dust. ___

Match It

Match each of the following words to its meaning.

1. cognizant
2. fundamental
3. abstract
4. corroborating
5. spurious
6. objective
7. dogma
8. suppress
9. dormant
10. phenomena

a. restrain
b. confirming
c. inactive
d. aware
e. belief asserted on authority
f. observable occurrences
g. forming an essential part of something; central
h. false
i. complex
j. unbiased

Axel Speaks

Greetings! I believe that you are now ready for something more intellectual. Choose the *best* word to fill in the blank in each sentence.

1. In his essay "Civil Disobedience," Henry David Thoreau took the extreme step of arguing that if the conflict of individual conscience and law is grave, the individual has not only a moral right to _____ the law, but also a duty to accept the punishment for his actions.

(A) scrutinize

(B) reiterate

(C) deduce

(D) suppress

(E) contravene

2. Supernovas that are visible without the aid of telescopes have occurred rather infrequently in recorded human history; 1006, 1054, 1572, 1604, and 1987 are the only years of occurrence for which _____ historical evidence is available.

(A) unprecedented

(B) corroborating

(C) varied

(D) spurious

(E) cognizant

3. Hindus believe that all who have not attained enlightenment must work, but that this work should be performed from a/an _____ motive and offered to God.

(A) irrefutable

(B) vestigial

(C) clairvoyant

(D) altruistic

(E) controversial

4. The standard set by the United States Supreme Court to allow censorship of material deemed to be of critical importance to the national security of the nation is that there must exist a "Clear and present danger," not merely a hypothetical threat that is not based on one _____ of evidence.

(A) iota

(B) paragon

(C) dogma

(D) mélange

(E) motif

5. The philosopher Friedrich Nietzsche believed that all of humanity's stories, even religious _____ and scientific theories, are essentially myths, in that they all attempt to explain reality on the basis of limited information.

(A) truisms

(B) dogma

(C) phenomena

(D) maxims

(E) euphemisms

Answers on pages 456–457.

And now, on with the story.

Episode 21

Invitation to a Barbecue

"UFOs?" Xela laughed.

"Yeah, she gets pretty far out there sometimes," Simon said. "She takes some ribbing from a lot of her friends, but she's **indomitable** when she's pursuing what she thinks is the truth. One of her **precepts** is never to follow **conventional** thinking without a healthy dose of **skepticism**."

"She sounds like quite a remarkable young woman. Where did she get all these **diverse** interests?"

"Probably a lot of it came from her dad. He's an amazing guy. I guess Jasmine just admired him so much that she pursued many of his interests," Simon said.

"What kind of interests?"

"Oh, well, he's a philosophy professor," Simon said.

"You know those philosophers," Xela laughed.

"Anyway, his **expertise** is Indian philosophy," Simon said. "He's working on really **recondite** subjects like the place of mind in the universe. He's trying to relate some of the Indian philosophers to guys like Plato and Kant and modern scientific theories like relativity and evolution and fields like cognitive psychology. He's very interested in how mind interacts with the rest of the world, how what we think tends to actually *be* the reality we live in. It's like the paradigms Jaz is always talking about that each person, each culture, looks at the world in terms of."

"Oh, now that's very interesting," Xela said. "I've read some of your ... . I mean, *the* Indian philosophers, and I find them often to be profound thinkers, in some ways closer to the **ultimate** truth than those in the Western philosophic tradition."

Simon looked at Xela with a somewhat **bemused** expression. Once again he found himself wondering, who *is* this girl?

He continued. "So I guess Jaz got her interest in all this stuff from her father. She says some of the yogis exhibit remarkable **psychic** abilities. They seem to use not only telepathy, she says, but things like clairvoyance and precognition, or knowing about something before it happens."

"So, what's your view about all this?" Xela asked.

"I guess I'm kind of skeptical. To me, seeing is believing."

"And you haven't seen anything yet."

"Right." Simon said. "Anyway, Jaz wants to find out more about it—how it works and if it can be **substantiated** empirically. Her hypothesis is that these yogi guys have sort of tuned their minds so they can access some sort of other dimension. If the universe is fundamentally mind, then it might make sense that minds could do that. Jaz thinks that maybe they do this by temporarily **fusing** our spacetime with this other one."

"You mentioned UFOs before, didn't you?" Xela asked. "How does Jaz fit them into her grand theory of the universe?" She seemed amused.

"That's where the UFO business comes in," Simon replied. "She says if there are people here who can do this kind of stuff, it seems reasonable to suppose that there are other sorts of **sentient** beings who can do it too. So maybe UFOs are the physical glimpses we periodically get of some sort of exploration of our world by processes that are predominantly psychic."

"Interesting. So how about this Axel? What's he like?" Xela asked.

"He's the same as Jaz. He's into everything too. He's a math and physics guy, so he's really into **rationality**. But he knows a lot about just about everything."

"Sounds like you get a pretty good education just being around those two."

"Yeah," Simon said, "it's pretty cool. My best friend and my best girl. I guess we are a pretty good little team."

Xela laughed.

"You know," Simon said, "sometimes I think if an alien landed, those two would love nothing more than to hop on its ship and go for a long **odyssey** through space studying everything they could."

"Sounds pretty good to me. How about you? Would you like to travel into space?"

Simon thought about it.

Xela gazed at him, thinking how cute he looked when he crinkled up his face to think about something. He was so **candid.** And so handsome. Suddenly, she felt herself powerfully drawn to him. He was so strong, so masculine, and yet also so *feeling.* She felt giddy. It wasn't supposed to be like this, she thought. This was not in the plan. Slowly, Xela gained control of her feelings and assessed the situation.

Simon was still pondering his answer (in that inimitable charming way he had, Xela noted). No, he hadn't sensed her feelings for him, she felt sure. Or had he?

Simon's expression changed. Once again, Xela felt a touch of **vertigo**. That wonderful smile was on his face. It was a smile that said, "I know you like me a lot, but, hey, it's OK."

Xela took a deep breath.

"Hey. Are you OK?" Simon asked. "You seem a little ... ." He stopped, unable to find the word to describe how she looked.

"I was just thinking how lucky you three guys are," she said.

"Lucky?"

"Yes, to have each other."

"Yeah, I guess we are."

"So, what do you think you'd find out there in space? Other civilizations? Like on *Star Trek*?" She laughed.

"Probably. But maybe no Federation."

197

"Mmm. So what does Axel think?"

"About what?" Simon asked.

"About space, about life, everything."

Simon shook his head up and down, thinking. "Well," he said finally, "Axel is one complex guy. He's into so much that sometimes it's hard to know exactly what he actually thinks about anything. The thing about Axel is that everything must be rational—empirically **verifiable**, as he says."

Xela smiled. "Well, that's understandable. That's how he thinks, I guess."

"Jaz says that he's the kind of person whose orientation toward the world is almost entirely cognitive. His life seems to be **predicated** on the view that logic is the best way of understanding things."

Suddenly, looking at Xela, Simon had a **revelation**; maybe this odd, brilliant, wonderful girl was the one for Axel.

"You know, Xela, I was just thinking, maybe you'd like to meet Axel," he said. "Hey! Why don't you come over tonight? We're having a little barbecue, and after that some people are coming over."

"Why not?" Xela replied. "He sounds fascinating."

Definitions

1. **indomitable** ADJ. incapable of being overcome
2. **precept** N. rule governing conduct
3. **conventional** ADJ. customary; ordinary
4. **skepticism** N. doubting or questioning attitude
5. **diverse** ADJ. various
6. **expertise** N. specialized knowledge
7. **recondite** ADJ. profound
8. **ultimate** ADJ. final; not susceptible to further analysis
9. **bemused** ADJ. confused
10. **psychic** ADJ. related to extraordinary mental processes
11. **substantiate** V. to support with proof
12. **fuse** V. to combine into one

198

13. **sentient** ADJ. conscious; aware
14. **rationality** N. exercise of reason
15. **odyssey** N. long adventurous voyage
16. **candid** ADJ. without pretense or reserve; straight-forward
17. **vertigo** N. dizziness
18. **verifiable** ADJ. capable of being proven true
19. **predicate** V. to base on
20. **revelation** N. something revealed

Simply Simon

Think you know the words? Then prove it! Choose the *best* word to fill in the blank in each of the sentences below.

expertise   vertigo   rationality   diverse   verifiable

recondite   ultimate   candid   bemused   fuse

1. _____ is important, but I don't believe that it alone can give us all the answers to our questions.

2. Professor Jones, my literature professor, once joked that some literary criticism has become so _____ that he'll have to go back to college himself pretty soon so that he can understand it.

3. Historians need _____ in a number of fields of knowledge.

4. I wonder what the world would be like if people were by nature incapable of being anything less than _____ about their feelings.

5. The further back in history you go, the harder it is to find _____ events.

6. Jaz said that if she could somehow _____ Axel's brains with my brawn she'd have the perfect man.

7. My intellectual interests have become far more _____ over the last few years; I read not only about politics and history but also about many other areas of knowledge.

8. According to astronomers, the _____ fate of the universe will be a contraction into a tiny point.

9. No matter how many times it's explained to me, I'm still _____ by the idea of time and space contracting into a little area billions of years from now.

10. Axel sometimes suffers from _____ when he's out in public, so he tends to stay at home.

Making Sense

Indicate whether or not each of the words in **bold** makes sense in the sentence. If it makes sense, put Y (Yes); if it doesn't make sense, put N (No).

1. I am so **indomitable** in my effort to improve in math that I fall asleep within minutes when Axel or Jaz tries to explain such concepts as "function of functions" and "set of sets" to me. ____

2. The **precepts** of democracy are fairly easy to state but very difficult to put into practice. ____

3. **Conventional** science is interested mainly in studying the mystical and the irrational. ____

4. **Skepticism** is an attitude that makes a person believe that everything in the world is exactly as it first appears and that nothing should be questioned. ____

5. Sometimes the longest journey a person makes is a spiritual **odyssey** through his or her own mind and soul. ____

6. The Theory of Evolution has been so well **substantiated** that there are hardly any respectable biologists who still believe it. ____

7. No **revelation** is complete without great music and tasty food. ___

8. Science is **predicated** on the assumption that the world is knowable through human inquiry. ____

9. Sometimes Jaz and I have fun trying to imagine what kinds of cultures and beliefs other **sentient** creatures in the universe might have. ____

10. Two notable people who were very interested in **psychic** research were Arthur Conan Doyle, the author of the Sherlock Holmes stories, and Harry Houdini, the magician. ____

Match It

Match each of the following words to its meaning.

1. precept	a. specialized knowledge
2. expertise	b. related to extraordinary mental processes
3. recondite	c. something revealed
4. ultimate	d. long adventurous voyage
5. psychic	e. capable of being proven true
6. substantiate	f. final
7. odyssey	g. support with proof
8. candid	h. rule governing conduct
9. verifiable	i. profound
10. revelation	j. without pretense or reserve

Axel Speaks

Greetings! I believe that you are now ready for something more intellectual. Choose the *best* word to fill in the blank in each sentence.

1. One of the central principles on which the American system of government is _____ is encapsulated neatly in Lord Acton's oft-quoted saying, "Power corrupts; absolute power tends to corrupt absolutely."

(A) conjured

(B) embroiled

(C) substantiated

(D) isolated

(E) predicated

2. Support for the theory that the universe is inhabited by _____ life in addition to that on Earth was recently found when astronomers discovered planetary systems in other solar systems; this is an important finding because it is difficult to imagine intelligent life existing outside of planets.

(A) sentient

(B) verifiable

(C) recondite

(D) indomitable

(E) settled

3. When beautiful paintings by early human beings of 20,000 years ago were discovered in France recently, some art critics expressed _____ that art of such power could have been produced by primitive people.

(A) vertigo

(B) precepts

(C) skepticism

(D) platitudes

(E) machinations

4. Combatants in guerilla warfare often resort to tactics such as kidnapping, which are unacceptable in modern _____ warfare.

(A) conventional

(B) sophisticated

(C) rational

(D) candid

(E) unorthodox

5. Many songs of praise were sung to the _____
spirit of the American pioneers as they moved westward, set-
tling the vast continent of North America.

(A) ultimate

(B) bemused

(C) candid

(D) indomitable

(E) reclusive

Answers on page 457.

And now, on with the story.

Axel's Song

Well, I'm riding towards the shore,
Gonna meet the one I love,
And we'll watch the golden sun,
And we'll feel the golden rays
Of the pale moon on the waves

"What a beautiful voice! So **serene** and **ethereal**." Xela said. "Who is that singing?"

Simon and Xela were walking across the lawn toward Simon's house. Xela had just gotten out of a taxi and Simon had met her at the gate. It was dark except for the light from the stars and from the windows of the house.

"That's my roommate, Axel," Simon answered. They stopped and listened. An acoustic guitar played the melody.

When we get there we'll feel right
As we turn to see the light,
Far away we hear the sound,
And we know we're nowhere near it,
But we'll try a little for it

"Amazing, huh?" Simon said. "I told you, he's quite a guy."

"There's something about that tune. It's so **evocative**. You know, I think I've heard it, but it's **elusive.** I reach for it, then it's gone." Xela said.

"Sounds like me trying to remember some **abstruse** mathematical theorem."

Xela laughed.

"But I know what you mean," Simon said. "His music has that effect on everybody. I don't know. It's like when you listen, you know he's written the song just for you. And everybody gets something different out of it—something that sort of speaks right to the heart. Everyone **construes** the words differently."

Xela looked puzzled. "Isn't that how all art works?" she asked.

"Well, I'm not a Lit or a Music major or anything, but I know there's a work of art, and then there's something beyond."

"Beyond the aesthetic?"

"Yes. With Axel, it's beyond just beauty. I mean, it's beautiful, but also ... ."

"True?"

"Yes. That's what I'm trying to say."

"So, what are the songs about?"

"Well, they're not really **ballads**. There's no narrative really. They're just so **lyrical**, they make you feel the most amazing things. But, you know, come to think of it, I can't really remember very many specifics. It's kind of **nebulous**. They give you intimations, a suggestion, a vision, that there's something *more*, something better ... more noble ... out there." He gestured toward the sky. Then he looked at Xela and added, practically in a whisper, "And here, too."

Xela was quiet, waiting to hear if Simon was going to say anymore.

He shrugged his shoulders. "I'm out of my depth," he said. "I'm a quarterback, not a critic or a poet, remember?"

She laughed. Simon thought that he had never heard a kinder laugh in his life.

"Simon, I thought you said Axel was"—she smiled—"a '100 percent cognitive dude'. If that's true, then why ...?"

She let him **infer** what the rest of her question was. Simon looked at the ground, **ruminating**, listening to another tune coming out of Axel's room into the night.

Out on the ocean
Trying to find
All things concerning
Peace of mind
In the music,
Oh, the music,
Cascading down
Through every soul

"Yeah," he said. "I know. It's kind of **paradoxical**. He's a complex guy. But what do you think?"

"Of the song?"

"Yes."

"It's incredible. It's kind of **doleful**, and yet at the same time it suggests that there is some sort of ultimate meaning to life, that there are eternal **verities** in the universe. And it's the most **dulcet**, soothing music I have ever heard. It is just so beautiful."

Simon noticed tears on Xela's cheeks.

"See, I told you," he said softly. "It's like he's another person when he's got that guitar and he's singing. Pure emotion. This incredible sensitivity." Simon paused and looked up. Hundreds of stars filled the sky.

"You know, Xela, sometimes I feel that when he's singing like this, he's gone," he said, pointing at the stars. "That he, or maybe his spirit, is out there searching for something."

"Like what?" she asked.

"Something he's lost. Happiness. His real home, maybe."

Xela saw that Simon was crying softly. She gently squeezed his arm. "It's all right," she said.

"Hey, sorry," Simon said. His voice was **tremulous**. "I just get a little choked up about the guy. He's great, but sometimes I just feel he's kind of sad, that he's really lonely, even with me and Jaz."

"I guess everyone is lonely. A little bit."

207

"Yeah," Simon said. "You know, he only plays when he thinks no one's around, or they're too busy doing something else to notice. Then sometimes he sits out on that balcony outside his room and plays and sings so softly you can hardly hear it. You have to listen really hard."

They listened again.

This dream leaves me peaceful
I lie inside a sleep
Sat out by the ocean
Under starlit skies

A single tone swept out of the sea
A late and lovely reckoning
The arrival of the real sound
Through the icy wilderness

How can I sing it—except like this?
Fill a hollow shell with something sweet as bliss

The song was different now. Less **melancholy**. As though the singer had felt an intimation of what he had been searching for.

The energy of peace is a channel
The story's in a crystal
The bursting universe is alive
In a brown cedar box

In the lofty old boughs
Supported above I see your eyes
And I know that they're my own
Moist gems blowin' back

"You know, Xela," Simon said. "I've just met you, yet I feel that I've known you forever."

"I like you a lot, Simon," she said.

208

"Xela," he said. "I wonder."

"What?"

He pointed to the sky, toward Jupiter, which was shining brightly. "I wonder if maybe you're from up there."

She laughed. Her eyes twinkled in the starlight.

"Where?" Xela asked.

Simon pointed to a constellation.

"Oh, the Orion constellation," Xela said. "Yes, I'm from Orion. And I'm on a mission to abduct you. Let me **mesmerize** you first," she said. And then she laughed.

"Hey, what law **stipulates** that aliens can't be sublimely beautiful?" Simon said. "It would be a great **ruse**, you know."

Xela laughed, but seemed more serious now.

Softly, Simon said, "Or maybe you're an angel."

Definitions

1. **serene** ADJ. calm; peaceful
2. **ethereal** ADJ. highly refined; spiritual
3. **evocative** ADJ. calling forth ideas or feelings
4. **elusive** ADJ. hard to grasp
5. **abstruse** ADJ. difficult to comprehend
6. **construe** V. to interpret
7. **ballad** N. narrative poem intended to be sung
8. **lyrical** ADJ. expressing feeling or emotion in an affecting manner
9. **nebulous** ADJ. vague
10. **infer** V. to conclude; deduce
11. **ruminate** V. to reflect upon; contemplate
12. **paradoxical** ADJ. contradictory; incongruous
13. **doleful** ADJ. sad; mournful
14. **verity** N. belief viewed as true and enduring
15. **dulcet** ADJ. pleasant sounding
16. **tremulous** ADJ. vibrating; quivering
17. **melancholy** ADJ. sad; tending to promote sadness or gloom

209

18. **mesmerize** v. to hypnotize
19. **stipulate** v. to specify as an essential condition
20. **ruse** N. trick; stratagem

Simply Simon

Think you know the words? Then prove it! Choose the *best* word to fill in the blank in each of the sentences below.

ballad   ruses   doleful   melancholy   tremulous

lyrical   dulcet   mesmerized   paradoxical   infer

1. Jaz and I are always coming up with _____ to trick Axel into meeting girls.

2. On long drives on the freeway at night it's easy to become _____ by the repetitive sights and sounds.

3. My favorite _____ is "The Lonesome Death of Hattie Carroll" by Bob Dylan, which tells the moving story of a black cleaning woman killed by a rich white man.

4. Many famous people—for example, Winston Churchill, Samuel Johnson, and Samuel Taylor Coleridge—had periods of their lives during which they were _____.

5. Sometimes I think it's kind of _____ that despite all their comforts, people in the modern Western world are in some ways less happy than they were before they had such luxuries.

6. On walks through the woods I love to listen to the _____ sound of the wind through the trees.

7. Jaz was _____ after she put the phone down; her father had just told her that her grandmother had just passed away.

8. Jaz says the poems of John Keats are the most deeply _____ works of literature she has ever read.

9. I learned in creative writing class that a skillful writer doesn't tell his readers everything; he allows them to _____ certain things for themselves.

10. In some cultures a funeral is not a/an _____ occasion but a joyous one, celebrating the person's passage into a new state of being.

Making Sense

Indicate whether or not each of the words in **bold** makes sense in the sentence. If it makes sense, put Y (Yes); if it doesn't make sense, put N (No).

1. Sometimes I love to kick back and relax to the **serene** sounds of a really loud heavy metal band. ___

2. Axel strongly supports a manned mission to Mars to examine the **verities** that astronomers believe line the surface of that planet. ___

3. For me, the fact that people often find the music of cultures other than their own to be **evocative** suggests that music is a sort of universal human language. ___

4. I find the meaning of complex poetry to be **elusive**. ___

5. A guy who wants to roll through college without taxing his brain too much should look for courses dealing with **abstruse** subjects that don't require an understanding of a lot of complex concepts. ___

6. Bertrand Russell is such a **nebulous** writer that every point he makes is related to all of his other points, so that his arguments are perfectly clear. ___

7. My college **stipulates** that students must take at least one course dealing with a non-Western culture. ___

8. The discovery of intelligent life elsewhere in the universe would give humanity a lot to **ruminate** about. ___

9. I was so **construed** by the symbolism in T. S. Eliot's poetry that I couldn't understand it. ___

10. Jaz and I love to listen to recordings of the **ethereal** sounds of Javanese gamelan orchestras; it transports us to another world of experience. ___

Match It

Match each of the following words to its meaning.

1. serene	a. belief viewed as true and enduring
2. ethereal	b. vague
3. elusive	c. difficult to comprehend
4. nebulous	d. spiritual; highly refined
5. ruminate	e. sad
6. paradoxical	f. specify as an essential condition
7. verity	g. calm; peaceful
8. melancholy	h. hard to grasp
9. stipulate	i. reflect upon
10. abstruse	j. contradictory

Axel Speaks

Greetings! I believe that you are now ready for something more intellectual. Choose the *best* word to fill in the blank in each sentence.

1. Along with the mushroom cloud signifying the atomic bomb, the double helix is one of the most _____ images of our times, calling to mind the complex workings of DNA.

(A) doleful

(B) serene

(C) evocative

(D) dulcet

(E) melancholy

2. A problem faced by soldiers in modern warfare is that they are frequently engaged in "total war"—that is, war between entire societies—in which the distinction between combatants and noncombatants is _____, since every productive member of the enemy's society contributes, directly or indirectly, to the war effort.

(A) pedestrian

(B) unorthodox

(C) intimate

(D) ethereal

(E) nebulous

3. The nineteenth-century Austrian botanist Gregor Mendel was able by logic and experiment, and with no knowledge of the biochemical mechanism of genetics, to _____ the fundamental laws of heredity.

(A) infer

(B) stipulate

(C) revise

(D) suspend

(E) ruminate

4. The _____ nature of mystical experience was expressed by Chinese sage, Lao Tsu: "Those who know do not speak; those who speak do not know."

(A) melancholy

(B) paradoxical

(C) common

(D) redeeming

(E) tremulous

5. The search for the _____ fundamental particle is the holy grail* of particle physics.

(A) lyrical

(B) impeccable

(C) elusive

(D) clandestine

(E) ubiquitous

Answers on page 458.

And now, on with the story.

* A "holy grail" is something greatly sought after.

The Girl for Axel?

Xela was silent. Simon sensed that she had lost just a little bit of her serenity. Though it was so subtle he could barely discern it, she seemed **pensive**. He felt that she had reached a decision about something important and was now going to act. What it was that she had decided, Simon had no idea.

"Well," she said finally, "this angel had better go inside and warm up or she'll freeze her wings."

She didn't laugh. They walked toward the house in silence.

By the time they got there, the music had stopped. "Axel must have heard us coming in, so he stopped playing," Simon explained. "Welcome to my humble **domicile**."

"Hey, not very humble," Xela said, laughing. She glanced around the room. It was comfortably, if eclectically, decorated with **artifacts** from many cultures. Thai **amulets**, Javanese ikats, and Japanese art scrolls ["makimono"— remember?] hung on the walls. Burmese woodcarvings, African masks, and statues of numerous Hindu deities lined the shelves of old teak bookcases. Peruvian blankets covered the sofa and chairs. Books were strewn about on tables and on the floor. Looking at several of them, Xela saw that they were on a large number of subjects, from the most arcane to the most **prosaic**. Books on General Relativity, **linguistics**, and **mysticism** mingled with books on plumbing, cooking, and carpentry. **Conspicuously** displayed in a case were Simon's football trophies. Xela walked to the display case and looked at them.

"It looks like you're one of the best at your chosen sports endeavor," she said.

Simon gave her a puzzled look. He had noticed that sometimes she used some pretty peculiar **diction**.

"Chosen sports endeavor?" he repeated.

"I mean, the male mock battle ritual in which you engage. I don't know much about such matters."

"Oh, you mean *football*," Simon said, laughing. "Hey, that's OK. A lot of girls—even some guys—don't follow sports. You know, this might sound funny coming from me, but I think too much is made of sports sometimes. Like football. I enjoy it, it's great, but it's just a game. It's not Shakespeare or Bach."

"No. But everything has its place," Xela said.

"Yeah, I guess. Hey, you look cold. I'll get you something warm. Hot chocolate?"

"Great," she replied. Xela waited for Simon to make her drink. She walked around the room, examining some of the many pieces of art. She looked closely at a painting of the Hindu god Krishna and his **retinue** of female devotees, the gopis. It was signed, "To my dearest Simon, from Jaz." Then she noticed some photograph albums lying on the floor and sat down on the rug next to them. She picked up one of the albums and began to look through it.

Several minutes later Simon returned with a mug of hot chocolate and handed it to Xela.

"Thanks," she said.

"Hey, that's Jaz coming back already. I hear her car."

"Wonderful," Xela said. "I can't wait to meet her."

***

A few moments later Jaz walked through the doorway.

"Hi, Jaz," Simon said.

"Hi!" Jaz replied. "I told you I'd be right back, didn't I?" She hugged Simon. "See, you *could* live without me for an hour," she said.

As she held him, Jaz had a feeling that there was some-one else in the room besides the two of them. Neither she nor Simon, as far as she knew, had expected anybody to arrive for the barbecue for several hours. She looked to her left. Sitting quietly on the floor in a corner of the room was a girl. A very pretty girl. In fact, an amazingly alluring girl, just sitting **demurely**, looking through photograph albums. Jaz stared at her. She looks sort of familiar, Jaz thought.

The girl lifted her head and smiled.

It was that incredible girl that Simon had been talking to so intimately in Pete's Place. Now here she was, sitting in *her* living room. This, Jaz thought, is *crazy*.

Hellooooo, she thought. Earth to Simon, Earth calling Simon. It's one thing to chat with a girl when you don't think I'm around, but it's a totally different scene to bring that girl to your house. I suppose next he'll introduce me to her.

"Jaz, this is Xela," Simon said **nonchalantly**, gesturing to Xela.

"Hi," Jaz said weakly.

Xela smiled so sweetly at her that Jaz was **disarmed**—almost.

"Simon," she said, "Why don't you come and help me light the charcoal for the barbecue? We'd better get it started." She looked at Xela. "Then we can socialize."

"OK," Simon said. "We'll be back in a minute, Xela."

"That's OK," Xela said. "Take your time. I'll just look around at all your interesting artifacts."

Simon and Jaz walked out to the patio.

"Simon, who is that girl?" Jaz asked.

Simon looked genuinely puzzled. "Huh?" he said. "I just introduced you. She's Xela."

"Yes, but ... ."

Simon gave Jaz an uncomprehending look. Then he saw what she was getting at. "Hey, you don't think ....? I always bring new people home, and she's the most amazing person."

Jaz relaxed a little bit. She knew Simon so well that she could tell instantly if he were dissembling, and clearly he wasn't. But that girl—whoa! She looked like the dream of every man on the planet **coalesced** into one package. She even took Jaz's breath away, and Jaz was not easily impressed by the appearance of other members of her gender.

"So, why is she so amazing?" Jaz asked.

"You'll see. Awesome, too," he teased.

"Yeah, I can see that," Jaz **retorted**. "But who is she? I mean, I've never seen her around campus or anything. Between us, we know practically everyone. Is she a student here?"

Simon looked puzzled. It was a rare occasion on which he didn't have a quick answer to a query that concerned people—his **forte.**

He pondered. "You know, she didn't say. We had the most fascinating discussion. It's kind of strange. I asked her all this stuff and she answered, but I can't seem to recall anything **tangible.**"

"Maybe you were so enthralled by her that your mind went blank. I've seen it happen very frequently with you, you know. Simon ... pretty girl .... vacant stare .... total blanksville," Jaz said.

"Very funny."

"Where did you meet her, anyway?" Jaz asked.

"Pete's Place."

Well, thought Jaz, he certainly isn't trying to cover anything up. I mean, I was *there*. Simon was, she knew, fundamentally incapable of **duplicity**. But that *girl*! She was like a princess out of a fairy tale. What man wouldn't find her beguiling?

Simon could tell by the look on Jaz's face that she was still a little **dubious** about the nature of his interest in Xela. "Jaz," he said, "come on, Xela's great, but I *really* don't mean like that."

"Really? She certainly is some girl," Jaz said.

"Yeah. But you know, a guy knows the girl for him." Simon kissed her.

As she held Simon, Jaz sensed that Simon was different in some subtle way. He was still the same Simon, but it was

219

like some additional dimension had been added to his personality.

"You know," Jaz said, "you seem a little different tonight, Simon. I can't put my finger on it, but ... ."

"Maybe it's meeting Xela," he said.

Jaz punched him hard on the shoulder.

"Ouch!" he said, "that really hurt."

"You dumb hunk," she said.

"Anyway, I got one of my famous flashes," Simon said.

"Oh, boy," Jaz said, "one of your **epiphanies**, huh?"

"Xela and I were listening to Axel's music, and I was looking at her and—Wham! It hit me. What if ... ."

Jaz was very quick on the deductive uptake. "What if we introduce Axel to Xela?" she practically shouted. And she knew, suddenly, that Simon was right. This strange, beautiful girl was the person that they had been seeking for Axel for so long.

They hugged each other happily. It was a moment that they would treasure for the rest of their lives.

"Hey," Jaz said, "you'd better get this charcoal lit. I'll go inside and talk to Xela."

Definitions

1. **pensive** ADJ. deeply thoughtful; thoughtful with a hint of sadness
2. **domicile** N. home
3. **artifact** N. item made by human craft
4. **amulet** N. ornament worn as a charm against evil spirits
5. **prosaic** ADJ. commonplace
6. **linguistics** N. study of language
7. **mysticism** N. spiritual practice seeking direct union with ultimate reality or God
8. **conspicuously** ADV. very noticeably
9. **diction** N. choice of words
10. **retinue** N. attendants

11. **demurely** ADV. in a reserved and modest manner
12. **nonchalantly** ADV. in a carefree and casual manner
13. **disarm** V. to overcome or allay suspicion; win the confidence of
14. **coalesce** V. to combine
15. **retort** V. to reply (especially in a quick, direct manner)
16. **forte** N. strong point or special talent
17. **tangible** ADJ. real; concrete
18. **duplicity** N. deception; dishonesty
19. **dubious** ADJ. doubtful
20. **epiphany** N. comprehension of reality through a sudden intuitive realization

Simply Simon

Think you know the words? Then prove it! Choose the *best* word to fill in the blank in each of the sentences below.

pensive   prosaic   conspicuously   demurely

duplicity   artifacts   epiphany   mysticism

retinue   disarms

1. Many of Axel's songs are _____, reflecting on serious themes such as the meaning of life.

2. Jaz says that a surprisingly large number of people have a/an _____ that totally transforms their view of reality.

3. Last summer, Jaz, Axel, and I went to the British Museum in London to see its amazing collection of _____ from all over the world.

4. One of Jaz's favorite books is William James' *The Varieties of Religious Experience*, which discusses _____ as well as other types of religious experience.

5. I've found that what is _____ to one person might be a source of wonderment to another.

6. Incidents of _____ are extremely rare in science, but cases have occurred in which researchers have gone so far as to deliberately tamper with their results to make them seem more significant.

7. Jaz sometimes _____ her opponents in a debate by saying something nice about them.

8. Professor James has a/an _____ of students who help him in his research.

9. In most cultures females are supposed to behave more _____ than males.

10. Jaz is so proud of my accomplishments in sports that she displays all of my trophies _____.

Making Sense

Indicate whether or not each of the words in **bold** makes sense in the sentence. If it makes sense, put Y (Yes); if it doesn't make sense, put N (No).

1. A person's **diction** is determined not only by what she wants to say but also by the habits of speech she has acquired. ____

2. Recently, I **nonchalantly** mentioned to Jaz that my father, who happens to be pretty wealthy, had agreed to donate $100,000 to our college's fund to help the poor children of India. ____

3. Scientists use **amulets** to build a rigorous and logical picture of the world. ____

4. Astronomers study how the universe, as it expanded, **coalesced** into large structures such as galaxies and supergalaxies. ____

5. My marks in College Mathematics—"F, F, D"—clearly indicate that my **forte** is higher mathematics. ____

6. Jaz wants to build **domiciles** for homeless children in India with the money donated by my father. ____

7. Quite a few of the scientists working on the Manhattan Project to build the first atomic bomb were **dubious** about the morality of playing a part in creating such a weapon; however, many of them were attracted by what the director of the project, Dr. S. Robert Oppenheimer, called the "sweetness" of the science. ____

8. **Linguistics** gives us deep insights into the nature of the physical world. ____

9. I can't understand how the physical world seems **tangible** when, according to physics, space is mostly empty. ____

10. Jaz basically believes that people should be nonviolent, so, when I asked her what people in a country should do if it were being invaded, she said "Pray." I **retorted**, "They'd better pray pretty hard." ____

Match It

Match each of the following words to its meaning.

1. pensive	a. choice of words
2. artifact	b. item made by human craft
3. prosaic	c. deeply thoughtful
4. mysticism	d. concrete
5. diction	e. strong point
6. nonchalantly	f. commonplace
7. forte	g. deception; dishonesty
8. tangible	h. doubtful
9. duplicity	i. in a carefree and casual manner
10. dubious	j. spiritual practice seeking union with God

Axel Speaks

Greetings! I believe that you are now ready for something more intellectual. Choose the *best* word to fill in the blank in each sentence.

1. Research on language acquisition has led many experts in the field of _____ to conclude that, although language ability is inborn, a child must be exposed to language and given ample opportunities to use it in order to unfold his or her abilities.

(A) linguistics

(B) mysticism

(C) duplicity

(D) diction

(E) ornithology

2. After the Big Bang, which occurred 12 to 15 billion years ago, the universe consisted of little except hydrogen and some helium, but after approximately 100 million years stars began to _____ out of this hydrogen.

(A) retort

(B) coerce

(C) engender

(D) coalesce

(E) replicate

3. If we consider not income but _____ assets, the gap in wealth between the rich and the poor in the United States is more spectacular than if we compare income: In 1973, for example, the poorer 50 percent of the population held only one percent of all wealth (property, stocks, bonds, savings, and so on).

(A) conspicuous

(B) tangible

(C) mundane

(D) empirical

(E) dubious

4. Fortunately for life on Earth, the Sun is a rather _____ star that is approximately halfway through its life, conserving its hydrogen quite well; this means that our planet should be habitable for about five billion more years.

(A) pensive

(B) prosaic

(C) demure

(D) sentient

(E) melancholy

5. In Arthurian legend it is believed that Camelot—with King Arthur and his _____—will rise like a phoenix, returning from Avalon to rule once more.

(A) epiphany

(B) protagonists

(C) retinue

(D) caricature

(E) pundits

Answers on pages 458–459.

And now, on with the story.

Episode 24

Axel's Origins

Xela looked up when Jaz came back into the room.

"Sorry we took so long. We had trouble getting the charcoal going," Jaz said. "Simon's got it going now, but he wants to monitor it. He's pretty **fastidious** when it comes to his barbecue. He's a pretty heavy-duty carnivore."

Xela laughed. "That's fine," she said. "I was just looking through your photograph albums. I hope you don't mind."

"No, of course not," Jaz said. She sat down on the rug beside Xela.

"Who is this?" Xela asked, pointing to a photograph in the album.

"That's Axel," Jaz replied. "As a baby, obviously," she added. "Simon mentioned Axel to you, I guess?"

"Yes." Xela replied. "He must be very close to Simon."

"Oh, they're practically inseparable, but they always let me tag along with them."

Xela laughed. Such a kind laugh, Jaz thought. Such a wonderful person. And suddenly, she knew for certain that wherever this wonderful, gentle creature had come from, she was here for Axel.

"When was that picture taken?" Xela asked.

"It's strange," Jaz replied. "It's the only childhood picture he has."

Xela was silent.

Jaz sensed that Xela had become pensive. "You know," she continued, "it's quite a story. Apparently he was abandoned at a very young age."

"How sad," Xela said.

Jaz looked at Xela. I have never seen, she thought, such a look of compassion in my life. It's an **amalgam** of a mother's tender love and the love of a man and woman. There was also something in it of a man's strong, protective love.

"No one knows where he was born," Jaz continued. "He says he remembers that they thought for a long time that he wasn't normal. Remember, he had hardly been socialized at all. But within a few months he had **assimilated** what he needed to know to function quite well. And he was the most amazingly **precocious** child. He was **proficient** in calculus at seven. By the time he was ten he seemed to know just about everything. He was a **prodigy**. He just amazed people with his erudition."

"I bet he did," Xela said.

"Soon he was doing college level courses," Jaz said. "Then it was graduate level stuff. He was clearly a genius. He began to make significant contributions to fields as diverse as mathematics, molecular biology, psychology, and art history."

"So, how did you two meet Axel?" Xela asked.

"Let's back up a little first. Simon's parents were driving along a country road one night. They were on a camping trip. On Route 13 they saw this little boy by the road. He looked like he was about five years old. Naturally, they stopped and asked him where he was going, and if he was all right. And, you know, all he said was, 'I need a home.' He could barely speak, Simon's father said. That's all he kept saying: 'I need a home.' It must have been so sad."

There were tears in Xela's eyes.

"Anyway, Simon's parents called the police—and this is really odd—nothing was ever found out about him."

"Nothing?" Xela repeated.

"No. Simon's parents are wonderful people. They had only Simon, so they decided to adopt Axel. Axel learned very quickly and in most ways he fit in fine. But in one area he had some difficulty. You see, Axel has always been—I don't think

228

he would mind me saying this to you—well, he's always been pretty reclusive."

Xela looked at Jaz as though she wanted her to continue.

"Axel's social skills are still a little **rudimentary**."

"I heard," Xela said, and laughed.

"But he's a *really* great guy." Jaz realized that she had said this more emphatically than she had perhaps intended to. Xela smiled.

"He's unique. He's very caring. In fact, he's always ready to help people. If anyone needs help with their work—even the professors, if they're not too proud—they come to Axel for help."

"So, he was raised with Simon?" Xela asked.

"Yes. And they've been close ever since," Jaz said. "Simon's sort of like his big brother, I guess. He watches over him and kind of helps him out with mundane things—food, clothing, all that—the **minutia** of everyday life."

Xela was quiet. She seemed to be pondering something. "You've been like a mother to Axel, haven't you, Jaz?" Xela asked.

Looking at Xela, Jaz felt a nearly overpowering feeling of love and appreciation from her. "Well, yes," Jaz replied. "I guess sort of. I mean, he's like Simon's brother."

"Yes, I can see that," Xela said. "So, I gather that Axel isn't attached to anyone?" She had just the faintest trace of a smile on her face.

"No," Jaz replied. "He most certainly does *not* have a girlfriend."

Simon walked into the room. Jaz sighed, remembering the debacle in the art museum. Yet another potential girl-friend for Axel scared off, she thought. Christine hadn't been seen since that night.

"Simon," Xela said, "Jaz just told me the saga of Axel. I'm curious. How did you and Jaz meet?"

"I'll let Jaz tell you that story," Simon said. "In fact, I have to go out and check on a few other things for the bar-becue. You two can get to know each other some more."

"I'm afraid it's another story that's a bit weird," Jaz said. "But I think we'd better save that one for later. All of these heavy-duty professors are coming over tonight and I want to have everything ready."

"I'm looking forward to tonight. I really appreciate your inviting me, you know, Jaz," Xela said.

"Hey, we're happy to have you. Anyway, any friend of Simon's is a friend of mine."

Xela laughed.

Watching her laugh, Jaz reflected on this person who had, out of nowhere, entered her life. What an amazing creature! I have never met anyone so completely **guileless**, she thought. And so serene. It's relaxing just being around her. There was something else about her too. It was elusive. The only way Jaz could verbalize it was to say that the girl seemed deep—no, *solid*, remarkably *here*—as though she were a part of something more: sort of like the visible part of something that was infinitely old and wise. Maybe, thought Jaz, deep down everyone is like this girl, but they just hadn't realized it yet. She would have to find out more about this woman later in the evening.

An idea occurred to Jaz. Why couldn't she invite Xela to the seminar? Somehow it seemed right. She could be an observer. Axel and Simon wouldn't mind; they totally trusted these weird hunches she got about people. Later in the evening, when the seminar got going, she and Xela could sit in the background while Simon and Axel led the savants in their discussion. Then the two guys could join them in a quiet little corner of the living room for some well-deserved R&R. Ax would be really chilled after all that intellectualizing. It was perfect. If this one doesn't work, Jaz thought, I'm **renouncing** any claim to the title of Queen of the Matchmakers.

"So, who are all these scholars coming over tonight?" Xela asked.

"Oh, they're the members of a kind of discussion group the three of us organized. We call it 'The Group.' We discuss all sorts of stuff—politics, economics, science, religion—just about everything.

"Is there a central theme to it?" Xela asked.

Jaz answered. "Well, I know this sounds pretty pretentious, but our ultimate aim is to bring together thinkers from all over the world to help solve humanity's problems. I mean, three college kids, it's kind of … . "

Xela looked very serious. She reached out her hand and held Jaz's arm. She looked into Jaz's eyes as she spoke. "Jaz," she said. "What you're doing is very necessary. Particularly at this critical **juncture** in this planet's history. It is **imperative** that you continue."

Jaz felt a sense of **tranquility** unlike any she had ever experienced before. She looked around the room. Things seemed clearer, more in focus, more *real*.

"Yes," Jaz said. "I guess you're right. It is important. I guess sometimes you wonder: Is it crazy thinking you can really change the world?"

"If you want to do it, you *can* do it," Xela said. "You will do it."

"Yes, I guess we have to start somewhere. You know, it's amazing what a group of people can do if they're focused and working together. Some nights we've had the group just crackling with energy, absolutely **scintillating** ideas everywhere. And it even starts to **cohere** into a pattern. When that happens, it's amazing. A few times I've felt we've been really close to something."

"To what?"

"I don't know how to put it. A solution I guess. And I don't just mean an intellectual solution. I mean like how to have an **equitable** society that's also **affluent**."

"That is a tricky one." Xela said.

"I guess I mean *people* solutions, human solutions. Spiritual ones, even."

"So, tonight's an especially important night?"

"Yes. We're going to try to bring this thing to some sort of **culmination**. We want this meeting to be much more

231

systematic. I guess we sort of feel it's time to move on to the next stage. It's going to be more formal. Some really important people—like Dr. James, the famous space scientist—will be on the **dais**. And Simon is even going to have a **rostrum**."

Xela smiled. "Simon?" she said.

Definitions

1. **fastidious** ADJ. very fussy
2. **amalgam** N. mixture; combination
3. **assimilate** V. to absorb
4. **precocious** ADJ. unusually advanced at an early age
5. **proficient** ADJ. skilled in a certain area
6. **prodigy** N. highly gifted child
7. **rudimentary** ADJ. not developed
8. **minutia** N. petty details
9. **guileless** ADJ. without deceit
10. **renounce** V. to give up; reject
11. **juncture** N. turning point
12. **imperative** ADJ. essential
13. **tranquility** N. peace; calmness
14. **scintillating** ADJ. sparkling; brilliant
15. **cohere** V. to come together; form an orderly whole
16. **equitable** ADJ. just; fair
17. **affluent** ADJ. wealthy
18. **culmination** N. climax
19. **dais** N. raised platform for guests of honor
20. **rostrum** N. platform for speech making

Simply Simon

Think you know the words? Then prove it! Choose the *best* word to fill in the blank in each of the sentences below.

tranquility   dais   coheres   juncture   guileless

proficient   amalgams   renouncing   scintillating

imperative

1. I'll never be a soccer star, but I'm a/an _____ enough player to kick the ball around pretty well with the guys on the men's soccer team.

2. Jaz says her father told her once, "You don't find _____; it finds you."

3. Novelists sometimes create characters that are _____ of people they know.

4. The Dave Matthews Band gave a/an _____ concert last week.

5. It's a common sight to see Professor James on the _____ at major international science conferences.

6. I believe it is _____ that more aid be given to developing countries.

7. One of the research interests of my astronomy professor is the process by which matter _____into structures such as galaxies and solar systems.

8. At this _____ of the football season we'd better be firing on all cylinders because these final two games will decide whether we get into one of the major bowl games.

9. I'm considering _____ my position as class president because I'm so busy with other things I can't do the job properly.

10. Axel is so _____ I sometimes have to kind of look after him a little so that people don't take advantage of him.

Making Sense

Indicate whether or not each of the words in **bold** makes sense in the sentence. If it makes sense, put Y (Yes); if it doesn't make sense, put N (No).

1. Jaz, Axel, and I are all **fastidious** about acknowledging any source from which we've taken ideas or information for our papers. ____

2. My anthropology professor says that if you want to really **assimilate** the way of thinking of another culture you have to experience it for a while. ____

3. As a child I was so **precocious** in math that I had a lot of trouble learning how to do division. ____

4. The **culmination** of the college term in September is always exciting because you can look forward to the masses of glorious knowledge you'll soon be soaking up. ____

5. Jaz believes that social science is at a **rudimentary** stage of development and so one should be cautious in making claims that a scientific understanding of humanity or society has been achieved. ____

6. A skilled novelist can convey a sense of realism without describing the **minutia** of every scene. ____

7. Jaz says she likes to have a **rostrum** when she's speaking in public. ____

8. The **equitable** distribution of the world's wealth can be illustrated by the fact that the several hundred richest people in the world possess half of it. ____

9. Many people in Africa are so **affluent** that they are close to starvation much of the time. ____

10. The English novelist Anthony Trollope was such a **prodigy** that he started writing novels in his forties. ____

Match It

Match each of the following words to its meaning.

1. tranquility   a. essential

2. precocious   b. give up; reject

3. proficient   c. turning point

4. prodigy   d. unusually advanced at an early age

5. renounce   e. peace; calmness

6. juncture   f. just; fair

7. imperative   g. come together

8. cohere   h. wealthy

9. equitable   i. highly gifted child

10. affluent   j. skilled in a certain area

Axel Speaks

Greetings! I believe that you are now ready for something more intellectual. Choose the *best* word to fill in the blank in each sentence.

1. The idea of evolution was current in _____ form in the middle of the nineteenth century before Charles Darwin published his *On the Origin of Species,* but Darwin provided, for the first time, a clear explanation and definitive proof for the process of the evolution of species by natural selection.

(A) imperative

(B) sublime

(C) rudimentary

(D) precocious

(E) proficient

2. A side effect of the Crusades of the eleventh, twelfth, and thirteenth centuries was that Europe was exposed to the cultures of Asia, and many Asian values and ideas were _____ into European culture.

(A) suppressed

(B) metamorphosed

(C) assimilated

(D) piqued

(E) resolved

3. Composite materials, such as concrete, are composed of a/an _____ of substances that combine the most useful properties of suitable materials.

(A) propinquity

(B) amalgam

(C) manifestation

(D) juncture

(E) pantheon

4. The long history of the development of the doctrine of human rights _____ in 1948 with the *UN Universal Declaration of Human Rights,* a document that has been endorsed by nearly every country.

(A) culminated

(B) progressed

(C) foundered

(D) rallied

(E) renounced

5. The success of capitalism and industrialization in Europe in the seventeenth and eighteenth centuries helped to create a large and _____ middle class, which in turn was a major factor in the rise of democracy.

(A) precocious

(B) affluent

(C) dubious

(D) fastidious

(E) guileless

Answers on pages 459–460.

And now, on with the story.

Episode 25

Jaz Confides in Xela

"Surprising, isn't it?" Jaz said. "Simon is a lot smarter than he lets on. And he's so amazing at bringing people together. And keeping them there. Sometimes an intellectual with a big idea is like the **proverbial** dog with his bone—he just won't let go of it."

Xela laughed. "So, Simon sort of **orchestrates** the whole show?"

"Yeah. I guess you could say he keeps everyone's feathers nice and smooth. He's really something to watch in action. Nothing **fazes** him. I'll give you a recent example. We had two guys having an **altercation** over whether it's worth spending money on looking for extraterrestrial life—the Search for Extraterrestrial Intelligence program (SETI) and all that. Now, both of these guys are basically **liberals**, favoring **lavish** spending of government money to solve—or at least **ameliorate**—social problems and help solve these **intractable** problems such as malnutrition that the world faces. But they totally disagreed about the space program, and especially about SETI. The one guy felt it was a ridiculous waste of scarce resources. 'Toys for boys' he called it. All that expensive equipment. Totally **profligate**. Just something for the **disaffected**, aimless **bourgeoisie** to amuse themselves with while Africa starves."

"I bet he wouldn't say that anymore if they actually found something," Xela said.

"Yeah. Well, he got the other guy pretty upset. You see, this other fellow is this really big pro-space guy. I mean he

238

could be the chief **apologist** for NASA's most **extravagant** programs. In this one area he's the **polar** opposite of the other fellow. His favorite quote is by the legendary Russian space scientist, Konstantin Tsiolkovsky: 'Earth is the cradle of mankind, but one does not live in the cradle forever.'"

"I like that," Xela said.

"And he's one important man. He's even been the science advisor to *presidents*. And he's been the head of some of the biggest think tanks in America. This guy has connections to everybody important in the scientific and governmental establishments."

Jaz paused and looked at Xela. She wondered if she should tell her what they had recently found out about Dr. James.

Xela waited for Jaz to continue.

No, she decided, there was nothing I can't trust this woman with. It was an intuition, but she had never felt more certain of anything in her life. "This is really hush-hush," she said. "It seems that this guy Dr. James turns out to be the person behind this powerful **consortium** of companies that is doing some secret work on UFOs for the government. And it seems that something really important is going to happen soon. We're hoping to find out more tonight."

"That sounds exciting," Xela said. "You know, Simon told me about your interest in telepathy. You believe it exists, don't you?"

"Yes. I think there's good evidence for it."

Jaz considered for a moment. Why had Xela just asked about telepathy? It was odd that Xela had just brought up the subject that was crucial to recent developments regarding the aliens. That was the other thing that was so exciting about what this consortium had discovered: Apparently, aliens were utilizing telepathy to contact people on earth. It sounded far out—like *The X-Files* or something. Simon was still skeptical. He thought it might be just more black ops (covert operations, basically) by certain elements in the **federal** government to throw people off the scent of the far-out stuff they were doing. But tonight, she felt, they would find out what was really happening.

"I have a **premonition** that you'll find out something very important over the next few days, Jaz," Xela said. "Professor James must stay in your group despite anything you might find out about him. He can be trusted completely. *Do not doubt him.*"

Jaz opened her mouth to respond, but stopped. How, she wondered, did this girl seem to know so much about Professor James? And, once again, she found herself asking, who exactly *is* this person? One thing was clear, however—she seemed to know something very important about the whole business.

"So, I guess you know this guy," Jaz said.

"I know of him."

"Well, then you probably know that he is not only a brilliant scientist, but also a superb politician. He knows his way around the **bureaucracy** in Washington—who the important people are, the influential **lobbyists**, how to get things done. And he always makes sure he doesn't get caught supporting one **faction** against another. He's a lot like Simon, in that way. They both are good at bringing people together—and bringing out the best in them."

1. **proverbial** ADJ. widely referred to
2. **orchestrate** V. to coordinate
3. **faze** V. to bother; disconcert
4. **altercation** N. noisy dispute
5. **liberal** N. person favoring civil liberties and the use of government to promote social programs
6. **lavish** ADJ. spending liberally or abundantly
7. **ameliorate** V. to improve
8. **intractable** ADJ. not easily managed
9. **profligate** ADJ. recklessly wasteful
10. **disaffected** ADJ. no longer contented
11. **bourgeoisie** N. middle class
12. **apologist** N. person who defends or justifies a cause, a program, and so on.
13. **extravagant** ADJ. excessive; beyond reasonable limits
14. **polar** ADJ. occupying opposite extremes
15. **consortium** N. association formed for joint ventures
16. **federal** ADJ. constituting the central government of a nation as opposed to states or other smaller governing units
17. **premonition** N. forewarning
18. **bureaucracy** N. government administration
19. **lobbyist** N. private person who tries to influence legislators in favor of a special interest
20. **faction** N. group of people within a larger group

Simply Simon

Think you know the words? Then prove it! Choose the *best* word to fill in the blank in each of the sentences below.

liberals   apologist   lobbyists   consortium

factions   lavish   intractable   ameliorated

altercations   fazes

1. Halftime shows at football games are becoming more and more _____, probably to entertain people not that interested in football.

2. When I'm in the "zone"—throwing perfectly, the offense running like clockwork—nothing the defense does _____ me.

3. To be successful, a president must first unite the _____ within his own party.

4. Coach Wilson advises his players to avoid getting into _____ with members of the opposing team.

5. _____ tend to be in favor of a lot of government involvement in areas like medicine and education.

6. C. S. Lewis was a respected British literary scholar and a leading _____ of Christianity.

7. I believe that poverty can be _____ but not ended.

8. Jaz believes that a/an _____ of governments and private companies should undertake the exploration and settlement of Mars.

9. Most major companies hire _____ to advance their interests in Washington.

10. Problems that appear _____ can sometimes be solved fairly easily by a systematic, step-by-step approach.

Making Sense

Indicate whether or not each of the words in **bold** makes sense in the sentence. If it makes sense, put Y (Yes); if it doesn't make sense, put N (No).

1. **Proverbial** observation using the Hubble Space Telescope has allowed astronomers to confirm many observations made by earth-based telescopes. ____

2. Jaz **orchestrates** me to study regularly. ____

3. During the Cold War the United States spent a **lavish** amount of money on its military in order to ensure its superiority over the Soviet Union. ____

4. Last night in a dream I had a **premonition** of my childhood. ____

5. A pretty good measure of the relative size of a country's government **bureaucracy** is the percentage of gross national product devoted to government. ____

6. The other day Professor Chandler remarked, half jokingly, that every congressman is dead set against **profligate** federal spending—unless it's in his district. ____

7. To stay in power, a dictator must ensure that the people are completely **disaffected** so that they don't become unhappy and decide to rebel. ____

8. Last summer Jaz and I went to France to study the amazing collection of **bourgeoisie** in the Louvre museum. ____

9. In comparative government class we studied the differences between the **federal** type of government of democratic countries such as the United States and Germany and the Westminster type found in the United Kingdom and many other countries. ____

10. You might expect identical twins to be **polar** opposites, but research says that they are more different than ordinary siblings in their personality and other areas. ___

Match It

Match each of the following words to its meaning.

1. proverbial   a. recklessly wasteful

2. altercation   b. widely referred to

3. lavish   c. middle class

4. ameliorate   d. noisy dispute

5. profligate   e. improve

6. bourgeoisie   f. forewarning

7. apologist   g. government administration

8. consortium   h. spending liberally or abundantly

9. premonition   i. person who defends a cause

10. bureaucracy   j. association formed for joint ventures

Axel Speaks

Greetings! I believe that you are now ready for something more intellectual. Choose the *best* word to fill in the blank in each sentence.

1. Many of America's Founding Fathers believed that it would be wise to accommodate _____ as well as individuals in the new system of government, since society consists of groups with common interests as well as individuals.

(A) factions

(B) camaraderie

(C) liberals

(D) apologists

(E) bourgeoisie

2. International laws such as the Geneva Conventions can only help to _____ the suffering caused by war; they cannot end such suffering.

(A) render

(B) orchestrate

(C) ameliorate

(D) preserve

(E) faze

3. For many people, Gothic cathedrals such as Chartres, far from being _____, are well worth the resources required to build them because they lift the human spirit toward the divine.

(A) extravagant

(B) proverbial

(C) fragile

(D) isolated

(E) oblivious

4. Despite government disincentives, such as a high tax on tobacco products, a stubborn minority of people in the United States (approximately 20 percent) are _____; they continue to smoke despite the best efforts of government to stop them.

(A) lavish

(B) disaffected

(C) intractable

(D) inevitable

(E) innumerable

5. In the American _____ system of government, each state government is essentially a smaller scale duplicate of the national government, having its own legislature, judiciary, and executive branch.

(A) profligate

(B) polar

(C) recondite

(D) federal

(E) enigmatic

Answers on page 460.

And now, on with the story.

A Girl-to-Girl Talk

"So, what happened?" Xela asked. "I mean, in your **anecdote** about the two guys arguing over expenditures on the space program."

"Yes, I'm sorry," Jaz said, "the anecdote. I got a little sidetracked there. It was pretty strange. I mean, as I said, Professor James is the most **imperturbable** man in the world. But this other fellow had him really **agitated**. The guy was practically calling SETI **diabolical**—the work of the devil or something. He was saying it was incomprehensible that money was being spent looking for little green men while there was so much suffering on Earth."

"What did Simon do?"

"He just went over to them, put his arms around these two guys, gave them that smile of his, and said something about baseball."

"Baseball?"

"Yeah. Weird, huh? Turns out that they're both like total baseball freaks. So Simon rattles off a long funny **monologue** about Babe Ruth."

Xela laughed. "That sounds like Simon."

"Well, it worked. After ten minutes these guys are laughing and exchanging baseball stories. He's got some kind of special touch with people. It's always different, but he always knows exactly what stratagems to use to bring people together and make them forget any **animosities** they might have."

"Sounds like he should run for president some day. So what does Axel do during these meetings?"

"Well, he generally listens a lot. Somehow, out of all the "noise"—that's what he calls it—he discerns a pattern. Some new, fruitful direction for the discussion. He says a few words to Simon and the discourse moves on to a whole new level. That's one of the main reasons that these people keep coming back. Axel is just uncanny. If it seems like there's no coherence to the discussion, he picks a few threads out of all of these complex, **meandering** discussions and pulls them together. Suddenly, totally new ideas and perspectives are being explored."

"And where do you fit into all this?"

"I generally mix around. I stay with the different groups for a while, encourage people to mingle. I guess I'm into building bridges between people, between different ways of looking at things."

"Yes, that's just as important as the purely intellectual side," Xela replied. "So," she said, "who are the other people coming tonight?"

"Well, of course Professor James, whom we've already talked about. As I said, it seems that he's very powerful in the consortium working on all that government stuff. But he's also one of the key members of our group. Besides him, there's a whole bunch of people. They are a very special group, you see. They represent the **elite** of just about every field of human knowledge, from the arts to the social sciences to the sciences, as well as the key people in business, finance, the military, government, and several other areas. And what makes them special is that they've been especially selected."

"How have they been chosen?"

"Well, Simon, Axel, and I have invited hundreds of people to these gatherings we've organized over the past several months. We have very carefully selected the men and women we believed to be in a position to be the **catalysts** for a major change of direction in the course of humanity. We believe that the folks coming tonight are the core—the critically important people."

"In what sense are they important?"

Jaz wondered if she should tell Xela any more. She had already **divulged** far more than she had intended to. Maybe this incredible girl from Heaven-knows-where would play some important part in their plans.

"They are the people who the three of us believe can work together. And with us. I guess we rely a lot on intuition."

Xela smiled. "There's nothing wrong with intuition," she said. "But aren't you sometimes a little **intimidated** by all these big name academics?"

"Maybe a little, sometimes. But I guess I'm too busy to be afraid."

"So, Simon and Axel are a real team, I guess," Xela said. "It must be something to watch them in action together."

"Yes. There's like this total chaos, but Simon is somehow always in *control*. It's just some sort of charisma or something he's got. He can be pretty persuasive. And he has this charm."

Xela agreed. "Simon is kind of like the force of gravity," she said. "It's always there and nobody can resist it."

Jaz looked at Xela. I really like this woman, she thought. There is so much **beneficence** and gentleness in her. There was something else too, she thought. Yes, *purity*. Maybe Simon was right: Maybe she really was some kind of angel, Jaz thought. And if angels were ranked according to their beauty, then Xela was an archangel. It was as if nature, or God, had decided to combine in her the quintessence of the femininity of all the races of humanity. Jaz looked at Xela in the way a very pretty girl looks at a woman who is so **surpassingly** gorgeous that she seems like a goddess visiting Earth—with awe that such beauty exists. But Jaz did not feel the slightest **tinge** of jealousy. And, looking at Xela, Jaz knew that this remarkable person would play an important part in her life—and in the lives of the two men she loved.

Xela looked into Jaz's eyes. Jaz felt as though her very soul was being scrutinized. Yet she did not feel that she was being judged. She felt again that wonderful **composure**, and something that she could only describe as love.

249

Xela smiled. "We've had a real girl-to-girl talk, haven't we?"

"Yeah, I guess we have," Jaz said. "But I guess 'woman-to-woman' would be more correct these days, at least according to the **dictates** of political correctness."

Xela laughed. "So, you promised to tell me how you and Simon met. Do we have enough time for that?"

Jaz looked at her watch. "We have plenty of time. The barbecue stuff is ready. And the other people aren't coming until later tonight. I can get the things for that ready later." She paused. "Xela," Jaz continued, "I wonder if you could stay for the seminar later. I think you'd enjoy it."

"Thank you. I'd love to. It would be an honor. But won't people wonder who I am and what I'm doing there?"

"I'll just say you're my friend. A friend I trust completely. One of the people I'm closest to."

Xela looked at Jaz. She reached out her hand and put it on Jaz's forearm. "Thank you," she said.

Simon walked into the room. "Everything is ready," he said. "And the charcoal is perfecto." He sat down on a chair by Jaz and Xela.

"I see that you two have been grokking," Simon said.

Xela looked puzzled.

"That's sixties lingo for 'exchanging vibes,'" Jaz said. "From some of the slang he uses, sometimes I think Simon would prefer to have been a flower child."

"I like to be able to speak the way I want to, Jaz," Simon said.

"Yeah, I know," Jaz said. "Anyway, Xela was just asking how we met."

"So, tell her. It's not that embarrassing, is it?"

Jaz and Xela laughed.

"OK. It's kind of weird," Jaz said. "As always with me and Simon, Axel was somehow **inextricably** linked to us."

"It must be your **karma**," Xela said

"What do you mean?" Simon asked.

"I mean, maybe the three of you were somehow linked in your previous **incarnations**. Maybe you're just continuing that pattern."

Simon laughed. "Maybe," he said. "Sort of like one unit, huh?"

"Axel is like this **recurring** motif in our lives, isn't he?" Jaz said. "Anyway, it was the first day of freshman year. I didn't know a soul here. I'm from India you see."

"So," Xela said, "do you mind if first I ask why you came to America to study?"

Definitions

1. **anecdote** N. short account of an event
2. **imperturbable** ADJ. not easily disturbed
3. **agitated** ADJ. disturbed
4. **diabolical** ADJ. wicked
5. **monologue** N. long speech by one person
6. **animosity** N. hostility
7. **meandering** ADJ. winding back and forth
8. **elite** N. most skilled members of a social group (also: a privileged group)
9. **catalyst** N. something causing change
10. **divulge** V. to reveal; make a secret known
11. **intimidate** V. to make fearful or timid
12. **beneficence** N. kindness
13. **surpassingly** ADV. exceptionally; exceedingly
14. **tinge** N. slight amount
15. **composure** N. mental calmness
16. **dictate** N. guiding principle
17. **inextricably** ADV. incapable of being disentangled
18. **karma** N. person's life force that determines his or her destiny in the next life
19. **incarnation** N. act of a soul taking on a body
20. **recurring** ADJ. happening repeatedly

Simply Simon

Think you know the words? Then prove it! Choose the *best* word to fill in the blank in each of the sentences below.

catalyst   tinge   monologues   divulge   karma

surpassingly   animosities   imperturbable

diabolical   agitated

1. Some people believe that the Internet will be a/an _____ for great social change, but I think that's an exaggerated view of the situation.

2. I once asked Coach Wilson how he remains so _____ despite all the pressures of big-time college football; I was surprised when he said, "Dude, I just chill."

3. Discussions about religion often get people really _____ .

4. A country at war often accuses its enemy of doing _____ things.

5. Comedians often base their _____ on events from their own lives.

6. It amazes me how historical _____ between groups are often passed from one generation to the next.

7. Under American law, torture cannot be used to force a person to _____ information.

8. Axel is so _____ brilliant that several universities have already offered him a full professorship.

9. People sometimes ask me if I ever feel envious of Jaz and Axel's intelligence; my honest reply is that I don't have the least _____ of jealousy.

10. Jaz says the law of _____ holds that all of a person's good deeds will be rewarded while all of his or her bad deeds will be punished.

Making Sense

Indicate whether or not each of the words in **bold** makes sense in the sentence. If it makes sense, put Y (Yes); if it doesn't make sense, put N (No).

1. The best **anecdote** to sore muscles after a hard practice is to practice yoga. ____

2. In studying political science I've found that politics and economics are **inextricably** linked. ____

3. In general, Asians believe it is important for a person to retain his or her **composure** even in upsetting situations. ____

4. Professor Chandler wrote a study of the great **dictates** of the twentieth century such as Adolph Hitler and Joseph Stalin. ____

5. Many Hindus believe that God has had a number of **incarnations** in the form of figures such as Rama, Krishna, and the Buddha. ____

6. I enjoy taking **meandering** roads through the country. ____

7. The **elite** of the world's population—approximately 20 percent of the people in the world—lives in poverty and often at near starvation levels of nutrition. ____

8. Many cultures believe in **recurring** cycles of creation and destruction of the world much like the cycle of destruction and rebirth in the natural world. ____

9. I'm so **intimidated** by a big pass rush that I stay as cool as a cucumber, waiting for a passing lane to open up. ____

10. Jaz says that there's a holy woman in India who is so filled with **beneficence** that she travels around hugging everyone she meets. ____

Match It

Match each of the following words to its meaning.

1. anecdote
2. imperturbable
3. diabolical
4. meandering
5. elite
6. catalyst
7. divulge
8. beneficence
9. composure
10. dictate

a. something causing change
b. mental calmness
c. reveal
d. not easily disturbed
e. guiding principle
f. most skilled members of a group
g. wicked
h. short account of an event
i. kindness
j. winding back and forth

Axel Speaks

Greetings! I believe that you are now ready for something more intellectual. Choose the *best* word to fill in the blank in each sentence.

1. A positive aspect of the increasing power and influence of multinational companies in the world is that people might put aside ancient _____ out of allegiance to their companies and the quest for profit.

(A) monologues

(B) dictates

(C) anecdotes

(D) animosities

(E) altercations

2. The English Romantic poet William Wordsworth believed that the human mind is _____ linked with nature.

(A) inextricably

(B) incorrigibly

(C) coyly

(D) euphemistically

(E) surpassingly

3. Once the young American government had established its dominance in the Western Hemisphere, it sought, through such thinly veiled threats as the Monroe Doctrine, to _____ European powers that were likely to threaten America's sphere of influence by establishing colonies in the region.

(A) sustain

(B) intimidate

(C) mollify

(D) chide

(E) coerce

4. Hindus believe that the law of _____ acts relentlessly and fairly, through reincarnation, rewarding virtue and punishing evil and allowing souls to experience what they need to so that they can uncover their divine nature.

(A) quintessence

(B) chemistry

(C) beneficence

(D) composure

(E) karma

5. The cloning of human beings raises in the minds of some people a vision of a cloned _____ that grows ever more intelligent and capable, ruling an underclass of normal humans.

(A) catalyst

(B) stereotype

(C) elite

(D) myriad

(E) incarnation

Answers on page 461.

And now, on with the story.

Globalization

"My dad wanted me to study in the United States," Jaz said.

"Why?" Xela asked.

"He thought I should study overseas. At the time I didn't think it was important. I was happy in my world. But with **hindsight**, I realize he was right. It was important for me to see things from a different **vantage** point. I was pretty **insular**, you see."

"In what sense?"

"I was really **imbued** with Indian culture. I was totally into it—Indian art, music, philosophy, everything."

"Isn't that good? Indian culture has so much depth and profundity."

"That's true. And I was into every aspect of it, but especially the philosophical tradition. You see, my dad is a philosophy professor."

"Simon told me," Xela said. "He's working on the connections between Western philosophy and Indian philosophy, right?"

"Yes. So, as a girl I got all these ideas from my dad. But maybe I kind of went overboard."

"In what way do you think you went too far?" Xela asked.

"For a while I was pretty **ethnocentric**. Anything—any other way of looking at the world—was inferior in my eyes. I was completely **doctrinaire**."

"But isn't it good to have a solid foundation in your own value system before you look too deeply into those of others?"

"That's a good point. Well, I certainly had that. But the problem was that I wasn't *questioning* anything. I was just accepting everything. Anything not in agreement with the Indian world view, I rejected."

"Jaz was becoming a real **reactionary**, weren't you?" Simon said.

"Yes, I guess I was something of a **fundamentalist**. You know, it's interesting how sometimes young people are more **conservative** than their parents. My theory is that it meets some kind of psychological need."

"Isn't that a little **reductionistic**, Jaz?" Simon said. "You're always warning me about reducing a person's motives to some simple cause. Isn't that what you're doing?"

"True. Well, at least in my case I think that was what was happening. You see, if you grow up in the West—Western Europe, the United States—you probably don't realize how pervasive and potent the influence of Western culture is now around the world. It's hard to appreciate that a lot of people resent this deeply. And, sometimes, people overreact. So there's this sort of irrational hatred of anything foreign that arises."

"**Xenophobia**," Simon said.

"Yes. Xenophobia. Some people start to see the West as some **monolithic** force consciously bent on getting everybody in the world to eat hamburgers, wear Nikes, watch CNN and *Mission Impossible* or whatever blockbuster is playing at the movies, spend all day making money, and think that the degree of individual freedom is the sole criterion for judging the success of a political system."

"But you guys are fighting back pretty well with Bollywood," Simon said. "Those musicals and other types of movies from India are *everywhere*."

"Yes," Jaz said. "I guess things tend to balance out eventually. So, anyway, I needed desperately to think my culture was the best, so I lashed out against the biggest threat I felt there was to it—the Big Bad West."

"Well, you certainly weren't alone," Xela said. "Isn't globalization a real threat to many cultures, especially the smaller ones that can't as easily withstand the onslaught of the media and the multinationals? I read that of the world's six or seven thousand languages, a couple disappear from the world every year. And if you lose your language, don't you basically lose your culture?"

"It sounds like the survival of the fittest," Simon said. "The strongest survive."

"Evolution can be a dangerous **analogy** when we're talking about culture and ideas," Jaz said. "Maybe the strongest isn't the best. Anyway, it looks like the world might be heading, for better or worse, toward one **homogenized** culture."

"OK," Xela said. "But if we want to be optimistic, we can say this culture will be made up of the best aspects of many cultures."

"Or the lowest common denominator between them," Jaz said. "A mongrel **hybrid**. In other words, whatever allows the big companies to keep selling stuff. Hundreds of millions of happy campers all over the world being told what they should want, consuming like crazy, never questioning anything. Capitalism triumphant. **Rampant** materialism. Conspicuous consumption the privilege of the elite and the dream of the masses. There are some pretty **ominous** trends."

"You see what happens around here when you ask a few simple questions, Xela?" Simon asked.

Xela laughed. "It's interesting, really," she said. "The story of Jaz's political awakening. Some of that sounds like Marxism. I thought that **ideology** had been completely **debunked**."

"Hey," Jaz said, "I'm certainly no Marxist. All I'm saying is that every system has its pros and cons. And if one system dominates the world, we'll have all of its pros and all of its cons. And no alternatives. Also, please remember that capitalism can be criticized from standpoints other than Marxism. I mean, some of what I've said would be **affirmed** by many

adherents of the world's major religious faiths. Did you know, for example, that in 1931 Pope Pius XII described capitalism as 'the economic **despotism** of a few'?"

"OK, I guess that about wraps *that* up," Simon said. "Any more questions, Xela?"

Jaz and Xela laughed.

"I guess I got a little carried away there," Jaz said. "Once I get going on this sort of subject I have a tendency to start **pontificating**. There's this **polemicist** inside me that's bottled up, but is always ready to come out if anybody is willing to listen."

"Actually, I find your perceptions very astute," Xela said. "And I don't think you're pontificating. These are important issues that the world must address."

"Yeah, Jaz doesn't have a **sententious** bone in her body, do you, honey?" Simon said.

Jaz laughed. "Maybe," she said, "I should save some of my brilliant ideas for later tonight."

1. **hindsight** N. perception of the significance of events after they have occurred
2. **vantage** N. position likely to provide superiority or give an overall view
3. **insular** ADJ. narrow-minded
4. **imbue** V. to fill
5. **ethnocentric** ADJ. based on the belief that one's group is superior
6. **doctrinaire** ADJ. rigidly devoted to beliefs
7. **reactionary** N. opponent of change
8. **fundamentalist** N. person who rigidly follows fundamental principles
9. **conservative** ADJ. favoring traditional values; tending to oppose change
10. **reductionistic** ADJ. attempting to explain complex phenomena by simple principles
11. **xenophobia** N. fear or hatred of foreigners
12. **monolithic** ADJ. constituting a single, unified whole
13. **analogy** N. correspondence in some way between two otherwise dissimilar things
14. **homogenized** ADJ. similar or the same
15. **hybrid** N. something of mixed composition
16. **rampant** ADJ. unrestrained
17. **ominous** ADJ. threatening
18. **debunked** V. discredited
19. **ideology** N. set of beliefs that are the basis of a political or economic system
20. **affirm** V. to maintain to be true
21. **adherent** N. follower
22. **despotism** N. absolute power
23. **pontificate** V. to speak with pompous authority
24. **polemicist** N. person skilled in polemics—the art of argument and controversy
25. **sententious** ADJ. given to pompous moralizing (also: terse and vigorous in expression)

Simply Simon

Think you know the words? Then prove it! Choose the *best* word to fill in the blank in each of the sentences below.

ominous   sententious   doctrinaire   reactionary

reductionistic   hindsight   insular   homogenized

vantage   rampant

1. Professor Chandler made a/an _____ remark last week: he said the Political Science final exam would be the toughest he's ever seen.

2. I wonder what our civilization today will look like from the _____ point of 1,000 years from now.

3. Professor Chandler believes that political and social commentary in America has become too tame and _____, leaving little room for the expression of a wide range of views that democracy thrives on.

4. _____ Marxists maintain that capitalism represents only a temporary stage in an historical movement towards communism.

5. After an unsuccessful play, our offensive co-coordinator sometimes says, "With twenty-twenty _____ I wouldn't have called that play."

6. To me it is _____ to argue that life is only an electro-chemical process.

7. Flu was _____ on campus last winter, so I asked my doctor if I should get a shot against it.

8. Globalization is making it difficult for countries to remain _____.

9. I've found that nearly anytime you express a strong opinion on a moral issue someone will accuse you of being _____.

10. Historians have observed that after a revolution there is frequently a counterrevolutionary movement by _____ forces in society.

Making Sense

Indicate whether or not each of the words in **bold** makes sense in the sentence. If it makes sense, put Y (Yes); if it doesn't make sense, put N (No).

1. Professor Chandler supported my argument that **despotism** is at the very heart of democracy. ____

2. The government of the United States takes steps to **imbue** citizens with patriotism through declaring national holidays such as Independence Day and instituting the Pledge of Allegiance in schools. ____

3. Jaz complains that I'm so **ethnocentric** that I'm always trying to get her to go with me to performances featuring artists from a wide range of cultures. ____

4. A person who wants to become an American citizen must **affirm** his or her loyalty to the United States and pledge to defend it. ____

5. A skilled **polemicist** is able to inflame public opinion so that a minor diplomatic incident is turned into a political crisis. ____

6. One of the **ideologies** we studied in political science is fascism, a political system in which there is very strict control of the people by government. ____

7. Professor Chandler says that there is a wide range of groups and views within Islam, and so it is a mistake to see it as a **monolithic** religion. ____

8. One of my favorite **analogies** is the story about two guys discussing what the longest homerun in baseball history was. ____

9. **Xenophobia** is defined as the irrational fear of warrior women. ____

10. The belief that the mainland of America could not be successfully attacked was **debunked** by the terrorist attacks on New York City and Washington, D.C. on September 11, 2001. ____

Match It

Match each of the following words to its meaning.

1. fundamentalist   a. narrow-minded

2. hybrid   b. correspondence in some way between two otherwise dissimilar things

3. adherent   c. person who rigidly follows fundamental principles

4. conservative   d. absolute power

5. pontificate   e. based on the belief that one's group is superior

6. insular   f. favoring traditional values

7. ethnocentric   g. fear or hatred of foreigners

8. analogy   h. speak with pompous authority

9. xenophobia   i. something of mixed composition

10. despotism   j. follower

Axel Speaks

Greetings! I believe that you are now ready for something more intellectual. Choose the *best* word to fill in the blank in each sentence.

1. The ancient Greek philosopher Socrates embodied in his life the ideal of philosophy as literally "love of wisdom": He refused to defer to authority in his search for truth, and constantly questioned _____ assertions made by people claiming to know the whole truth about a subject.

(A) conservative

(B) offensive

(C) doctrinaire

(D) monolithic

(E) insular

2. Zoroastrianism is an ancient Persian monotheistic religion that has few _____ today, but whose influence can be seen in Judaism and Christianity.

(A) ideologies

(B) precepts

(C) dogmas

(D) adherents

(E) vogues

3. Fascism is considered a right wing political philosophy because it favors state power over individual power, and is supported by _____ elements in society, mainly wealthy capitalists and landowners.

(A) rampant

(B) adoring

(C) reductionistic

(D) loyal

(E) reactionary

4. The large increase in agricultural productivity that occurred in the second half of the twentieth century (known as the Green Revolution) occurred in large part as a result of the work of scientists such as Dr. Robert Borlag in developing new _____ of hardier and higher-yield grains.

(A) fundamentalists

(B) machinations

(C) hybrids

(D) prodigies

(E) despotisms

5. Naturalists are greatly concerned about a/an _____ recent trend: Worldwide, species are being lost at a rate of about 50 times greater at present than at any time in the past 100,000 years.

(A) ominous

(B) homogenized

(C) spurious

(D) enigmatic

(E) sententious

Answers on pages 461–462.

And now, on with the story.

COMING TO AMERICA

"So, you came to the States to study because your father wanted you to?" Xela asked.

"Yes," Jaz said. "Basically, I had no choice."

"Isn't that like fascism or something?" Simon asked.

"Some of my friends thought that," Jaz said. "But, you know, it's such a different value system over there. A child is supposed to do what her parents want. There's not this emphasis on rights like there is here. There's more stress on responsibilities."

"Well," Simon said, "we have the commandment, 'Honor thy father and mother.'"

"True," Jaz said. "But maybe that's followed more in theory than reality. I mean, here you're supposed to almost *rebel* against your parents, establish your own identity, be **autonomous**. Otherwise you're not quite a real person in this society."

"You know, it's sort of **ironic**," Simon said.

"What?" Jaz asked.

"I mean, the conservative value of **filial piety** was what made you follow your father, who was, presumably, trying to make you more open in your outlook."

"It must have been quite a culture shock," Xela said.

"Yeah, right into the belly of the beast," Simon said. "The **citadel** of democracy and capitalism—Burgers, hot dogs, football, Hollywood, cable, MTV, 1,000 brands of breakfast cereal, guns—and, of course, guys like me."

"So, what was your first impression?" Xela asked.

"This place is *freezing!*"

Simon and Xela laughed.

"I mean, I was like, how do people *survive* here? These people must be crazy. Or they must all have Eskimo blood or something. I came in September and I thought it was pretty cold. Boy, did I have a lot to learn!"

Xela was still laughing.

"I mean, it just kept getting *colder*. There's cold, then there's frigid. And then there's insanely cold, where your cells stop functioning at the molecular level. I mean it's like they're in **stasis** or something."

"Yeah, that's how we met," Simon said. "I found this poor girl frozen solid in the street. And, being a kind soul, I took her home and thawed her out."

"Seriously," Jaz said, "Simon really did help me out. There are so many little things that seem **inconsequential** when you grow up in a place, but to an outsider they're really critical to know."

"I've always prided myself on my **pragmatism**," Simon said. "Like buy the best gloves you can afford."

"And layers!" Jaz continued. "That was a *major* break-through. Simon told me you have to dress in layers. I was like, 'Layers of *what*? What is this guy talking about?' And then I experimented and saw what he meant. He was right— you have to dress so you're covered in many **strata** of clothes. That way you can adjust to the temperature around you by taking stuff off or putting it back on so you maintain **thermal equilibrium**."

"And you really learned that lesson, didn't you Jaz?" Simon said. "So, how many layers do you have on now?" Simon turned to Xela. "It's pretty warm in here, so she's probably down to, what, about two dozen, right Jaz?"

Xela laughed.

"It seems funny now, but I was completely clueless, wandering around in my sari and a little sweater, wondering why my life force seemed to be **inexorably** ebbing away, and

269

why everything always seemed kind of blurry. The cold was completely **debilitating**."

"So that's how you met?" Xela asked.

"Well, maybe a little **hyperbole**," Simon said.

"Hyperbole! Without Simon I wouldn't have *survived*. I remember thinking a few days after we met, *girl, you can make it*. With a little luck and a lot of prayers, you might even be alive at the end of your first winter in America."

"So *that's* why you acted so friendly to me."

"Hey, I was *cold*. I was just using every survival skill I had."

"I thought it was against the **creed** of modern women to use their charms on a guy to get something."

"Forget women's lib. It was every girl for herself. At that point I'd use anything as long as I could be *warm*."

Xela looked at Jaz. "So, I guess you're pretty warm now?" she said.

"Yeah. We're pretty comfortable here, aren't we Simon?"

"Yep," Simon said, "everything is great. So, now you know why Jaz came to America to study and how we met. Fascinating, isn't it?"

"Yes, it is," Xela said. "You know, I was just wondering. Is your roommate in the **proximity** of this room? That was him we heard singing before, wasn't it Simon?"

"Right," Simon said. He looked at his watch. "Axel should be coming down pretty soon. When he smells the barbecue, he'll appear out of nowhere, like magic. In the meantime, why don't we keep talking? It'll help get us ready for the seminar later. Axel can join us when he comes downstairs."

"Jaz," Xela said. "I'm curious about one thing. You said your father wanted you to challenge the beliefs—the **orthodoxies**—you had been taught, right?"

"Yes. You see, my dad has this belief—well, actually it's practically a dogma with him—that a person needs to continually develop, to grow. His basic tenet is that a person needs to challenge his or her **presuppositions**, to inquire about the world, to ask *why* things are a certain way, to ask if his or her beliefs are congruent with reality.

"Yes," Xela said, "I can see the importance of that. But, as we were discussing before, wasn't he afraid that in doing that you might lose your moral foundation, an unshakable **edifice** of values that you don't question, beliefs that are **immutable** truths and that give your life meaning?"

"That is an excellent question. You know, I've never asked him that. I guess he must have been aware of the risk that I would lose my values. But he must have felt that it was worth the risk. After all, values that can be lost can't be that great, can they?"

Xela nodded.

Definitions

1. **autonomous** ADJ. independent (N. autonomy)
2. **ironic** ADJ. constituting a difference between what might be expected and what actually occurs
3. **filial** ADJ. pertaining to a son or daughter
4. **piety** N. devotion and reverence to parents (also: devotion and reverence to God)
5. **citadel** N. fortress
6. **stasis** N. motionless state
7. **inconsequential** ADJ. insignificant; unimportant
8. **pragmatism** N. practicality
9. **strata** N. layers (*sing.* stratum)
10. **thermal** ADJ. pertaining to heat
11. **equilibrium** N. stable, balanced state
12. **inexorably** ADV. relentlessly; unyieldingly
13. **debilitating** ADJ. making weak
14. **hyperbole** N. exaggeration
15. **creed** N. principles
16. **proximity** N. nearness; closeness
17. **orthodoxy** N. traditional belief
18. **presupposition** N. something assumed in advance

19. **edifice** N. structure
20. **immutable** ADJ. unchangeable

Simply Simon

Think you know the words? Then prove it! Choose the *best* word to fill in the blank in each of the sentences below.

autonomous   ironic   stasis   thermal   proximity

debilitating   filial   edifice   creed

inconsequential

1. In his novels about the future colonization of Mars (*Red Mars*, *Green Mars*, and *Blue Mars*) the science fiction writer Kim Stanley Robinson portrays a future in which multinational companies have become _____ political units.

2. Some people find it _____ that the Vietnamese, who sacrificed so much to defeat America in war, are now being so greatly influenced by the culture of that country.

3. Dr. Miller, my English teacher, says that many students seem to believe that commas are _____ little marks meant to be sprinkled at random around an essay, kind of like salt and pepper on a steak.

4. Life on Earth depends on the _____ energy of the Sun.

5. I believe that a person's religious _____ is something that is between her and God.

6. Jaz says that Hindu teaching is that the universe will reach a point of _____ and then begin to vibrate and expand, in an endless cycle.

7. The _____ of my TV to the kitchen means that when I'm watching a game, I can easily grab a snack during a commercial.

8. Chinese culture places great emphasis on _____ obligations.

9. It's amazing how modern medicine can allow athletes to return from _____ injuries that a generation ago would have ended a person's career.

10. Axel says we should stand in awe of the _____ of knowledge that scientists have systematically built over the centuries.

Making Sense

Indicate whether or not each of the words in **bold** makes sense in the sentence. If it makes sense, put Y (Yes); if it doesn't make sense, put N (No).

1. From the human point of view, a plant doesn't visibly change over an hour's observation; however, over 24 hours the plant appears **immutable**. ____

2. Each individual must find an **equilibrium** between the social roles he is expected to play and his own "inner" life. ____

3. Religious leaders in Europe are concerned about increasing levels of **piety** among the population. ____

4. The **citadels** of Los Angeles and San Francisco have a friendly rivalry as to which city is California's more important city. ____

5. **Pragmatism** tells us that we should follow our dreams, even if they are unrealistic. ____

6. I learned in sociology class that the vast majority of Americans, when asked to identify themselves as belonging to the low, middle, or high **stratum** of society, place themselves in the middle level. ____

7. Many people are afraid of accepting **orthodoxies** because they believe that too much disagreement and uncertainty will undermine the stability of society. ____

8. Axel believes that science will march on **inexorably**, until it has understood everything. ____

9. **Presuppositions** are essential in order to prove our assumptions about a particular topic. ____

10. My creative writing teacher says that we should use **hyperbole** only when we want to describe something with complete accuracy and realism. ____

Match It

Match each of the following words to its meaning.

1. autonomous	a. practicality
2. piety	b. independent
3. pragmatism	c. exaggeration
4. equilibrium	d. traditional belief
5. inexorably	e. something assumed in advance
6. hyperbole	f. devotion and reverence
7. creed	g. unchangeable
8. orthodoxy	h. stable, balanced state
9. presupposition	i. relentlessly
10. immutable	j. principles

Axel Speaks

Greetings! I believe that you are now ready for something more intellectual. Choose the *best* word to fill in the blank in each sentence.

1. Important to the development of democracy was the concept of the social contract—the idea that people voluntarily give up a certain amount of individual _____ to a state in return for that state undertaking certain duties.

(A) methodology

(B) autonomy

(C) piety

(D) orthodoxy

(E) skepticism

2. It is _____ that earth satellites that had been developed mainly for military purposes subsequently made many valuable contributions to human well-being in such areas as communications, weather monitoring, and resource finding.

(A) debilitating

(B) inconsequential

(C) ironic

(D) immutable

(E) persuasive

3. To promote public support for science in America in the late nineteenth century, scientists appealed to the _____ of the American public by encouraging the idea that all technology is an outgrowth of scientific research, whereas in reality most technology has been developed independently of science.

(A) piety

(B) creed

(C) acumen

(D) pragmatism

(E) ideologies

4. Today, environmentalism has become such a/an _____ that even many industries whose activities cause extensive pollution have embraced it.

(A) edifice

(B) conundrum

(C) hyperbole

(D) orthodoxy

(E) amalgam

5. The greatest single determinant of climate is latitude; this factor is affected by others, such as _____ to land masses and bodies of water, altitude, ocean currents, and prevailing winds.

(A) opposition

(B) analogy

(C) proximity

(D) equilibrium

(E) impediments

Answers on pages 462–463.

And now, on with the story.

Mind Games

"Xela," Jaz continued, "you said 'immutable truths.' But immutable for *whom*? I mean, some 80-year-old philosopher might have one truth and I might have another."

"Yeah, like Dr. Swenson, the **eminent** computer scientist," Simon said. "He's convinced that the world consists of information. To him the truth is binary: on, off, 0, 1. That's it. That's *his* truth."

Xela smiled at Simon. "OK," she said. "But there can't be more than one truth, can there? I mean, logically."

"Yes," Jaz said, "it's true there can be only one truth. But the question I always have is, how do we know whose version of the truth is true?"

"Maybe they're each true in their own way," Simon said.

"That's an interesting point, Simon," Xela said. "Isn't it possible that each individual perceives only one aspect of a reality that is multifarious?"

"So each person builds his philosophy on that," Simon said.

Xela nodded.

Jaz was silent, pondering. "Possibly," she said. "But I think that our premise must be that there is an objective truth we can all reach some sort of consensus about. I mean, otherwise, it's chaos."

"Nicely put," Xela said. "We can't get very far if we say everything is **subjective**, can we?"

"So," Simon said, "what you two are saying, if I can attempt a summary of it in my own words, is that no matter how we feel about some sort of ultimate truth—whether it exists, whether we can know it—we should **provisionally** assume that we can find an objective truth."

Xela smiled at Simon again. "That was beautifully **paraphrased**," she said.

"So, then what?" Simon asked.

"I guess whoever builds the most **cogent** case for his philosophy should be the one we **tentatively** follow," Jaz said.

"So, it's like a *game*," Simon said. "The most articulate team wins. Whoever makes the most **compelling** case gets to say what we all should believe. So, if the pragmatists, the guys who say we should look for meaning in observable practical consequences of ideas, are really on top of their game this season, we follow them rather than the existentialists, who've been kind of **depleted** by injuries to key personnel recently."

Xela and Jaz laughed.

"I'll tell you one thing," Jaz said. "In Simon's scenario I'd be really chuffed."

"Chuffed?" Simon said.

"Yeah, *chuffed*. It's British English for 'pleased.' I thought it had crossed the ocean."

"It must have sailed right by me," Simon said.

"Anyway, I'm glad to hear that the pragmatists would win the battle of the brains," Jaz said.

"Why?" asked Xela.

"Because if I had to endure very much of that existentialist stuff, about how each of us is alone in an uncaring universe, I'd blow a circuit or something. I mean, they're completely depressing. Why were those guys so *unhappy*? Something must have ticked them off, big time. Dread, anguish, **ennui**, despair, meaninglessness, anxiety. What a **litany** of woe!"

"I had to read some of that stuff in lit class," Simon said. "I mean, compared to Kierkegaard and his soulmates, Hamlet was a raving party animal with nothing but nonstop revelry on his mind."

Xela was laughing hard. It was the first time Simon had seen her really kick back and laugh out loud.

"Can you imagine one of their meetings?" Simon said. 'No, Marcel, you cannot be in our club,' the chairman says. 'You're just not melancholy enough. Come back when you're *seriously* unhappy. We cannot accept even the smallest trace of mirth in our members.'

"Or, 'Sorry, Martin, you're not doing badly. You seem really depressed. Excellent. Practically suicidal. Keep up the good work. But you're not completely **alienated** yet. Go home and immediately break off with all of your so-called friends. You've got to become more **cynical**. Don't you know that they're like everybody else, just acting friendly so they can get something out of you?'

"How about, 'Karl. What a disappointment you are! You're a disgrace to existentialists everywhere. What are you, some kind of **maverick**, actually trying to live an authentic, truly meaningful existence? What kind of existentialist *are* you? You're an **apostate**, that's what you are. You'll **undermine** our whole game. Who wants an ebullient existentialist? It's an **oxymoron**. The reading public wants long, **lugubrious**, inde-cipherable, tedious, pretentious books on being and not being, the pointlessness of existence; how we're all alone in this vast, cold, impersonal universe—totally **estranged** from all other creatures; how we come into it for a moment, have a brief, horrible existence that lasts just long enough to give us a chance to think about how pointless and absurd it is, and then leave, nobody really caring whether we're still around or not.

"Stuff like that. **Mammoth** tomes they can fall asleep at night reading, thinking how lucky they are to not be as depressed as the author of the book must be. Something a guy can leave on the coffee table so girls will think, 'He *reads* this stuff. He must be some kind of sensitive, heavy-duty intel-lectual. I can't understand a word those people say. But I love guys who can. There's just something irresistibly appealing about **cerebral** men who really try to understand life.'

280

"What they do *not* want from us, Karl, is some life-affirming, optimistic book that actually makes *sense* and helps them find meaning in life. Think of the *market*, the public. They have rights too, you know. They *want* to be depressed. Or at least pretend to be. Your job is to give them what they want.'"

Definitions

1. **eminent** ADJ. distinguished
2. **subjective** ADJ. particular to a given individual; personal
3. **provisionally** ADV. for the time being
4. **paraphrase** V. to restate in other words
5. **cogent** ADJ. logically convincing
6. **tentatively** ADV. not definitely; provisionally
7. **compelling** ADJ. having a powerful effect; convincing
8. **depleted** ADJ. reduced in quantity; exhausted
9. **ennui** N. boredom and dissatisfaction
10. **litany** N. repetitive recital
11. **alienated** ADJ. feeling separated from others
12. **cynical** ADJ. distrustful of the motives of others
13. **maverick** N. rebel; nonconformist
14. **apostate** N. one who abandons his or her beliefs or principles
15. **undermine** V. to weaken
16. **oxymoron** N. combining of terms not suited to one another
17. **lugubrious** ADJ. sorrowful; mournful
18. **estranged** ADJ. alienated
19. **mammoth** ADJ. gigantic
20. **cerebral** ADJ. intellectually sophisticated

Simply Simon

Think you know the words? Then prove it! Choose the *best* word to fill in the blank in each of the sentences below.

cogent eminent mammoth depleted litany

maverick oxymoron undermine provisionally

alienated

1. When someone says that something is impossible, Jaz likes to remind people that in the nineteenth century _____ scientists said that machines that fly could never be built because they would violate the laws of physics.

2. My Freshman English instructor told the class that since we make the same errors on every assignment he might as well make a tape of his _____ of complaints about our writing to play for us.

3. The economies of many developing countries are being _____ because of talented people leaving to work in the rich countries.

4. Some people say the term "smart jock" is a/an _____, but I think I've pretty much proved how wrong that view is.

5. Every team I've been on seems to have one _____—a guy who often is an excellent player but who just has to do things his own way.

6. In Japan, increasing numbers of young people are becoming _____ from society.

7. Coach Wilson has _____ decided that we'll switch to the West Coast offense next season because he thinks we'll have the speed to make it work.

8. Some strategists believe one of America's aims is to _____ China's political stability so it does not become a major competitor later in this century.

9. Did you take my advice and get yourself a/an _____ dictionary?

10. In comparative religion class I read three particularly _____ essays: C. S. Lewis arguing brilliantly for Christianity, Swami Vivekananda persuasively outlining the beliefs of Hinduism, and Bertrand Russell clearly stating the atheist position.

Making Sense

Indicate whether or not each of the words in **bold** makes sense in the sentence. If it makes sense, put Y (Yes); if it doesn't make sense, put N (No).

1. Every church needs a core group of **apostates** so that it has a solid foundation. ___

2. Scientists primarily study **subjective** experience, using powerful instruments such as telescopes. ___

3. Good dance music is upbeat and **lugubrious**. ___

4. Jaz's anthropology professor says she thinks that people living in industrialized countries are becoming **estranged** from nature. ___

5. Sometimes in life it's hard not to be a little bit **cynical**, but I do believe that people are basically good. ___

6. Senator Barry Goldwater made such a **compelling** case for his position when he was running for president in 1964 that he lost in a landslide. ___

7. Dr. Miller asked us to **paraphrase** a passage from a work of literature to help us see the differences between literary language and everyday language. ___

8. In philosophy class we learned that Karl Popper believed that scientific theories can never be conclusively proven, only **tentatively** accepted until they're either disproved or a competing theory becomes more convincing. ____

9. There's nothing like a little **ennui** to really liven up a dull party. ____

10. Professor Jones says that in his view a lot of modern poetry has become so **cerebral** that reading it is a kind of intellectual game rather than the deep human experience that reading a work of literature should be. ____

Match It

Match each of the following words to its meaning.

1. cogent	a. weaken
2. subjective	b. rebel
3. tentatively	c. intellectually sophisticated
4. alienated	d. combination of terms not suited to one another
5. cynical	e. not definitely; provisionally
6. maverick	f. sorrowful
7. undermine	g. feeling separated from others
8. oxymoron	h. particular to a given individual; personal
9. lugubrious	i. distrustful of the motives of others
10. cerebral	j. logically convincing

Axel Speaks

Greetings! I believe that you are now ready for something more intellectual. Choose the *best* word to fill in the blank in each sentence.

1. In his book *Escape from Freedom,* the distinguished psychologist Erich Fromm put forward his theory that people living in modern society experience more anxiety than did people in earlier societies because they live in a world in which they are _____ from the traditional values and institutions that formerly gave life meaning.

(A) alienated

(B) depleted

(C) cajoled

(D) importuned

(E) repressed

2. DNA tests are acceptable evidence in all 50 American states, but in 48 states prisoners who have been convicted do not have a legal right to them, even if _____ evidence of their wrongful conviction is introduced.

(A) subjective

(B) provisional

(C) tentative

(D) ambiguous

(E) compelling

3. In contrast to psychoanalysis, behaviorism attaches no importance to _____ reports of the mind, but rather relies solely on observable behavior.

(A) subjective

(B) cynical

(C) lugubrious

(D) cogent

(E) cerebral

4. _____ astronomers such as Carl Sagan have argued that if intelligent life exists outside the earth, it would probably make use of radio to alert other intelligent life forms of its existence, and that since science is a universal language, its message would probably refer to universal laws of nature.

(A) Apostate

(B) Estranged

(C) Pedantic

(D) Eminent

(E) Lethargic

5. The psychologist Erich Fromm believed that though people in the modern world have more freedom to develop themselves than did people in the past, the price of this freedom is that they feel _____ from the deeper meaning of life and from their fellows.

(A) animated

(B) estranged

(C) dispassionate

(D) enthralled

(E) skewed

Answers on page 463.

And now, on with the story.

METAPHORS

Xela had laughed nearly nonstop through Simon's little monologue. Yes, she was thinking, Jaz had been right when she had said that Simon is a lot smarter than he usually let on. He had a wisdom beyond his years, a sort of intuitive understanding of life. And he could be delightfully **iconoclastic** and independent in his thinking.

"But it's true, isn't it?" Xela said. "Isn't it kind of the way Simon just described it, a game? I mean, aren't there intellectual fashions we all follow?"

"Oh boy," Simon said, "here come the paradigms again."

"Well, it's true," Jaz said. "I mean, it's pretty obvious in terms of vogues like existentialism. But it's not so obvious over longer time scales. You kind of have to step back and get some perspective. A few centuries ago Idealism was all the rage. Everything was the mind, universals, ideas. Then, it was this materialistic worldview that became **preeminent**—and still is. If you can't see it, it must not exist. Or if it does, it's irrelevant. Only **utilitarian** thinking has any validity."

"That's true," said Xela. "You have to get an overview."

"And it seems that there's a dominant sort of **metaphor** for describing the world in every era," Jaz continued. "In the mechanistic eighteenth century they had this fascination with the clock. Everything could be seen in terms of time, kept by all these clocks just merrily ticking away. The whole universe must be like a clock, people thought. Yeah, some **omnipotent** person made this clock—our universe—gave it a good winding,

288

put it on a shelf where it's been gathering dust, and it's been there ever since, tick tock, tick tock, year after year, eon after eon."

"Well, let's hope it *keeps* running," Simon said. "So does this guy *look* at the watch? I mean if he's so powerful and **omniscient** he must be able to tell the time without looking at his watch."

"It's just a metaphor," Jaz said.

"OK. But then tell me why this guy would bother to make a watch in the first place. And if he took the trouble to make it, why doesn't he bother to take a look at it? Wouldn't he ever think, 'Hey, I wonder if that watch I made a couple of billion years ago is still running? Maybe I'll take a look and see if it's still ticking away, see if it's lost any time or anything.'"

"Maybe he misplaced it," Xela said.

"Oh, great," Simon said. "He took it out to show his girl—I mean this must be one impressive watch—but for some reason she had no interest in it, and so he forgot all about it."

Jaz and Xela laughed. "Maybe he doesn't care enough about it to even bother looking for it," Jaz said.

"Now that's a depressing thought," Simon said. "But really, Jaz is right. I learned about it in history. The clock was *humongous* back then. Sort of like the computer to us. People desperately needed a way to keep accurate time. Without such a device they would have been lost—literally. I mean, it was the holy grail of the eighteenth century, the elusive thing everyone was searching for. Without a really accurate timekeeper, a ship's navigator can't determine his longitude very well. And if you can't tell your longitude pretty accurately, you don't know where you are in the ocean. **Cartography** wasn't exactly a precise science back then either, so maps were wildly distorted and weren't much help. Now, it's pretty obvious that if you can't tell where you are, you have a little bit of trouble sailing all over the world. You're always getting lost."

289

"And," Jaz said, "if you can't sail around the world without getting lost, the **mercenary** bit doesn't work out too well. You can't make a lot of **lucre** for Church and King if you spend most of your time sailing in circles."

"OK," Simon said, "we've established that that era was really into the clock idea. So, what's the hot metaphor in our time?"

"Maybe what you mentioned before—the computer," Jaz said. "It's *perfect*. It's totally mechanistic, so it doesn't involve any violation of the materialistic view we're so **enamored** of. And it *thinks*."

"Or at least it *seems* to think," Xela said.

"That's close enough. To most people, it thinks. It *must* think. Heck, it's smarter than us most of the time. It's a *machine that thinks*. It shows there can be a mind in a soulless universe."

"So that means that our existence makes some kind of sense after all," Simon said.

"Right. If a machine can think like us, or even better than us, it must mean that mind is a natural, reasonable outcome of mechanistic processes, not some scary 'ghost in the machine'—a soul in a body—that must be **exorcised** at all costs."

"So you're saying we tend to look at the world through this metaphor of the computer?" Simon asked.

"Yes. Simon, a while ago you mentioned Professor Swenson. You said that to him the world is essentially information. Well, that kind of view is just an extreme version of what I'm talking about," Jaz said. "We tend to think that if we just have enough data, we can find out the truth. Just keep feeding information into the computer, let it keep crunching those numbers, and eventually the truth will pop up on the monitor."

"And don't a lot of psychologists spend a lot of their time building models of the brain based on the metaphor of the brain as a computer?" Simon asked.

"Yes," Jaz said. "And there's this obsession with artificial intelligence—AI, to use the **acronym**—now too. Simulate

290

thinking, you have thinking. Logical. Simple. Simulate rain; you have rain."

"You just have to use your imagination," Simon said. "So Jaz, what do you think *your* metaphor for looking at the world is?"

"Well, I guess according to my view I would be the worst person to answer that question because I'm arguing that it's difficult for a person to see past the main idea he or she uses for interpreting the world. I mean, how can I look at it objectively, from the outside, and see what I fundamentally see things in terms of? It seems like a kind of **futile** exercise."

"Come on, Jaz. You're the smartest person I know—except for Axel, anyway. Can't you by a **Herculean** effort **emancipate** yourself from your world view?"

"OK. I'll give it a shot. Well, it might be the very fact that I see everything in terms of paradigms for looking at the world."

"So, how about more generally," Simon said. "Do you think there's anything besides the computer, and maybe these paradigms, that's a dominant way of viewing the world in contemporary America?"

"Oh, that's a much easier question to answer. Its influence is ubiquitous. It sets our society's **agenda**. It decides what is important in our culture, even what is real. Homeless people? No way. Not in The Land of the Free. It's at the heart of our reality. Studies have shown that a huge number of people would rather give up their *spouse* than this trusty friend. To most people, life without it would be unimaginable."

"The tube?"

"Bingo, Simon. If it isn't on the tube, it isn't real. If it wasn't on *Oprah,* it can't be worth much, can it, although some of the books she used to recommend are really **maudlin**."

"Seriously," Jaz said, "when historians hundreds of years from now look back and analyze the worldview of twentieth-century America, I bet they look mainly at a lot of tapes of old television shows."

Simon thought of these guys watching endless reruns—*The Little Rascals, Flash Gordon, The Honeymooners, I Love Lucy, I Dream of Jeannie, Bewitched, Dallas, Happy Days, The Flintstones, All in the Family, Bay Watch, The Days of Our Lives, Melrose Place, The X-Files, The Simpsons, Charmed, Buffy the Vampire Slayer, Friends,*— scribbling on electronic tablets, trying to make sense of it all.

"That's a little depressing, Jaz," Simon said. "You mean, you think that'll be our biggest **legacy**? The *box*?"

"Yep. That's where we seem to be at. That's where we *live*. The Entertainers. Life as one gigantic soap opera. Or an endless sit-com, the same laugh track endlessly playing, those same cackling women and guffawing men, for eternity."

"You know," Simon said, "I can imagine these historians a millennium from now watching our TV shows, trying to figure us out. Suddenly one of them leaps up and cries, 'That's it! I've found it. The twentieth-century Americans achieved the **zenith** of civilization and discovered the ultimate truth. But like the ancient Egyptians, Atlanteans, and Lemurians before them, they cleverly disguised their deepest wisdom teachings. These guys were really wily, you see. They acted stupid, created a truly **vapid** mass culture that any casual, intelligent observer would see as the product of fourth-rate minds. Well, my friends, I have discovered the **occult** mystery hidden in these programs. Here, take a look at this still video frame.

"*That's* what they knew and that we have lost. *Any resemblance between this program and reality is purely coincidental.* All these shows were fantasies—completely **fictitious**. Even the most obtuse of them must have known this. We have taken the programs as real, and tried to build an elaborate account of these people based on fantasy, explaining inconsistencies away with clever but facile scholarship. How could Larry Hagman be an astronaut in the early 1960s on *I Dream of Jeannie* but in the 1980s be a tycoon on *Dallas*? You see, the truth is, these guys had discovered the ultimate secret—the road to perfect contentment, how to really *chill out*, as they so aptly put it. In short, my friends, they perfected the art of being couch potatoes. Just watch the box all day. Live in an artificial, alternative reality of caring moms and doting dads, where all the girls are blond cheerleaders and everyone is middle class with a **colossal** house in the suburbs and an SUV in the driveway the size of a tank. No drugs, no poverty, no racism, no ghettoes. No huge **disparities** in wealth between people. Where violence has been **eradicated** and Americans have no enemies in the world because everyone just *loves* them."

Definitions

1. **iconoclastic** ADJ. attacking cherished beliefs
2. **preeminent** ADJ. notable above all others
3. **utilitarian** ADJ. stressing the value of practicality (also: functional; useful)
4. **metaphor** N. figure of speech that compares two different things
5. **omnipotent** ADJ. having unlimited power
6. **omniscient** ADJ. having infinite knowledge
7. **cartography** N. science of making maps
8. **mercenary** ADJ. interested in money or gain
9. **lucre** N. money
10. **enamored** ADJ. captivated
11. **exorcised** V. to drive out evil spirit; free from bad influence
12. **acronym** N. word formed from the initial letters of a name or series of words
13. **futile** ADJ. fruitless
14. **Herculean** ADJ. calling for great strength
15. **emancipate** V. to free
16. **agenda** N. list or program of things to be done
17. **maudlin** ADJ. overly sentimental
18. **legacy** N. something handed down
19. **zenith** N. highest point
20. **vapid** ADJ. dull and uninteresting

21. **occult** ADJ. secret
22. **fictitious** ADJ. imaginary
23. **colossal** ADJ. huge
24. **disparity** N. difference
25. **eradicated** V. wiped out

Simply Simon

Think you know the words? Then prove it! Choose the *best* word to fill in the blank in each of the sentences below.

preeminent   omniscient   maudlin   futile

utilitarian   legacy   agenda   zenith

exorcise   lucre

1. Many experts believe that Albert Einstein was the _____ scientist of the twentieth century.

2. In designing a building, an architect should put _____ concerns first.

3. Jaz has come to the conclusion that teaching me to cook is a/an _____ exercise, so I just get pizza or something when she doesn't feel like cooking.

4. Some historians believe that Western civilization has already reached its _____ and is now beginning a long period of decline.

5. Being _____ would be cool for a college student because he wouldn't have to study.

6. I notice Jaz has written "clean house" on tomorrow's _____ that she puts on the bulletin board in the kitchen.

7. Jaz described my favorite soap opera as "hopelessly _____ ," so I was surprised to come home one day and find her totally absorbed in it.

8. The _____ of ancient Greece lives on in much of the language, art, and thought of Western civilization.

9. I am one of those people who believes that _____ is beginning to dominate sports in America.

10. Professor Chandler says that Germany is still trying to _____ the memory of its actions in World War II.

Making Sense

Indicate whether or not each of the words in **bold** makes sense in the sentence. If it makes sense, put Y (Yes); if it doesn't make sense, put N (No).

1. The United States government has such a **colossal** public debt that it spends billions of dollars a year paying interest on the money it owes. ____

2. Scientists generally try to employ as many **metaphors** as they can in formulating laws of nature so that their language is precise and logical. ____

3. Some writers have said that one of the rewards—or perhaps dangers—of the craft of fiction is the feeling you get of being the **omnipotent** ruler of a universe that you alone govern. ____

4. I believe that education has broadened my outlook on life and **emancipated** me from many of the prejudices I used to have. ____

5. I have a little device in my Nissan Patrol that a **cartographer** or navigator of the eighteenth century would have given his two front teeth for; it uses three satellites orbiting the earth to determine my position accurately to within about 30 feet. ____

6. The Greek philosopher Socrates was a most **mercenary** kind of person; he always refused to accept money for his teaching because he was afraid it would influence his pursuit of the truth. ____

7. "Lucent," a word meaning "shining" in Latin, was the **acronym** chosen as the name of a company. ____

8. I once read a science-fiction novel that portrayed a society in which virtually all the differences between the sexes had been **eradicated**. ____

9. My English professor, Dr. Miller, says he has great admiration for the **Herculean** effort made by Dr. James Murray, the first editor of the Oxford English Dictionary, to create a dictionary illustrating the origin and history of nearly every word in the English language. ____

10. People throughout history seem to have had a strong need to make up **fictitious** characters and tell stories about them. ____

Match It

Match each of the following words to its meaning.

1. iconoclastic	a. difference
2. enamored	b. attacking cherished beliefs
3. occult	c. figure of speech that compares two different things
4. disparity	d. interested in money or gain
5. vapid	e. captivated
6. metaphor	f. free
7. omnipotent	g. secret
8. mercenary	h. highest point
9. emancipate	i. having unlimited power
10. zenith	j. dull and uninteresting

Axel Speaks

Greetings! I believe that you are now ready for something more intellectual. Choose the *best* word to fill in the blank in each sentence.

1. The fact that serious books are now being written discussing various methods of sending explorers, and perhaps, one day, settlers, to Mars, suggests that the issue of a manned mission to Mars is now on the American political _____.

(A) tableau

(B) zenith

(C) legacy

(D) agenda

(E) edifice

2. The American poet Walt Whitman was a notable practitioner of free verse; he was a/an _____ writer who challenged the poetic practices of his day, using free verse to convey his theme of the freedom and nobility of the individual.

(A) omniscient

(B) iconoclastic

(C) vapid

(D) utilitarian

(E) maudlin

3. Despite the tremendous advances in medicine that were made in the twentieth century, doctors are far from _____; for example, they remain ignorant of the causes of most diseases.

(A) enamored

(B) preeminent

(C) Herculean

(D) omniscient

(E) mercenary

4. The Internet was invented by an agency of the United States Department of Defense, the Advanced Research Projects Agency (known also by the _____ ARPA) as a system to connect research computers around the country.

(A) agenda

(B) appellation

(C) acronym

(D) metaphor

(E) euphemism

5. Freudian psychotherapy can be likened to _____ the "demons" in one's subconscious mind so that one is freed from their influence.

(A) debunking

(B) emancipating

(C) chiding

(D) exorcising

(E) censuring

Answers on page 464.

And now, on with the story.

How Jaz Bumped Into Axel

"That was quite a **diatribe**, Simon," Jaz said. "It must have been really **cathartic** for you. I didn't know you felt so strongly about TV."

Simon grinned sheepishly. "I got carried away there. Actually, I don't believe most of what I just said. But I think it demonstrates something important."

"What's that?" Jaz asked.

"How a guy can let his own **rhetoric** take him away from the truth."

"That was pretty sensational toward the end there," Jaz said. "Really polemical. And **vitriolic** too. Maybe you should go on the tube."

Jaz turned to Xela. "What do you think, Xela? Should Simon go on TV? He can go on TV and be a sensation," Jaz said. "He could have his own talk show."

"Yeah, well there's some truth in what I said. It's not all hot air."

"I would never accuse you of being full of hot air, Simon. Would I?"

Xela started laughing. "Hey you two, break it up. I'll go find some boxing gloves if you guys want to take up **pugilism**."

"Well, we've certainly covered a little ground, haven't we?" Simon said. "Globalization, philosophic truth, paradigms and metaphors for thinking about the world, the influence of the media. Can anyone think of anything we left out?"

"It's good preparation for later tonight," Jaz said. And I'm enjoying hearing some new points of view. Xela, you certainly seem to have given a lot of thought to things."

"From what I heard," Xela said, "Axel always keeps a pretty good eye out for the truth too. I'm really looking forward to meeting him and hearing what he has to say."

"When he comes down," Simon said.

"*If* he comes down," Jaz said.

"Well," Xela said. "Look, I'm a pretty patient girl. I've been hearing about Axel for the past couple of hours. I'm beginning to wonder if he's some kind of mythical creature that you guys **concocted**. I mean, where *is* he?"

Simon and Jaz looked at each other.

"Listen," Xela said. "I'll just go freshen up. Maybe he'll come down while I'm gone." She got up to leave.

"Through there," Jaz said.

"Thanks," Xela said, and walked out of the room.

"OK," Jaz said, nodding her head. "Is it just me, or was that just a little strange?"

"It was a little odd," Simon said. "It's like she suddenly decided to become another person. She was probably just hamming it up. We all know how you girls sometimes like to put on your little acts."

"Yeah. A lot of females do seem to be into **histrionics**."

"Isn't that stereotyping and generalizing, Jaz?"

"Some generalizations are true, you know. Anyway, since I'm a female myself, I'm less likely to incur the **wrath** of the thought police. But anyway, what I want to know is, who is that woman?"

"She's Xela. I met her at Pete's Place."

"Yeah, yeah. I know. But who *is* she? Where is she from? What does she *do*?"

"You know, it's funny. Several times I started to ask her that and somehow I never do," Simon said.

"That happened to me too," Jaz said. "It's like I'm going to ask her where she's from and what she's doing, but somehow I seem to forget to. But there's something about her."

"There's a *lot* about her," Simon said.

"Yeah, that's just it. She seems—I don't know how to describe it exactly—sort of more real than real is the only way I can express it. Not that she's weird or anything. Exceptional, yes. But she's also completely human. You know what I mean? It's just a feeling I get."

"I know, I know," Simon said. "And we both feel so close to her and we've only known her a little while. I thought she must be some kind of angel when I first met her."

"Yeah, me too. She seems so pure and good. But not in some **intangible** way."

"She's certainly a fully **corporeal** girl. And one thing's for sure, she certainly is keen on meeting Axel," Simon said.

"It's like she has some kind of intuition about him."

"I know. Well, we both certainly built him up as one amazing guy. I hope she isn't disappointed."

"Disappointed?" Jaz said. "I'm shocked that you could even suggest that Axel won't meet her expectations."

"Oh, I forgot. Axel has such a great record with girls. Especially gorgeous, scintillating girls like Xela," Simon said. "He'll just sweep her off her feet, as usual."

"Just wait," Jaz said. "You'll see."

Xela walked back into the room. Simon watched her as she sat down on the carpet. Why, he reflected, do virtually all attractive girls sit on the floor like that? Was it **inherent**, a genetic trait that is a **concomitant** of beauty? Or is there some school they go to that teaches it? Whatever the reason for the behavior was, they all did it; they sort of curled up like cats, looking totally **winsome.**

"So, Jaz," Xela said, "while we wait for the grand entrance of the elusive Axel, maybe you could fill me in on how you met Simon. I mean, you did promise to tell me, remember?"

"OK," Jaz said. "But first I have to tell you the story of how Axel and I met. That came first, you see."

"OK, shoot," Xela said.

"It was my freshman year, the first day of Astrophysics. I was really looking forward to this class because the professor is like world class. He's at the **pinnacle** of the astrophysics field. The only other people in the class were a few graduate students."

"Yeah, that's because there are only a few people around who can understand that stuff," Simon said.

"Well, I guess it was sort of an advanced class. Cosmology, General Relativity. Kind of technical. Anyway, I notice one guy. He's sitting by himself at the back of the room. He looked sort of lonely. I felt kind of sorry for him."

"Jaz feels sorry for everybody," Simon said. "She's the original Good Samaritan."

"Anyway," Jaz continued, "I'm looking at him, and he notices me. Of course, he totally avoids my look and kind of hides behind this big pile of books on his table."

"Axel always carts these huge tomes around," Simon said. "He says they're indispensable."

"Well, at least he gets some exercise," Xela said.

"So, during class," Jaz said, "I occasionally try to take a peek at him. Of course, every time I turn around, he sees me and hunkers down behind his books. Anyway, this little game goes on for quite awhile. Then, one time I turn suddenly. Professor Naxos was just coming to the end of quite an **intricate** line of reasoning in quantum theory. I look up and I see the most amazing look on Axel's face."

"What was it like?" Xela asked.

"It was like he was in *love*. I mean, he was completely transfixed. I could see he really liked this stuff. That look really made me want to talk to him."

"But he's not exactly the most gregarious guy around," Simon said. "Meeting Axel is not the easiest thing in the world to do."

"It was strange. The class was over and we were walking out the door, starting down a few steps of stairs out to the lawn. And he sort of bumps into me a little."

"You're sure it wasn't more like you sort of got in his way a little so he couldn't help bump into you? Girls are always doing that to me," Simon said.

"No," Jaz said. "Really. No **nefarious subterfuge** was involved. I mean, if I didn't know he was so totally timid and introverted, I would have sworn he did it on purpose. Like he knew he wanted to meet me."

"So, then what happened?" Xela asked.

"Well, it was pretty funny. I'm in front of him on the steps, and I hear, 'Aarrgh.' I turn, and, suddenly, Axel is in my arms. I mean we're *really* face to face. I'm not the biggest person in the world, so his momentum carries us both to the ground. I'm on my back with him on top of me."

Simon and Xela were both laughing. "So that's how you bumped into Axel," Xela said.

"Yes, as I told you before, his social skills are a little rudimentary. Anyway, we untangle ourselves and get up. Of course, he's completely **flustered** and apologetic. Notes and books are strewn all over the place."

"I've got to hand it to the guy, though," Simon said. "It might be a little **gauche**, but that is one heck of an original way to meet a woman."

"So he's apologizing like crazy, and the more he apologizes the more I laugh. Talk about your stereotyped absent-minded professor! I mean it was too hysterical for me to be mad. But suddenly I notice this book on the ground. *New Frontiers in General Relativity.* I said, 'Wow! That looks like an amazing book. Are you into Minkowski spacetime or more recent formulations?' Well, he kind of froze. He looks at me and said, 'Yes. General Relativity is currently one of my research areas with Professor Nexus.'" Jaz paused and smiled. "Now, I happened to have done a little bit of work in that area."

"Jaz is incorrigibly modest," Simon said. "What she means is that she's had articles published in *Physical Review Letters,* the most **prestigious** journal in the field," Simon said.

"Anyway," Jaz continued, "I say, 'I think Professor Nexus' tensor field analysis is excellent, but it needs some refinement. Can I make a little suggestion? Maybe you guys should look more at the Bianchi identity in relation to Einstein's field equation.' Axel's jaw dropped a little when I said that, I must admit. I mean, he could see I knew quite a bit about this stuff. He says, 'What do you think of the Reimann tensors? Are they still valid?'"

"And I said, 'Well it's still the most **tenable** approach we have. Based on Dr. Luxor's recent work in Holland, however, the paradigm might have to be revised.' Axel just looks at me. He just says, 'That's amazing. It never occurred to me that there might be something wrong with the entire paradigm. How did you come up with that? Nobody's been able to make any progress at all in that area. The whole field has been practically **moribund**. This gives us a chance to attack the problem in a whole new way.' Anyway, he invited me back to his house and we discussed relativity and astrophysics all night."

"And they've been doing that ever since," Simon said. "They work together on a lot of stuff."

"I bat ideas around in cosmology and other areas with Axel. And he often gives me ideas for my psych projects. Our interests are very **complementary**. We're both into cosmology, the origin of life, evolution, the place of mind in the universe. Axel is more into the physics of it, while I'm more interested in the psychological and even **metaphysical** aspects of such areas."

"Yep, those two like the simple things in life. Real down-to-earth things, like the **genesis** of consciousness and the fate of the cosmos," Simon said.

Xela laughed. "So, Jaz, what kind of stuff are you working on with Axel now?" she asked.

1. **diatribe** N. bitter verbal attack
2. **cathartic** ADJ. purifying; cleansing
3. **rhetoric** N. pretentious language
4. **vitriolic** ADJ. sharp; bitter; scathing
5. **pugilism** N. boxing
6. **concoct** V. to invent
7. **histrionics** N. exaggerated behavior for effect (also: theatrical arts)
8. **wrath** N. anger
9. **intangible** ADJ. incapable of being perceived by the senses
10. **corporeal** ADJ. material; tangible
11. **inherent** ADJ. firmly established by nature or habit
12. **concomitant** N. something that exists concurrently with something else
13. **winsome** ADJ. charming; engaging
14. **pinnacle** N. peak
15. **intricate** ADJ. complex
16. **nefarious** ADJ. wicked
17. **subterfuge** n. deceptive strategy; trick
18. **flustered** ADJ. nervous; upset; confused
19. **gauche** ADJ. lacking social grace
20. **prestigious** ADJ. esteemed
21. **tenable** ADJ. defensible; reasonable
22. **moribund** ADJ. about to die
23. **complementary** ADJ. supplying mutual needs; completing
24. **metaphysical** ADJ. pertaining to speculative philosophy
25. **genesis** N. origin

Simply Simon

Think you know the words? Then prove it! Choose the *best* word to fill in the blank in each of the sentences below.

genesis   pinnacle   diatribes   pugilism   wrath

intricate   prestigious   gauche   concomitant

winsome

1. Radio phone-in show hosts generally cut off people who launch into long _____ against what they think is wrong with the world.

2. A/An _____ of economic progress in a developing country seems to be a weakening of traditional family bonds.

3. Tokyo University is one of the most _____ universities in Japan.

4. Axel once tried to explain the _____ workings of the central processing unit in a digital computer to me, but I lost him after about a minute.

5. _____ is one of the oldest sports in the world.

6. I can't remember the exact quote, but William James, the great philosopher, said something like, "If a young person applies himself steadily to his work he will one day find himself at the _____ of his chosen field."

7. I'm certain that Axel is not deliberately _____; he just seems unaware of the little things that make up social grace.

8. To avoid incurring Jaz's _____, I decided to skip my old friend's bachelor party.

9. Some scientists believe that the _____ of life is a rare event in the universe, while others argue that it probably occurs routinely.

10. Axel says that from a purely scientific viewpoint the _____ look of the human female is merely a clever device developed through evolution to attract as many potential mates as possible; it sure seems like a lot more than that to me though.

Making Sense

Indicate whether or not each of the words in **bold** makes sense in the sentence. If it makes sense, put Y (Yes); if it doesn't make sense, put N (No).

1. Many people find confessing something they've done wrong to be a **cathartic** experience. ____

2. My parents taught me that the most important thing in life is to always be honest and to use **subterfuge** at every opportunity. ____

3. Even a great statesman like Sir Winston Churchill allowed himself flights of **rhetoric** at times, but he always returned quickly to solid ground. ____

4. I've found a big dose of **vitriolic** sweet talk can get you out of some pretty tight spots. ____

5. Jaz is generally a serious person, but as Axel found out in the art museum, she can **concoct** some pretty amusing pranks. ____

6. Scientists say that the sun is a middle-aged star in such a **moribund** state that it will keep burning for billions of years. ____

7. The ancient Greeks seemed to have believed in gods and goddesses who took **corporeal** form, often hanging out with guys or girls they thought were cool. ____

8. Nothing is more **inherent** to me than finding out that one of our top receivers has been declared academically ineligible. ____

9. Coach Wilson and his offense coach have come up with some plays for the game against State that are so clever they're almost **nefarious**. ____

10. Back in high school I told Alice, a girl who had already been accepted by Princeton and MIT, that although she was an extremely attractive woman, my interest in her was purely of a **metaphysical** nature. ____

Match It
Match each of the following words to its meaning.

1. histrionics   a. incapable of being perceived by the senses

2. intangible   b. defensible; reasonable

3. flustered   c. material

4. tenable   d. deceptive strategy

5. complementary   e. origin

6. cathartic   f. exaggerated behavior for effect

7. corporeal   g. supplying mutual needs

8. subterfuge   h. about to die

9. moribund   i. purifying

10. genesis   j. nervous; confused

Axel Speaks

Greetings! I believe that you are now ready for something more intellectual. Choose the *best* word to fill in the blank in each sentence.

1. Some historians have maintained that the economic cost to Britain of maintaining India as a colony outweighed the gains, but others argue that Britain gained important _____ benefits from its colonies.

(A) tenable

(B) nefarious

(C) corporeal

(D) metaphysical

(E) intangible

2. The satire of the English Victorian novelist Anthony Trollope can be described as Horatian because it is mild and amused, unlike Juvenalian satire, which is _____ and outraged.

(A) subtle

(B) flustered

(C) vitriolic

(D) sublime

(E) cathartic

3. Hinduism, in contrast to Christianity, believes that human beings are not _____ sinful, and that people do bad things only out of ignorance and unhappiness.

(A) inherently

(B) intricately

(C) lavishly

(D) rationally

(E) concomitantly

4. It appears that bureaucracies are today a necessary evil—a _____ of modern society.

(A) subterfuge

(B) concomitant

(C) diatribe

(D) legacy

(E) pinnacle

5. Over the last several years astronomers have accumulated indirect evidence for planets in orbit around stars other than the sun through observations of irregularities in the movement of stars hundreds of light years away, making a belief in extraterrestrial life more _____ .

(A) utilitarian

(B) prosaic

(C) nefarious

(D) gauche

(E) tenable

Answers on pages 464–465.

And now, on with the story.

Bingo!

"Right now," Jaz said, "Axel and I are working on some really fascinating stuff. In fact, we've just completed some amazing extrapolations based on recent findings showing that there have been changes in the fine structure constant of the universe. That means the laws of the universe are not immutable, but changing over time. The **implications** are quite astounding, really."

"What do you mean?" Simon asked.

"Okay, it seems very possible—indeed very likely—that there are many different planes of reality that exist besides this one."

"Planes?" Simon said.

"Look at it this way. Everything that exists is kind of vibrating, right?"

"Yeah, I guess."

"Well, it seems that this vibration is a constant in the universe. At least in this universe. Everything that exists in it vibrates at this rate."

"But I thought things had different frequencies?"

"They do, but that's only on one level. Listen, if you want this in "dude" **terminology** I can't go into higher mathematics and the more recondite ramifications of the discovery. The best way to put it is to say that at a deeper level it's all the same. That's why, for example, you can see me and I can see you. We're on the same plane."

"Okay, I'm with you so far."

"So, now imagine there are other places that are vibrating at a different sort of rate. These places—let's call them planes—each would probably have its own **distinctive** appearance and so forth, right?"

"That makes sense. If something so fundamental is different, other things would probably be different too. So, what kind of folks do you think live on these other planes?" Simon asked.

"Now, that is a good question,' Jaz said. "I mean, that gets us into minds ... consciousness."

"Do you think they would be like us? I mean, would they love barbecues, tell a lot of jokes, struggle to pass College Math, have a wonderful girlfriend, like to flirt a little?"

Jaz laughed. "And play football? I have no idea. But the evidence suggests that mind is the unifying and fundamental force. If that's true, then maybe thought is pretty much the same everywhere. It's just the physical universe that would be different."

"Something just occurred to me," Simon said. "Jaz, isn't one of your theories that a lot of paranormal stuff that happens is the result of these other planes sort of bumping into ours? Angels and other spirits, ghosts, even UFOs, could be things on other planes that are kind of **protruding** from their own plane, poking a bit into ours. So, they appear to us to be kind of coming from out of nowhere. They just seem to pop into existence and then pop back out. At least from our perspective."

"So, Jaz," Xela said. "If these planes do exist, it might be possible, at least theoretically, for beings on one plane to contact those on another. Maybe even visit, right?"

Jaz pondered. "Theoretically, yes. Practically, it would be hard to imagine. I told you before about the evidence that some extraterrestrial **entity** has been contacting people using telepathy. That makes sense to me if the being is in our physical universe. I know the evidence is that telepathy transcends the laws of **causality**, as well as our ideas of space and time. But I've been working on the **presumption** that

314

these guys are in our universe, not some hypothetical other plane. I have to stress that although the planes are well-supported theoretically, there is no evidence of their existence."

"But if ESP is independent of space and time, it's **conceivable** that this communication could be from one of these planes," Simon said.

"Yes. But in science you're trained to first take the most straightforward hypothesis."

"Occam's Razor, right?" Simon said.

"Right," Jaz said. "The principle that says you should cut through convoluted explanations and theories like a razor and choose the simplest and least exotic one. Explain the unexplained in terms of things you already know. As I said, these planes could exist. Sentient creatures could even live in them. But there's no corroboration for either possibility. It's just interesting, though quite well supported, speculation in an area of physics called string theory. On the other hand, the evidence for telepathy is **conclusive**. So why **posit** the existence of these planes when you're trying to explain telepathy?"

"But," Xela said, "if the planes do exist, communication between planes certainly seems like a possibility at least."

"I suppose."

"How about actual travel?" she asked.

"Now that seems really hard to imagine," Jaz said. "Even if we provisionally accept that an object could be sent from one plane to another plane, the question of what would happen to a passenger—a living creature—arises. I mean, if different laws control each plane, you would think that a traveler would face some pretty **insuperable** difficulties. For example, the laws of chemistry would no doubt be different, so you have to wonder how an organism from another plane could function in ours. Even time could be different. Maybe it flows in a different direction on each plane. Or, maybe instead of being **linear**, it's circular."

"It sounds like he would be one confused guy," Simon said.

"If he could stay alive long enough to be confused," Jaz said. "It just doesn't seem to be a **viable** way to travel."

"But is it at least conceivable that some sort of way to protect a traveler could be **fabricated**?" Xela asked.

"Well," Jaz said, "there would have to be some way to counteract the disparities between his world and the one he's visiting. Or some way to at least **mitigate** the effects."

"How about some sort of capsule," Simon said. "It would protect him, allow him to function like he's in his own world."

"OK," Jaz said. "Let's say that it's possible. But even if it's **feasible**, how could he interact with the environment around this capsule?"

"The capsule would be designed so he could have some contact with the other plane," Simon said. "Sort of like a plastic bubble around him that's **impermeable** to things that would harm him but would allow in certain things. He could see and perceive—maybe not perfectly, but well enough—and he would be protected. His life processes could function normally." Simon paused. "You know, Jaz," he said, "I'm still a little confused about one thing. You said before it seems pretty clear that mind is the fundamental force, right?"

"Yes."

"Well, then isn't it true that these planes are ultimately mental constructs? I mean, everything seems to be a result of consciousness. So, if consciousness *creates* the world, consciousness can *change* the world too, can't it?" Simon said.

"Maybe," Jaz replied. "You were talking before about planes possibly rubbing against each other, interacting sort of at the periphery. Well, my research on UFOs supports that. Very often they're described by observers as sort of 'popping into' our reality, totally violating the laws of motion, time, and so forth in our universe, and then popping back out again. The famous **psychiatrist** Carl Jung thought that UFOs might be creations of the human **psyche**, something we create because we live in this extremely rational world to fulfill our need for the magical, the nonrational. Maybe he was

316

right in that they're mental constructs, but wrong about whose constructs they are."

"You mean they're somebody *else's* sort of mental projections?" Xela asked.

"Yes," Jaz said. "And not necessarily just shadowy, intangible mental constructions either—fancies of somebody's brain. Sometimes I wonder if these UFOs—or at least some of them, are some sort of actual 'mental' craft like we were positing just now."

"So, it could be possible for these travelers to use *thought* to modify the plane around them enough so they could survive and interact?" Xela asked.

"Bingo!" a voice said. It came from the landing on the stairs to the second story.

"Axel!" Simon cried.

Simon got up and went up the stairs to the landing where Axel was sitting. "How long have you been here, Ax?" Simon asked.

"I've been enjoying the discussion. Quite a high level of discourse, I must say."

"Come on Ax, come and join the party."

Axel strode into the room.

"Axel, it's great to see you," Jaz said. "I guess you heard what we've been discussing."

"Yes. And I was most impressed." He looked at Xela. "And," he said, "I was particularly impressed with that last observation." He gazed steadily at Xela. He was, thought Jaz, like someone who had been sleepwalking for a long time but who was now fully conscious. Jaz was dumbfounded. Axel looked almost like a different person. He **exuded** absolute confidence and control. He was looking at Xela with an expression she had never seen before. It was a look of total love. And Xela was gazing back at Axel, completely **enraptured**. Axel and Xela, Jaz thought, were like lovers who had been reunited after some unimaginably long separation.

"Your name is Xela," Axel said.

"Yes."

317

"So, what do you think? Do you think it's possible for beings to travel from one plane to another?"

"Purely theoretically?"

"Of course. Purely theoretically."

Xela smiled. Simon had seen Xela smile quite a few times, and each one was etched **indelibly** in his memory. But this smile transcended all the others. It was the smile of a **cherub** before the Almighty. Her eyes shone with total adoration. He was speechless. And Axel seemed *huge*, a towering figure surveying his kingdom with godlike **detachment**. Aloof to everything. Except his Queen.

Jaz too watched the couple in awe. What had happened to Axel, the **timorous** little boy? she wondered. Here was a *man*. A man in total control. She thought of King Odysseus returning from his long voyage to claim his kingdom, coming home to the arms of his faithful, adoring wife, Penelope. It was as though some virtually **impervious** protective layer had been removed from him and she was seeing him for the first time as he really was. She had never thought of Axel as particularly handsome. Now he looked like a god—the most purely masculine man she had ever seen. Xela continued to look at Axel. He was her object of devotion. Rays of joy seemed to be **emanating** from her, like some powerful **cosmic** phenomenon.

Jaz sensed waves of emotion so intense that the synapses of her brain seemed to be firing overtime. Somehow, she was drawn into these emotions, sharing the intimate feelings of these two beings. What they had endured! *Longing. Endless longing. Waiting. Love. So much love. Worry. Loneliness. And, now, joy.* **Ineffable** *joy.* Waves of emotion were surging across Axel's face. *Helplessness. Loneliness. Longing. Relief. Joy. Tenderness.* And then a new look came over him—certainty and resolve.

Axel looked at Jaz and smiled. He then turned to Xela and took her hand. Jaz felt that she could hear the thoughts that passed between them.

It has been so hard.

I know. I'm here now. I've come to bring you home.

So long. It has seemed like eternity.

Dearest, dearest. I've waited for millennia. So hard, watching you, not being near you.

Union. Union soon.

It is nearing completion. They are evolving.

Yes, I've seen it. It is so hard. I saw through their eyes. So alone. So lonely. Separate individuals. But they love too.

I know, dearest. I was with you, but you could not know.

Union soon.

They are the ones?

Yes. The boy and the girl. I'm coming home soon, dearest.

Dearest, dearest.

They will survive? I love them.

Your work has been perfect. They are ready. I think they already know, each in their own way.

They are so young. To bear such a burden.

They are seeds. Their race will grow from them. Others will evolve too.

Can we not give them a little more time?

The threat is too great. The Dark Ones control too much of their planet already. Through the Consortium they control the minds of the most important people in every sector. Simon and Jaz must move now—tonight and tomorrow. It is their only hope, however small it has become. They must teach their people to work together to break the grip the Pleiadesians have on them. Only these two can do it. They are ready. They must be ready. There is no other way.

Can we not stay a little longer? To help them?

You know, dearest, the Dark Ones have already nearly discovered us. And now that we have

319

*contacted the two humans in their own plane
there is very little time. The Observer will locate
our thought waves. At any moment they will find
us. We cannot stand against them alone. I have
come for you. We will return as one.*

But they will be alone.

*They will fight. We have done all we can. Simon is
strong. He will lead them well. And he will have
Jaz at his side.*

A feeling of appreciation and love swept over Jaz. What
these two had suffered for humanity! Separated for millennia.
So another species could grow. To shield it from danger to
give it a chance to survive.

She looked at Simon, who was gazing, awestruck, at the
transmogrification his friend had undergone. Axel smiled at
Simon and stood next to him, still holding Xela's hand in his.
Gently, he put his other hand on Simon's shoulder. He
seemed to tower over Simon.

"My dear friend," he said.

Simon was silent. Tears were in his eyes.

"You're not so simple, are you Simon?" Axel said.

Simon smiled. He nodded slowly.

"So it's true, after all?" Jaz said.

Neither Xela nor Axel spoke.

"We are not alone in the universe, are we?" Jaz said.

Simon heard a voice speaking clearly in his mind. *You
know who I am, don't you?* It was Axel, now totally com-
manding. It was a voice that sounded almost infinitely old and
sagacious. Yet there was something else, something feminine—gentle and tender—in the voice. Xela. And Axel.
Together at last.

"You are Lexa, aren't you?" Simon said.

Axel and Xela, hands still joined, stood side by side. They
smiled at Simon.

"Hey, Ax," Simon said. "I guess you found what you've
been looking for, haven't you?"

I'm home already, in a way. Axel kissed Xela.

"Do you really have to leave?"

Yes.

Jaz got up and stood next to Simon. She put her arms around his big shoulders and kissed him. Then she stood by Axel.

"You really do have to go home, don't you?" she asked Axel.

Axel nodded. "You guys always thought I was a little weird, didn't you?"

"Yeah," Simon said. "But cool. Definitely cool."

Definitions

1. **implication** N. something suggested
2. **terminology** N. specialized vocabulary
3. **distinctive** ADJ. characteristic
4. **protrude** V. to stick out
5. **entity** N. something that exists
6. **causality** N. relationship between cause and effect
7. **presumption** N. belief based on reasonable evidence
8. **conceivable** ADJ. believable; credible
9. **conclusive** ADJ. decisive; ending all controversy
10. **posit** V. to assume to be true; postulate
11. **insuperable** ADJ. insurmountable
12. **linear** ADJ. like a straight line
13. **viable** ADJ. practicable
14. **fabricate** V. to construct
15. **mitigate** V. to make less severe; moderate
16. **feasible** ADJ. possible
17. **impermeable** ADJ. not permitting passage through its substance
18. **psychiatrist** N. doctor who treats disorders of the mind
19. **psyche** N. mind

20. **exude** v. to give off
21. **enraptured** ADJ. filled with delight
22. **indelibly** ADV. permanently
23. **cherub** N. angel
24. **detachment** N. feeling of being emotionally removed; aloofness
25. **timorous** ADJ. fearful
26. **impervious** ADJ. not penetrable; impermeable; incapable of being affected
27. **emanate** v. to issue forth
28. **cosmic** ADJ. pertaining to the universe as distinct from Earth (N. cosmos)
29. **ineffable** ADJ. incapable of being expressed
30. **sagacious** ADJ. wise

Simply Simon

Think you know the words? Then prove it! Choose the *best* word to fill in the blank in each of the sentences below.

terminology   presumption   feasible   insuperable

cosmic   impermeable   distinctive   conceivable

protrudes   exude

1. When Jaz goes to one of my football games in bad weather, she wears several layers of raincoats that are _____ to water.

2. I've found that before you study a subject you're not familiar with it's helpful to learn some of its commonly used _____.

3. Miss Bridget, my creative writing instructor, says that each student should try to develop his or her own _____ style of writing.

4. Christine told me that Dr. Paunch, her English instructor, has a gut that _____ so far from his body that he uses it to put his lecture notes on during class.

5. Axel believes that what are now regarded as _____ barriers to faster than light travel may one day be overcome with the steady advance of science.

6. Most scientists believe that faster than light travel is not _____; they might be right, but we should remember that it wasn't long ago that leading scientists were saying the same thing about the use of nuclear energy.

7. A leader must _____ confidence to win the support of the community.

8. It amazes me to think that the light rays from a/an _____ event that occurred a billion years ago could be just reaching Earth now.

9. Axel has tried every _____ approach to improving my math skills, but he's beginning to think someone forgot to fit me with a math-processing chip.

10. I like teachers who act on the _____ that college students are mature young adults.

Making Sense

Indicate whether or not each of the words in **bold** makes sense in the sentence. If it makes sense, put Y (Yes); if it doesn't make sense, put N (No).

1. The **implications** for life on Earth of a large asteroid striking the planet every 26 million years or so are pretty depressing. ____

2. People in our culture tend to see time as **linear**—sort of like an arrow moving through the air, occupying one position in space after another. ____

3. One thing college has taught me: if you look at something with **detachment** you'll never be able to get a fair and unbiased view of it. ____

4. Several scientists, including Professor Richard Muller, have **posited** the existence of a companion dark star to the Sun that periodically causes comet storms that result in mass extinctions of life on Earth. ____

5. I'm such a **timorous** guy Coach Wilson always sends me to give talks in high schools and to various groups all over the state to help recruit good athletes. ____

6. After a lot of planning, I came up with a new play and showed it to Coach Wilson; he studied it and said that it was **viable** but that it just wouldn't work. ____

7. When I was young I thought old people were naturally **sagacious**; since then, however, I've met some pretty dumb people over 50. ____

8. The writer G. K. Chesterton expressed the view that the truths of the individual **psyche** are more difficult to find even than the truths of nature: "The self is more distant than any star," he said. ____

9. The first time I met Jaz is **indelibly** printed on my mind. ____

10. I like things that are clear and **ineffable** so you don't have a problem getting your head around them. ____

Match It

Match each of the following words to its meaning.

1. entity   a. decisive; ending all controversy
2. causality   b. construct
3. conclusive   c. angel
4. fabricate   d. something that exists
5. mitigate   e. make less severe
6. psychiatrist   f. not penetrable
7. enraptured   g. issue forth
8. cherub   h. doctor who treats disorders of the mind
9. impervious   i. relationship between cause and effect
10. emanate   j. filled with delight

Axel Speaks

Greetings! I believe you are now ready for something more intellectual. Choose the *best* word to fill in the blank in each sentence.

1. Some commentators have _____ the existence of a parallel to the Protestant work ethic in Chinese culture, which they call the "Confucian work ethic," to explain the economic success of some countries with large Chinese populations.

(A) cherished

(B) fabricated

(C) posited

(D) mitigated

(E) exuded

2. The _____ Carl Jung believed that humanity shares what he called the "collective unconscious," out of which arise particular symbols and images that appear in dreams, myths, and certain types of literature.

(A) interlocutor

(B) humorist

(C) exemplar

(D) psychiatrist

(E) cherub

3. According to the philosopher Karl Popper's view of the scientific method, since it is not possible to possess complete knowledge of anything it is never possible to obtain _____ proof of a theory; however, it is possible, according to Popper, to compile evidence that tends to confirm a theory or show it to be incorrect.

(A) conclusive

(B) conceivable

(C) prudent

(D) explicit

(E) sagacious

4. Proponents of experimentation on living animals (vivisection) argue that strict laws ensure that animals are subjected to suffering only when there is no _____ alternative.

(A) impervious

(B) cosmic

(C) utilitarian

(D) distinctive

(E) feasible

5. Moore's Law, which says computer processing power doubles every 18 months, proved remarkably accurate from the 1960s through the end of the twentieth century, but experts at Intel (a major microchip manufacturer) believe that this law may be broken, because seemingly _____ obstacles to progress arise as transistors on the microchips get as small as 100 atoms thick.

(A) viable

(B) cryptic

(C) ineffable

(D) insuperable

(E) abstract

Answers on pages 465–466.

And now, on with the story.

Lexa

So, thought Jaz. *It's true after all.*

Yes.

Telepathy? Aliens? Different planes of existence?

There is a lot you don't see. There's so much else all around. Your mystics and poets sometimes see a little of it.

Does Lexa see all?

None sees all. Each sees only a small fraction of reality. Lexa sees much.

Who are you? It was Simon.

If you like, you can think of us as guardian angels. We help young species like yours at critical times in your development. At times like this we even intervene directly—telepathically mostly—so that you stand some chance against others who seek to enslave or destroy you.

Are there many who seek to harm us?

There are many such.

How do you protect us?

*We intervene in certain critical situations, such as this one. Certain alterations have been made in your brain, as well as in Jaz's. We are sorry. It is wrong to intervene in this way. We beg your forgiveness, but it is the only way. These changes have greatly **enhanced** your intuition and your ability to understand and empathize with others of your kind. They have also awakened your dormant telepathic **faculties**.*

*To allow your **nascent** abilities in this area to develop, they had to be protected from the Observer.*

The Dark Ones?

Yes, those from the Pleiades star cluster. And certain others who are not an immediate threat. If your communications had been detected before you could shield them, you would have been found and destroyed. Even now there is grave danger.

I feel it, Simon thought. *I can sense it lurking out there, watching and waiting.*

Yes. There is someone searching for us. And for you and Jaz. They are coming near.

Dearest Simon, do not be afraid.

Xela. Is that you?

Yes. Though we are Lexa, we are also Axel and Xela.

Simon, you must let your mind go completely. You are coming to me. Become part of me. Yes. Now you are Xela. I am Simon. We are Lexa now.

Jaz.

Axel? Jaz thought.

You are so close to me already, Jaz. Come. Just a little further. Now, we too are Lexa.

This is pretty awesome, Simon thought.

Xela laughed. *Relax. Four consciousnesses fused into one. Now you will learn everything you need to know.*

Is there any risk that the Observer can read our minds now? Simon thought.

There is no danger when we are merged like this. No thought can be detected outside our minds.

You will have no conscious recall of this later. Or of who we are. But you will discover that you have abilities that no one else has. They will help you to help your people. You have much work to do. The future of your race is in your hands. We have given you hope. We have given you the tools to build a fire to protect yourselves and to help you evolve. It is up to you to build that fire. And whether it brings your race to a higher level or destroys it, that also is in your hands. People will follow you, Simon. Lead them well.

"Hey, the barbecue!" Simon shouted. "The steak is burning. How the heck did that happen? I must be totally out of it today. I never burn good steaks."

"We must have gotten really **engrossed** in our discussion," Jaz said.

"What were we discussing, anyway?" Simon asked.

"Theories about planes of existence. Pretty far-out stuff," Axel said.

"Well, maybe not that far-out, Axel," Jaz said.

"What do you mean?" Axel asked.

"I mean, I feel there is a definite threat that must be countered **expeditiously** and **decisively**."

"What kind of threat?" Xela asked.

"Remember I told you that aliens had made telepathic contact with people on earth?" Jaz said.

"Yes."

"Well, I just have this really strong hunch those guys are the ones controlling the consortium, the consortium that's controlling the world."

"Jaz is right," Simon said. "Tonight we must organize a powerful opposition and begin to reclaim this planet. *Our* planet."

"Simon," Axel said. "You seem so certain—so **resolute**."

"Trust me. Please. I've never been more sure of anything."

"I would never doubt you, Simon. Your hunches are **sacrosanct**. If you're that sure something is true, it's true. Just tell me how I can help."

"Me too." Xela said. "If there's anything at all I can do to help, I'll do it. But Simon, first you'd better get those steaks off the barbecue, don't you think?"

"You're right! I must be really into this stuff if I keep forgetting the steaks."

Simon looked at Axel. Somehow, he seemed different. He seemed much more relaxed and confident. He was sitting next to Xela as if he had been her boyfriend practically forever. He saw that this had not escaped Jaz's notice either. She was smiling a smile that said, *This is the girl for Axel, at last*. He had never seen Axel so happy. Nor Jaz. He got up and left to get the steaks.

"So," Xela said. "Simon has a pretty big job on his hands tonight, doesn't he Jaz?"

"Yes," Jaz replied. "He must convince all these big shots that the threat is **imminent**, and that immediate, drastic steps must be taken. The true nature of the consortium must be uncovered and its leaders identified. Hopefully, we can sever their contact with the aliens."

"Jaz, I was wondering," Axel said. "If these aliens are contacting these key people telepathically—controlling them—then how do you know they can't read your minds, and the minds of others at the Seminar?"

"You'd better hope you have a guardian angel, or some sort of **tutelary** spirit, shielding your Seminar from observers," Xela said.

"Actually, that's an excellent point, Axel," Jaz said. "I am very happy to announce, however, that I have made excellent progress in developing my latent telepathic abilities over the last few months. I must say, I am no longer a **tyro**."

Simon came back carrying the steaks.

"I now am," Jaz said, "a reasonably proficient practitioner of the art and science of telepathy. It's far from perfect but I am able to read most people's minds when I go into a special type of meditation."

"You didn't tell me you had progressed that far," Simon said.

Jaz laughed. "Maybe it's in my genes," she said. "My family has a long line of psychics, clairvoyants, and yogis. I just **augmented** it with some modern science. It's remarkable how complementary that tradition is to modern Western science when you really get into it."

"So," Xela said. "Can you read my thoughts, Jaz?"

"Well, I don't know. I'd have to go into my little trance and all."

Axel looked at Jaz. "Jaz, I think you'll be able to tell if something is watching."

"You know, I think you're right, Axel. I don't know why, but I feel it's gotten so much stronger just recently."

"Thank goodness," Xela said. "That's really good timing, considering the threat that you and your group have uncovered. So, maybe you can read my thoughts. Let me think of something, OK?"

An image came into Jaz's mind. It was Simon standing at a rostrum. He was giving the Seminar's opening address later in the evening. Jaz shook her head. "That was really vivid. It was like reality. It's Simon, isn't it?"

Xela nodded.

"It's so clear. And so realistic. I felt like I was actually seeing the future."

Xela laughed. "My friends say I sometimes seem kind of clairvoyant."

"Maybe you can help me train, help me improve my ESP."

"Sure. You know, Jaz, the future will be what you want it to be, what you visualize. So, try to think about it clearly."

"Like Simon's speech tonight?"

"Yes. See him as getting things off to a wonderful start with that speech. Setting the **keynote**. Saying exactly the right things in precisely the right way to motivate people. Pushing all the right buttons—an almost telepathic understanding of people." She looked at Simon and smiled. "He has charisma," she said. "People will follow him."

"Thank you, Xela" Simon said. "I'm glad you have so much confidence in me. Now if I only knew what I was going to say."

"You'll think of something, Simon," Xela said. "I heard that you're very good at **extemporaneous** speaking."

"That's not what I'm worried about," Jaz said. "I have complete faith in Simon."

"I agree," Xela said. "Someday he'll probably be president. At least."

"That would be cool," Simon said. "Air Force One, your own movie theater ... ."

"And all those groupies chasing after him at the **apex** of the power **hierarchy**," Xela said. "Females all over seem to love males with power. It's like some law of the universe."

"That's true," Simon said. "In my political science class Professor Chandler once quoted Henry Kissinger, the powerful secretary of state in the 1970s. He said something like, 'Power is the ultimate love potion.'"

"Guys," Jaz said. "I'm worried how we are going to get this thing *done*."

"Get what done?" Axel asked.

"I mean, it's clear we have to break the power these aliens have over all of these important people. At this rate, they'll totally control the world."

"You're right," said Axel. "Action must be taken."

"OK," Jaz said. "We've been working on awakening the awareness of this group of people we've carefully selected. They must become more cognizant of what's happening in the world, and be much better organized. They will have to learn to really work together. We've brought together all their expertise representing the **gamut** of human knowledge: politics, economics, law, business, science. We want to find ways to end poverty, war, racism, all the social ills that have **bedeviled** humanity for so long."

"It's been kind of like the World Economic Forum, which brings all these experts together from business, politics, and the academic world to try to agree on solutions to the world's problems," Simon said. "But this is different. We really are going to do something decisive and comprehensive that will make fundamental changes in the way the world is run."

"Yes," Axel said. "All that is wonderful. But it won't mean much if we can't break free from these aliens."

"So," Simon said, "what do you think we should do? Announce to the Seminar that key people in the world are being controlled telepathically by aliens, messing everything up, siphoning off vast wealth, **exploiting** our species and our planet—and that we'd better get hopping to put a stop to it?"

"No," Jaz said. "We don't announce it. Look. Professor James and the other people in the Group know how critical the situation is. We've got to get them ready to help us fight."

"Fight how?" Simon said.

"Telepathically. That's how these guys are controlling us. So that's where we hit them. We find the central controlling agency and **neutralize** it. We'll use our new powers to search the world for the most powerful psychics, not just from the Group, but also from all over the world. We'll tell them about the threat."

"Tell them," Simon said, "'now, if you guys just put your heads together ... .'"

"It's not funny, Simon," Jaz said.

"Maybe you don't have to do that," Xela said. "I mean, it would take time. And such a wide search might be detected."

"So what do you propose we do?" Jaz asked.

"Look at us, right here. You're a telepath. I seem to have some such powers. And maybe Simon and Axel can be trained."

"Didn't you say everybody has ESP in latent form, Jaz?" Axel asked.

"Yes," Jaz said. "But, like Xela said, this is pretty time-critical. Xela, do you think Axel and Simon can be trained in just a few hours?"

"Why not try?" Xela said.

"You have a good point, Xela," Simon said. "What's the other alternative? Contact the Group? What's that going to do in such a short time?"

"And if we contact the Group, there's the risk of panic," Jaz said. "Also, keeping all those people under control would be pretty tough. I mean, they're all wonderful people as individuals, but any time you have a group there are social dynamics involved. If even one person were to freak, it would blow the whole thing. The Observer would probably find us just like that."

"And then we'd all be toast," Simon said. "If they didn't destroy us telepathically, they could easily arrange for us to sort of disappear."

They were silent, each considering the situation.

"So what you're saying, Xela," Simon said finally, "is that if the four of us can work together we can maybe find out what exactly this threat is. Who these nasty critters are that are messing around with people's minds?"

"Yes," Xela said. "And then, maybe, we can even take them out."

"Now *that*," Simon said, "would be truly awesome. The world will be a much better place without those space cadets jerking us around."

"I think that we might very well have the advantage of surprise," Jaz said. "It's just a hunch, but these guys seem a little **complacent**. I don't think they're sitting around worrying, expecting Earth to counterattack any time soon. They've had it their way for so long they might think it's the natural order of things. Just sit on this planet forever, sucking practically everything out of it and its **indigenous** inhabitants."

"Listen." Xela said. "Why don't we try this first? We find them and try to destroy them. If we take them by surprise and **annihilate** them, great. It's all over. If it doesn't work, we go to stage two; we scan Earth for people with developed powers. Then we fuse all these minds into one really awesome force."

"And then," Simon said, "those guys had better watch out. The sheriff is coming. He's got a huge piece of iron strapped on his hip. And he is definitely not the happiest camper on the planet."

Xela laughed. "I've always liked the sheriffs in those Westerns. Kind of like **avenging** angels."

"What's that country song by Marty Robbins—'Big Iron'?" Simon said. He sang softly: 'He's an Arizona Ranger ... He's here to do some business, with the big iron on his hip.'"

"Hey," Axel said, "didn't one of the Grateful Dead-connected groups cover that tune?"

"Yeah, Kingfish," Jaz said. "You're such a Deadhead, I'd thought you'd know that. But guys, can we get back to the program, please?" Jaz said. "So, it's agreed?"

"OK. What do we do, all hold hands or something?" Simon asked

Xela smiled at Simon. "Don't worry, everything will work out great, Simon." She reached over and touched him on his arm. "Yes, everything will be just fine."

Simon felt completely calm. A feeling of total well-being came over him. He felt drowsy. But happy. So happy.

Simon.
Xela?
You are the one who will do it.
What?
Soon. You will destroy the Observer.
It's here?
Yes. We will guide you to it. You will know It, but It will not suspect you.
Won't it know when you contact me by ESP?
Yes. But it will be too late for It. You will kill It. It is the link. Break the link and a lot of misery will leave your world.
I will do it.
Make the speech tonight. But act like everything is wonderful. No problems. Everything is great. There must be nothing to make It suspect.
Where do I find this creature—this thing?
DelMonico's Cafe. Outside. Tell people you're going there to work on your creative writing assignment. You just want to relax, look at people, get some ideas.
Yeah, I've **procrastinated** a long time about doing Miss Bridget's assignment. I guess I'm not the creative writing type.
Don't worry. You'll have a lot to write about soon.
When does this thing go down?
Tomorrow. At noon.

336

Will I know what's happening?

No. Your mind will be shielded by us. It must have no way to read your thoughts. You will not be conscious of any of this. You must do everything by instinct. Trust yourself. You are the last chance we have to stop It. Act completely from your heart. You are the one person who can do it. You will wake up, have a leisurely Sunday morning breakfast, and read the newspaper. After a while, you will feel inspired to begin that creative writing assignment you've been putting off, the one that's due tomorrow morning. The one you've so carefully avoided thinking about. You'll think, hey, why don't I go to DelMonico's? Have a bite to eat, an espresso or two, and watch the people to get some ideas going.

You will just be some college guy doing a little writing, eating, drinking some coffee, just hanging out.

And then the deal will go down?

Yes. And then the deal will go down.

1. **enhance** v. to improve
2. **faculty** N. ability; power
3. **nascent** ADJ. starting to develop
4. **engrossed** ADJ. occupied fully; absorb
5. **expeditiously** ADV. quickly and efficiently
6. **decisively** ADV. conclusively
7. **resolute** ADJ. firmly determined
8. **sacrosanct** ADJ. beyond criticism
9. **imminent** ADJ. about to happen
10. **tutelary** ADJ. protective
11. **tyro** N. beginner
12. **augment** v. to increase
13. **keynote** N. main underlying theme
14. **extemporaneous** ADJ. unrehearsed
15. **apex** N. highest point
16. **hierarchy** N. body of persons organized according to authority
17. **gamut** N. entire range
18. **bedevil** v. to plague
19. **exploit** v. to make use of selfishly or unjustly
20. **neutralize** v. to make ineffective
21. **complacent** ADJ. overly contented; smug
22. **indigenous** ADJ. native
23. **annihilate** v. to destroy completely
24. **avenging** ADJ. taking vengeance
25. **procrastinate** v. to postpone

Simply Simon

Think you know the words? Then prove it! Choose the *best* word to fill in the blank in each of the sentences below.

engrossed **bedeviled** **tutelary** **imminent**

keynotes **hierarchies** **avenging** **decisively**

apex **tyro**

1. When Axel is _____ in a scientific problem it is as though he has totally tuned out everything around him.

2. In wartime, government propagandists sometimes portray the military as a/an _____ army that will bring evildoers to justice.

3. We human beings tend to think of ourselves as members of a species representing the _____ of the process of evolution.

4. Although democracy is a form of government that is frequently _____ by problems, it nevertheless appears to be by far the best system of government humanity has devised.

5. A crisis tests the ability of a leader to act _____ and to rally public support.

6. It's interesting to study how human groups tend to form _____ based on power and other factors.

7. One of the _____ of that president's administration was identifying manageable problems of ordinary people and taking measures to help solve them.

8. Considering that Christine was a/an _____ at the flirting game, I think she handled herself really well.

9. When final exams are _____ I head for the library, taking nothing but the books I'm studying, some writing paper, and a few pens.

10. Many religions believe in _____ spirits that watch over people, guiding and protecting them.

Making Sense

Indicate whether or not each of the words in **bold** makes sense in the sentence. If it makes sense, put Y (Yes); if it doesn't make sense, put N (No).

1. **Nascent** works of literature such as *Hamlet* and *Moby Dick* are so complex that they can be interpreted in several different ways. ____

2. A president who is not **resolute** in accomplishing his or her goals will probably be considered a poor leader. ____

3. Marxists believe that capitalists **exploit** the labor of the working class, extracting far more value from it than the value of the salaries they pay. ____

4. I spent a week planning, researching, and writing the **extemporaneous** talk Professor Chandler asked me to give last week. ____

5. Physicists use computers to **augment** the power of the human brain, allowing them to perform incredibly complex calculations. ____

6. Axel says that the impact of a large asteroid or comet with the earth would not **annihilate** the planet, but that it could cause the extinction of all life on it. ____

7. The United States maintains several methods of delivering nuclear weapons, so that if one is **neutralized**, the others can be used. ____

8. Many of the **indigenous** people of Australia, the Aboriginals, have not been able to integrate successfully into the culture of the European settlers in that country. ____

9. Axel enjoys browsing through the *Encyclopedia Britannica* because it contains clearly written articles on the whole **gamut** of human knowledge. ____

10. It's good to become **complacent** because sometimes you need something to motivate you to change. ____

Match It

Match each of the following words to its meaning.

1. faculty	a. improve
2. expeditiously	b. postpone
3. enhance	c. overly contented
4. sacrosanct	d. ability; power
5. procrastinate	e. beginner
6. imminent	f. native
7. augment	g. quickly and efficiently
8. complacent	h. increase
9. indigenous	i. beyond criticism
10. tyro	j. about to happen

Axel Speaks

Greetings! I believe that you are now ready for something more intellectual. Choose the *best* word to fill in the blank in each sentence.

1. The Romans did not derive all their beliefs from the Greeks; for example, unlike the Greeks, they believed that each person has a/an _____ spirit *(Genius)* that guides him or her from birth to death in a way similar to the guardian angels mentioned in the *Bible* (Matthew 18:10).

(A) avenging

(B) resolute

(C) complacent

(D) tutelary

(E) sacrosanct

2. Gene therapy—substituting normal genes for abnormal ones—is in a/an _____ stage of development, but the technique holds promise for the treatment of hereditary diseases.

(A) extemporaneous

(B) nascent

(C) indigenous

(D) dubious

(E) imminent

3. An example of unsuccessful government interference in the economy is the government borrowing money to finance spending to stimulate growth, thereby raising the cost of money, and thus, paradoxically, _____ the effects of the stimulus.

(A) enhancing

(B) neutralizing

(C) procrastinating

(D) ameliorating

(E) augmenting

4. Sigmund Freud believed that in every person there is a constant struggle between the desire to fulfill instinctual desires (the pleasure principle) as _____ as possible, and the duties one has as a member of society, embodied in the superego.

(A) sporadically

(B) enticingly

(C) expeditiously

(D) succinctly

(E) reproachfully

5. During World War II, the German, Soviet, British, and American governments each _____ artists to create propagandist art to portray the enemy as evil, and their own cause as righteous.

(A) annihilated

(B) emancipated

(C) mesmerized

(D) bedeviled

(E) exploited

Answers on page 466.

And now, on with the story.

CREATIVE WRITING

The Seminar, Simon thought, had gone spectacularly well. People were ready to change the world. Groups of key people had come together to deal decisively and comprehensively with all the major problems of the human race. In fact, things had gone so well it was almost unbelievable. It seemed almost as though someone had been behind the scenes, subtly influencing people's minds so they cooperated fully. Jaz and Xela might have ESP, Simon thought, but there was no way they could have done this. It had to be the result of Jaz's brilliance in organizing everything and Axel's genius in the discussions. And his own charisma certainly seemed to have helped, he had to admit. But he had a feeling that something else had played a big part too.

So, everything was pretty great. OK, there was still this crazy alien business, but somehow he felt that it would be dealt with. Jaz seemed so powerful now. And with Axel and Xela helping it should be a piece of cake. The planet was finally waking up.

It was a perfect fall morning—clear, crisp, and sunny. Sunday. A day designed for a guy to relax after a week of toil. Sunday. NFL day. Time to sit back and do some serious football watching. Maybe he could get Jaz to watch at least part of a game with him. She needed to relax too. Man, she was really into some far-out stuff: different planes of reality, ESP, aliens. And it couldn't be denied that he also had a lot of intense things to deal with. But there was nothing that had to be done immediately, after all—at least, nothing that couldn't wait until tomorrow.

Or was there? Uh oh. There's one little problem, Simon thought. There was that **vignette** due for Miss Bridget tomorrow morning at ten. Not only hadn't he *written* it, he hadn't *thought* about it, in fact, he had deliberately *refused* to think about it. Two weeks ago Miss Bridget had cornered him after class and told him, "Simon, I think you have **aptitudes** you're not using. I do not accept that in my students. You have something to say and you're going to learn how to say it. Now, your writing is getting better. But on your next piece I want to see a quantum leap. I want your words to sing to me, make me laugh, cry, scream—anything. Just make me *feel*. Or make me see something I've never even imagined before. And, Simon, I don't want to see anything imitative. Don't go to the bookshelf and pull out Asimov or Trollope or somebody and try to write like them. Find your *own* voice. The real Simon. I want *you*—your voice, your style, your ideas—not something **derivative** or a mere **pastiche**."

Simon divided his teachers into two broad categories: the dedicated and the not so dedicated. Miss Bridget was definitely in the first category. No question about that. Within this category he had perceived two subgroups: the truly dedicated and the **fanatically** dedicated. Unfortunately, Miss Bridget belonged to the latter of the subgroups—a small group of teachers whose main purpose in life seemed to be hounding students until they had no *choice* but to improve. Fortunately, there were not too many of this type around. Charm was completely **ineffectual** on them. Any excuse outside of death was considered a **rationalization**—and even the Big D had to be well documented and justified, **posthumously**, of course, in clear, concise language, or your grade wouldn't appear on your transcript. Of this dedicated type, Miss Bridget was the **archetype**.

For the first assignment Miss Bridget had given to his class, he had pleaded writer's block. She had looked at him for a long time after he had said that. Finally, she had said,

"Simon, you are not a real writer. You cannot, therefore, have writer's *block*. Extension denied."

The next time he had pleaded that he needed more time because his mind was completely focused on the big game against the Lions. He was the *quarterback* after all! "Coach says I have to completely master all the new defensive alignments the other guys will be preparing to throw at us," he had said. "Videos, scouting reports, playbooks—a **multiplicity** of things to study. The whole college is depending on me. My reads have to be perfect." Again Miss Bridget had looked at him for a long time. "Simon," she had said, "I wouldn't care if it were the Rose Bowl you were preparing for. Or the Super Bowl. Or Armageddon. Focus on giving me a piece of writing that *sizzles*. Make it so scintillating I'm blinded. And tell Coach you have more pressing assignments to complete before you'll have a chance to look at his football playbook. Extension denied."

So, what could he try now? "Oh, Miss Bridget, by the way, I need just a little more time. You see, I've been kind of busy dealing with this alien threat to Earth. These fellows are pretty serious customers. In fact, they're really bad news. They're very close to cutting *Homo sapiens* right out of the deal. You see, Miss Bridget, we still have to **obliterate** them, and we have absolutely no idea whether the way we're planning to do it will do the trick. If we don't work this thing out, it looks like curtains for our species as we have come to know and love it. So, you see, I really do have some legitimate distractions in my life right now making it hard for me to focus on my writing assignment."

Not bad. Coherent. Well-argued. Persuasive. A really solid case. It would work with anybody. Except with Miss Bridget. No, it just wouldn't fly.

"Aliens," she would probably say. "That's no excuse, Simon. Oh, I accept that what you say is the truth. I trust your veracity completely. I even admit that in this case there are some **extenuating** circumstances. However, you'll have to learn to plan your time more **judiciously**. You will have to find time in your schedule to deal with them—*after* the vignette is on my desk, neatly typed. Hey, and good luck with the alien business. And, by the way, Simon, do these aliens have a *literature*? Oh, and has it occurred to you to ask *them* for some ideas? You've got to get *outside* yourself, Simon. You have to see humanity from a more detached point of view. Use this as an opportunity to gain a whole new perspective for the writing task. Ask them how they look at us. Maybe we're **vermin** to be exterminated, as in *Independence Day*. They're probably totally **devoid** of concern for our species. This is an opportunity sent from heaven. I expect you not to waste it. With this amazing stimulus to creativity you've had, Simon, I expect to read something so original it'll take me to the stars. On my desk. 10 A.M. Extension denied."

Yes, he'd better get the writing thing squared away first. He sighed. Writing was really hard work. It actually made his brain ache. It was so much easier to imagine it already done—and graded. He could see it, five neatly printed pages, lying on his desk. He could even see the grade—"A+"—and Miss Bridget's comments: "An exquisitely beautiful piece of writing, Simon. Truly sublime. It took me to the stars. I pay **obeisance** to you in the name of Dickens, Twain, Fitzgerald, Faulkner, Hemingway, Mailer, and all the saints, both living and dead. With your permission, I will personally submit this to a publisher I know. The whole world must read this."

The only problem was he still had to write it. And first he had to think of something to *say*, something that wasn't completely lame. Didn't Professor Jones, his literature teacher, always make it a point to tell his students that everything important had already been said? OK, not the most encouraging words for someone trying to write something creative, but probably true, nevertheless. And hadn't no less a **luminary** in American literature than Willa Cather **opined** that, "There are only two or three great human stories, and they go on repeating themselves as fiercely as if they had never happened before."? Since he had absolutely no idea

348

what those few choice stories were, he was kind of out of that picture. Maybe they were handed down from Great Writer to Great Writer who were members of some kind of exclusive club, keeping average guys like him out of the loop. "Hey, Norman," Ernest says, "Can't get any ideas for a novel? You want a really hot story? It's been used by Homer, Shakespeare, Dickens. All the big boys. It's been a sure thing down through the ages. Readers always dig it. They just keep lapping it up. Same basic story, again and again. They always keep coming back for more. It's foolproof. You're a member of the Great Writers' Club, right? Then take it. Go write the Great American novel."

So, anyway, why keep trying to think up something totally new? Then again, some other guy had said that everybody has one novel in him, waiting to come out. Well, if that were true, his novel must be really **subterranean**, so far down in his psyche that it might as well not exist. A *novel*? He'd be lucky to write a decent *page* that wasn't totally **banal** and insipid.

A girl—ah yes, Daphne—who sat next to him in class had tried to help him. She had suggested that he first try to write a good descriptive paragraph. *Describe something you find interesting.* So he had started with a girl. What could be more interesting than that? Especially when she was described in powerful, dramatic, unadorned **prose**: "The pretty girl was sitting across from me in class. She looked at me. I looked at her. Our eyes met. I smiled. She smiled too. We were both smiling like crazy. Maybe, I thought, this girl digs me." And with finely observed detail, using carefully chosen adjectives, just as Miss Bridget had told him to use: "Her hair was blond—no, really an incredible light brown with just a touch of red. She was wearing this really pretty, sort of satiny blue top and she was, in the truest sense of the word, awesome." And with realism. "Her name was beautiful. Daphne. So beautiful I had to say it a few times to myself: Daphne, Daphne, Daphne. I felt that I was the luckiest guy in the world to have such a cool girl helping me."

He had thought it had been pretty good. Really honest and direct, like all good writing. No **superfluous** words or **figurative** language to distract the reader from the subject. It gave a vivid picture of the young woman. And Daphne seemed to have genuinely liked it. She had smiled at him after she read it and said, "That is really honest writing. I liked your description of me. It's good to write what you feel. You really have an eye for detail—a real gift. I didn't think that star quarterbacks could write such powerful prose! Maybe we could talk about this some more over some lunch. You could teach me a thing or two." Unfortunately, Miss Bridget had not been as encouraging. She had written on it: "F. Be advised that my class is listed in the college catalog as Creative *Writing*—not Creative *Flirting*."

Jaz had suggested that a good way for him to find inspiration would be to go to DelMonico's and observe people. "What in the world could be more interesting than people?" she had said. As usual, Jaz was probably right. Excellent advice. OK, the describing people bit hadn't worked so well the last time he had tried it, but maybe he had gone off on the wrong track. He had been diverted by Daphne's allure. It wouldn't happen again. Yes, he would take his notebook and study people. There had to be *something* to say about people. What, after all, was more inspiring, more likely to spark creativity in a dude, than a *person*? Of course, for the average guy, in this **context** "persons" basically meant girls. But he would make a genuine effort to observe the whole range of humanity. He would be Balzac, **keenly** observing Parisian life. Yes, he wouldn't let himself get sidetracked again. He would seriously observe and describe what he saw fully and honestly. Maybe inspiration would come.

1. **vignette** N. short literary composition
2. **aptitude** N. ability
3. **derivative** ADJ. unoriginal; derived from another source
4. **pastiche** N. imitation of another's style in writing
5. **fanatically** ADV. with excessive enthusiasm or zeal
6. **ineffectual** ADJ. not effective
7. **rationalization** N. self-satisfying but incorrect reason (v. to rationalize)
8. **posthumously** ADV. occurring after death
9. **archetype** N. original model after which others are patterned
10. **multiplicity** N. large number
11. **obliterate** v. to completely destroy
12. **extenuating** ADJ. reducing in severity by providing a partial excuse; mitigating
13. **judiciously** ADV. wisely
14. **vermin** N. small animals or insects that are destructive or injurious to health
15. **devoid** ADJ. totally lacking
16. **obeisance** N. homage
17. **luminary** N. notable person in a specific field
18. **opine** v. to express an opinion
19. **subterranean** ADJ. hidden
20. **banal** ADJ. lacking originality; commonplace
21. **prose** N. ordinary writing (as opposed to verse)
22. **superfluous** ADJ. unnecessary; excessive
23. **figurative** ADJ. using figures of speech; metaphorical
24. **context** N. circumstances in which an event occurs (also: part of a text in which a word appears)
25. **keenly** ADV. perceptively

Simply Simon

Think you know the words? Then prove it! Choose the *best* word to fill in the blank in each of the sentences below.

pastiche   archetype   prose   context

subterranean   extenuating   opine   devoid

banal   posthumously

1. One of my English teachers in high school said that it is not possible for a mind that's full of _____ ideas to produce an interesting work of literature.

2. Miss Bridget once told me that if I were as creative in my writing as I was in coming up with _____ circumstances to justify handing assignments in late, I would be a candidate for the Nobel prize in literature.

3. Scientists are sometimes portrayed as being _____ of feeling, but if you read about their lives you'll find that most of them have been passionately dedicated to the search for the truth.

4. Miss Bridget once assigned us to write a/an _____ based on a passage by our favorite writer so that we could get a better understanding of what makes up a writer's style.

5. Sigmund Freud believed that _____ impulses and feelings powerfully influence us without our being aware of them.

6. In literature class we learned not to merely _____ about a work of literature, but to analyze it rigorously.

7. Professor Jones often reminds us that we need to be able to see a work of literature in the _____ of its time.

8. In English class last year we looked at the writing of some famous scientists such as Charles Darwin and Albert Einstein and concluded that many of them wrote wonderfully clear and balanced _____.

9. Some public figures want their memoirs to be published _____.

10. Scholars believe that there is no single _____ for the modern novel, but rather that the form developed from a number of different types of literature.

Making Sense

Indicate whether or not each of the words in **bold** makes sense in the sentence. If it makes sense, put Y (Yes); if it doesn't make sense, put N (No).

1. In my capacity as Jaz's assistant chef, I often ask her to add more **vignettes** to Mediterranean dishes. ____

2. Jaz said she's amazed by the huge incomes of **luminaries** in the sports and entertainment world. ____

3. One of the reasons I have a pet cat is to discourage **vermin** from hanging out in my house. ____

4. **Obeisance** should be granted by the United States and other developed countries to victims of severe political repression. ___

5. Despite my most **ineffectual** efforts to rally support for the charity concert, the turnout was disappointing. ____

6. An **aptitude** test can help determine the subjects for which you have a flair. ____

7. One thing I've learned about public speaking is that you need to say enough about a topic to hold the audience's interest but not go into a lot of **superfluous** details so they get bored. ____

8. A competent novelist can **obliterate** a world scene by scene so that it seems almost real to the reader. _____

9. Humanity must not use its nonrenewable resources **judiciously** so that there will be plenty left for future generations. _____

10. Professor Jones says that all serious works of literature are **derivative** in the sense that every writer is influenced by the tradition within which he or she works. _____

Match It

Match each of the following words to its meaning.

1. aptitude	a. self-satisfying but incorrect reason
2. fanatically	b. using figures of speech
3. multiplicity	c. perceptively
4. rationalization	d. ability
5. archetype	e. lacking originality
6. judiciously	f. large number
7. banal	g. original model after which others are patterned
8. superfluous	h. with excessive enthusiasm
9. figurative	i. wisely
10. keenly	j. unnecessary; excessive

Axel Speaks

Greetings! I believe that you are now ready for something more intellectual. Choose the *best* word to fill in the blank in each sentence.

1. It is now generally accepted that the impact of a meteor 65 million years ago, while it did not _____ the earth, had a disastrous effect on the planet's ecosystem, destroying 95 percent of species, including the dinosaurs.

(A) circumvent

(B) stipulate

(C) emancipate

(D) obliterate

(E) rebuke

2. In the eighteenth century, the American colonies of Britain grew tired of paying _____ to the motherland, and albeit reluctantly, turned to civil disobedience and, eventually, armed rebellion to establish a separate nation.

(A) vignettes

(B) archetypes

(C) obeisance

(D) pastiches

(E) piety

3. Although there was considerable opposition to slavery on moral grounds in colonial America, slaves were so inexpensive and efficient that colonists _____ the practice of slavery by the argument that the slaves enjoyed a better life in America than they did in Africa.

(A) evinced

(B) rationalized

(C) eschewed

(D) debunked

(E) suppressed

4. In a landmark decision, the Supreme Court ruled in 1966 that the community has a right to censor material it considers obscene if it is _____ of "redeeming social value."

(A) devoid

(B) derivative

(C) oblivious

(D) disaffected

(E) negligent

5. It is sometimes argued that language has a tendency to move, over time, from the literal and concrete to the _____, and that metaphor has its origins in this tendency.

(A) derivative

(B) ineffectual

(C) banal

(D) superfluous

(E) figurative

Answers on page 467.

And now, on with the story.

DelMonico's

Simon was **ensconced** at a table at DelMonico's. A cold drink was in his hand. A truly gargantuan bucket of chili mussels awaited his attentions. Flanking them were two long baguettes of garlic bread. **Gustatory** paradise. **Hedonistic** heaven. **Glutton's** delight. In some ways, Simon thought, this was the best part of the experience—looking forward to those first few wonderful mouthfuls of mussels and garlic bread, **olfactory** senses going full bore. He took a long draw on his drink. The mussels could wait a few more minutes. They weren't going anywhere anytime soon.

This sure is some restaurant, he thought. He certainly was no mathematician, but DelMonico's excellence had inspired him in an area in which he had never before showed much ability. With some help from Jaz one evening he had, right here in this very restaurant, managed to produce a significant contribution to higher mathematics. It was not something that would shake the edifices of the mathematical establishment, but it was a pretty piece of mathematical **legerdemain**, a beautifully balanced equation:

$$DelMonico's = Heaven.$$

Who said pleasure could not be **quantified**? Axel had called it, "An elegant piece of mathematical reasoning." Granted, it wasn't as impressive as the equations Jaz and Axel scribbled over every piece of paper in sight. But look at $e = mc^2$. That wasn't much longer, and it was supposed to describe some really important stuff, like the fundamental nature of the universe. OK, Einstein's baby did have two mathematical symbols whereas his only had one. But that was no problem. That could be **rectified**. Mathematics, after all, was a process of endlessly making refinements to statements that were basically true, but that could be made, by indefatigably inserting more symbols, to convey ever more subtle and obscure truths. He was a master. He didn't need to use all those complex symbols. Just one more would do the job nicely. Yes, he still had the touch: $DelMonico's = Heaven^2$. The equation was still balanced. Perfect.

Yes, DelMonico's was his favorite Italian restaurant. No, his favorite restaurant—*period*. The best dishes from all of Italy, perfectly prepared and presented. Several weeks ago he and Jaz had been here celebrating after the team had won a big game. He had been so moved by the **cuisine** that he had felt compelled to seek out the chef and personally express his gratitude. This occasionally happened to Simon; he got an overpowering desire to find the genius behind the food and thank him. And it wasn't like Simon to just find the guy and say, "Hey man, thanks for one really fantastic meal—an **epicurean** delight, a transcendent culinary experience, a bodacious repast." How could you thank someone for that kind of meal with cold, impersonal words? No, with Simon an expression of gratitude would have to take some **palpable** form. When Simon had really enjoyed a meal, Jaz usually waited with some **trepidation** to see exactly what form his "thank you" would take.

The last occasion on which Simon had really enjoyed a meal had been here in DelMonico's. And the chef had—to Jaz's **chagrin**—received the full treatment. Suddenly, a look of **rapture** was on Simon's face. Then he asked a waitress, "Where's the head chef? It is imperative that I talk to him." When the chef, Angelo—a **burly** man who spoke mainly Italian and very little English—appeared, Simon had drawn him close and held him. It must have been, Jaz thought, an intensely emotional moment for both of them. Simon had limited proficiency in Italian, but he used the two words he knew quite skillfully: "Mama mia, mama mia," he said. "Mama mia, mama mia." Angelo was slightly more proficient in Simon's language than Simon was in Angelo's. He knew three words of English. But, like Simon, he used the words he did know **efficaciously**. He said, again and again, "My best dude, my best dude," as he patted Simon on the back. Weird. Jaz had searched the psych literature for information on this phenomenon, but to no avail. One of her hypotheses was that it was some exotic form of male bonding ritual. Interestingly, Simon and the chef had been able to communicate with little knowledge of one another's language and across the barrier of culture. Her deeply considered conclusion about the behavior was, while not likely to be cited as a major contribution to psychology, relatively straightforward and admirably free of technical **nomenclature**: "Guys can be pretty weird sometimes."

So, Simon was now almost perfectly chilled. Except for the fact that Jaz had convinced him to go **incognito**. That was a little strange. But she was into this kind of stuff. She, like many girls he had known, loved nothing more than dressing up, often to the point of practically changing their identities, at least for a while. Masquerade balls were best, of course, but they were kind of hard to find these days. So most girls had to settle for the occasional opportunity that occurred in everyday life. He remembered the knockout at the art museum. Jaz had outdone herself with that one. And *Christine*. Talk about a performance. He would be forever in awe of that one. Yes, they had seemed really comfortable acting like people they weren't.

However, it made Simon uncomfortable. He felt like some kind of spy with his false beard and sunglasses. And he felt detached from other people, like he was invisible. On the other hand, Simon thought, if you got into it, it might be kind of cool. Maybe he looked like a visiting mathematics professor from Germany or something. And, as Jaz had said, it did make sense. How was he going to observe the flow of life **impartially** if people kept **ogling** him and he heard them saying, "Hey, that's the big football star! Did you see the *game* he had on Saturday? That guy can *bring it*."?

1. **ensconced** V. to settle comfortably
2. **gustatory** ADJ. pertaining to the sense of taste
3. **hedonistic** ADJ. believing that pleasure is the chief good in life (N. hedonism)
4. **glutton** N. one who eats and drinks excessively
5. **olfactory** ADJ. concerning the sense of smell
6. **legerdemain** N. slight of hand; trickery
7. **quantify** V. to express as a quantity
8. **rectify** V. to correct
9. **cuisine** N. food prepared in a certain style
10. **epicurean** ADJ. suited to the tastes of an epicure (that is, a person devoted to the pleasures of the senses)
11. **palpable** ADJ. capable of being touched; tangible
12. **trepidation** N. apprehension; dread
13. **chagrin** N. embarrassment
14. **rapture** N. ecstasy
15. **burly** ADJ. husky
16. **efficaciously** ADV. effectively
17. **nomenclature** N. terms used in a particular discipline
18. **incognito** ADV. in disguise
19. **impartially** ADV. fairly; without bias
20. **ogle** V. to stare at

Simply Simon

Think you know the words? Then prove it! Choose the *best* word to fill in the blank in each of the sentences below.

ogle   quantify   cuisines   incognito   olfactory

burly   impartially   rapture   trepidation

efficaciously

1. I wonder if cavemen used to _____ cavewomen wearing the latest fashions in animal skins.

2. Our offensive line has performed _____ this season; they've opened up big holes for our running backs and given me plenty of time to get my passes off.

3. Scientists try to analyze data _____, but it must be difficult for them to not sometimes favor interpretations that support their own theories.

4. I'll always remember the look of _____ on Xela's face when she saw Axel again after their long separation.

5. Jaz says that stimulating the _____ centers in the brain of a subject can trigger off old memories associated with certain smells.

6. Not too many people would be inclined to pick a fight with Jack, our _____offensive tackle; he weighs 300 pounds and our trainer says he's never seen an athlete with less body fat.

7. In psychology class I read about a scientist who attempted to _____ the intelligence of great geniuses in various fields; I think that Bach, Newton, Einstein, and Shakespeare were among the people at the top.

8. Jaz said sometimes I should try going out with her _____ so we're not hounded by people wanting to shake hands with the big football star.

9. My three favorite _____ are Mediterranean, Indian, and traditional American.

10. When I'm assigned a long and difficult novel I start to read it with some _____ because I'm afraid that I won't be able to understand it, but usually once I get into it everything is cool.

Making Sense

Indicate whether or not each of the words in **bold** makes sense in the sentence. If it makes sense, put Y (Yes); if it doesn't make sense, put N (No).

1. Axel seems happiest when he's **ensconced** in the laboratory working hard on his research. ___

2. Jaz says that experiments show that women possess superior **gustatory** senses to those of men; that may be true, but I'm a guy and I certainly love the taste of food. ___

3. In studying the lives of the great saints in religion class, I noticed one trait that stood out above all others—they were all really **hedonistic**. ___

4. After the **legerdemain** passes a bill it generally doesn't become law unless the president signs it. ___

5. One of the problems with being a **glutton** is that you tend to put on weight pretty quickly. ___

6. In last week's game one of the clocks was so **rectified** that it couldn't be fixed, so the officials just turned it off. ___

7. Axel has such **epicurean** tastes that he would probably live on bread and water if Jaz didn't cook some decent food for him. ___

8. The amazing illusions of David Copperfield illustrate the fact that you can't always trust your senses completely—in them **palpable** objects such as the Empire State Building seem to disappear. ____

9. Some familiarity with Latin is a big help in understanding scientific **nomenclature** since much of it is in that language. ____

10. Axel has so much **chagrin** he's always the life of the party. ____

Match It

Match each of the following words to its meaning.

1. hedonistic   a. capable of being touched

2. glutton   b. express as a quantity

3. legerdemain   c. embarrassment

4. quantify   d. fairly

5. rectify   e. one who eats and drinks excessively

6. palpable   f. ecstasy

7. trepidation   g. correct

8. chagrin   h. believing that pleasure is the chief good in life

9. rapture   i. apprehension

10. impartially   j. slight of hand

Axel Speaks

Greetings! I believe that you are now ready for something more intellectual. Choose the *best* word to fill in the blank in each sentence.

1. Many experts have concluded that the most _____ way to improve living conditions in underdeveloped countries is to educate women so that they become more aware of family planning and are able to help provide their children with more up-to-date information about the world.

(A) palpable

(B) cerebral

(C) gustatory

(D) efficacious

(E) tangible

2. Near the end of *The Odyssey*, the hero of the story, Odysseus, returns home _____ after many years away and discovers that his wife Penelope has remained faithful to him.

(A) impartially

(B) generously

(C) incognito

(D) palpably

(E) indelibly

3. Binomial _____ is the system of biological classification developed by Linnaeus that requires every species to be assigned a bionem—a genus and species name.

(A) expertise

(B) euphemism

(C) appellation

(D) nomenclature

(E) legerdemain

4. Every person who writes science fiction must write with some _____, knowing that nearly every theme in the genre was anticipated by the great Olaf Stapledon in classic books such as *Star Maker.*

(A) rationalization

(B) hyperbole

(C) trepidation

(D) serendipity

(E) skepticism

5. The Buddhist attitude toward asceticism is that it has some merit, but that it is undesirable to practice it to an extreme; Buddhists believe that a middle way should be found between extreme self-denial, on the one hand, and _____, on the other hand.

(A) anachronism

(B) legerdemain

(C) chagrin

(D) hedonism

(E) rapture

Answers on pages 467–468.

And now, on with the story.

The Gabfest

Simon looked at the three women sitting several tables from his. Christine—yes, it was good old Christine, now also known as Nausikaa. She was the center of attention. The other women were looking at her as she talked, **gesticulating** expressively. Now they were all laughing at something Christine had said. It looked like a really heavy-duty gabfest. Do I know the other two women? Simon wondered.

Hey! That's *Miss Bridget*! She looks different. She certainly is enjoying her chat with the girls. Miss Bridget was looking intently at Christine, and seemed to be following the most **minute** changes in Christine's facial expressions. You could see her whole body **resonate** to Christine's expressions. Christine smiled. A moment later, a similar look appeared on Miss Bridget's face. Similar but not the same—transformed slightly, subtly different. Miss Bridget had, presumably, received Christine's emotion, processed it by whatever complex **alchemy** females process feelings, and then returned it, with her own feelings added. Now, Simon thought, if a guy listened to another guy like that—actually tried to listen—he'd be totally **stigmatized**, maybe even **ostracized**, for violating the onerous, totally unyielding **statutes** of Guy World.

This was a fascinating perspective, he thought. Observing women talking to each other. Maybe, Simon thought, listening to so many of Jaz's psychology discussions had affected him more than he had realized. He could really get into this observing people thing. The only problem was he didn't know if he would be able to capture it in words. And even if he could get it down on paper, there would still be a few technical hurdles to overcome. Like, he couldn't turn in a vignette to Miss Bridget in which she was one of the characters. "So, Simon, you were observing me, incognito, at DelMonico's the other day to get ideas for your assignment." It was **preposterous**.

Simon looked at Miss Bridget. Yes, she certainly had changed her appearance. She was wearing the most amazing white dress. But there was something else. What else made her look so different from the way she looked in class? Of course. *Makeup*. Simon had never seen Miss Bridget with makeup on.

Christine had apparently stopped her monologue. All three women were laughing. They were, indeed, practically hysterical. That must have been some story, Simon thought. He smiled. Maybe humor was contagious, he thought, or something that could be experienced vicariously.

The laughter gradually ended. The three women were quiet for a little while, sipping their coffees and taking a few forkfuls of the cakes they were eating. Then Miss Bridget leaned forward. She was on. *Show time*. Now she started in on what seemed to be her monologue. Again Simon observed the careful following of the story by the other two women, the high-speed exchange of glances, gestures, smiles, frowns, as well as some expressions that were too complex even for Simon's well-developed ability to decode. It was dizzying. And the *intensity*! It seemed almost aggressive, even **rapacious** at times, the listening. It must be exhausting, Simon thought—completely **enervating**.

After several minutes, Miss Bridget seemed to be finishing her story. Again, the three women exploded in laughter. Gradually the laughter subsided, the three women still exchanging glances a mile a minute. Simon felt like he was watching one of those action movies with really fast cuts from scene to scene. No wonder most women didn't really bother much with those movies—they had their own far more **harrowing** movies.

Christine was still chuckling when a waiter appeared carrying a tray of coffees. The waiter was a tall, solidly built fellow. His features were strong and perfectly chiseled. His shirt was open, showing much of his **hirsute** chest. The women were silent as he set the drinks on the table.

All three women had a look of total aloofness, like all they were thinking about in the whole world was what they were going to discuss after this little **hiatus** in the action. Maybe not completely aloof, however. Christine had a tiny smile on her face. A casual observer would not have perceived the glance that Christine threw at Miss Bridget. Miss Bridget smiled slightly.

How, Simon wondered, did Christine and Miss Bridget know each other? What did they have in common? Yes, they both knew him. But that smacked of **megalomania**. He couldn't be that important, could he? He strained to catch what Christine was saying. No luck. DelMonico's was, as usual, packed, so there was a **din**. He looked at Christine, who seemed to be into another monologue. He looked at her mouth. Simon was not an expert lip-reader, but he could make out a few words **intermittently**—*quarterback, nice, so he*—but nothing continuous. Who was the other woman? His view of her was partially blocked by some hefty fellows at another table. As **inconspicuously** as he could, he craned his neck. He could see her better now. She was looking down at the table. There was a big piece of chocolate cake in front of her. Simon could see that her hair was brunette. The woman looked up, laughing at something Miss Bridget had said. It was Dr. Beaufort, the curator from the art museum. Well, Simon thought, that's par for the course. Another woman from the college.

So what were these women up to? Just eating their cake, drinking their coffee, chatting away like crazy? If his past experience were any guide, they were probably just getting warmed up. People at gabfests seemed to have a **propensity** for saving the really juicy bits for later so they could look forward to them. They were left unspoken, kind of hanging in the air. That way, when they finally got around to them, which, it appeared, could be several hours from now, they could be **relished** all the more. He could probably go home, catch an early pre-game show, watch the entire game, cop a few Zs on the sofa, come back here, and they'd still be at it. OK, by then they would probably have that happy look people got toward the end of such a session. A *really* happy look because the juicy bits were coming out now: "He did *what*?" "She said *that*?" "I told you, you can't *trust* him."

The weirdest thing about it was that they didn't seem to regard an event as real unless they had told at least one of their friends about it in detail. There was nothing better than talking about something. Doing it was fine. But not nearly as satisfying as analyzing it in depth, examining every **nuance**, every scenario, every implication. After all, nothing was truly real unless it had undergone this process: Do I really like Diane? *I have no idea.* Until I talk it over with Ted and Camille.

Definitions

1. **gesticulate** v. to make gestures
2. **minute** ADJ. tiny
3. **resonate** v. to vibrate; echo
4. **alchemy** N. seemingly magical process of transforming
5. **stigmatize** v. to brand as disgraceful
6. **ostracize** v. to exclude from a group; shun
7. **statute** N. law; rule
8. **preposterous** ADJ. ridiculous
9. **rapacious** ADJ. taking by force; greedy
10. **enervating** ADJ. draining energy; weakening
11. **harrowing** ADJ. extremely distressing; terrifying
12. **hirsute** ADJ. hairy
13. **hiatus** N. interruption; break
14. **megalomania** N. delusion of importance
15. **din** N. ongoing loud noise

16. **intermittently** ADV. stopping and starting at intervals
17. **inconspicuously** ADV. in a way that is not readily noticeable
18. **propensity** N. inclination; tendency
19. **relish** V. to greatly enjoy; savor
20. **nuance** N. shade of meaning

Simply Simon

Think you know the words? Then prove it! Choose the *best* word to fill in the blank in each of the sentences below.

din   hiatus   rapacious   gesticulating

megalomania   ostracized   nuance   alchemy

inconspicuously   intermittently

1. Once during a game I looked up into the stands and saw Axel _____ like crazy; he had spotted a subtle weakness in Big State's defensive alignment and was trying to let me know about it.

2. In order to enjoy a work of literature a reader does not have to understand every _____ of the text.

3. Sometimes I ask Jaz if there might be just a little _____ in our plans to transform the world.

4. Professor Walters, my art teacher, once called art "a/an _____ that transforms the ordinary into the extraordinary."

5. In the fall I play on the football team, in the winter I play on the basketball team, in the spring I play on the baseball team, and in the summer I relax and enjoy a/an _____ in my competitive sports schedule.

6. Jaz says that in many traditional societies people who are _____ are considered to be, essentially, dead.

7. Famous people sometimes like to be able to move around _____.

8. Our _____ defense forces a lot of turnovers that often give our offense great field position.

9. When Axel is working he is _____ interrupted by phone calls from professors who are stuck on a problem and need his help.

10. I'll always remember the _____ in the stadium after I ran in a two-point conversion as the clock ran out, giving us a victory over State.

Making Sense

Indicate whether or not each of the words in **bold** makes sense in the sentence. If it makes sense, put Y (Yes); if it doesn't make sense, put N (No).

1. Physicists study nature from the smallest elementary particles to the most **minute** galaxies. ____

2. One thing I hate about politics is the tendency to oversimplify: for example, conservatives brand liberals as unrealistic spendthrifts who love big government, whereas liberals **stigmatize** conservatives as hard-hearted defenders of Big Business. ____

3. Jaz showed me a study that concluded that a surprisingly large number of Americans have a **propensity** for deep, spiritually transforming religious experiences. ____

4. Darwin's theory that organisms evolve through the process of natural selection is so **preposterous** that it has been almost universally accepted by scientists. ____

5. It is important to eat **enervating** foods before a game so that you have enough energy to go all out for the whole game. ____

6. Last Sunday Jaz and I spent a **harrowing** lazy afternoon in a rowboat on the lake, just drifting along and chilling out. ____

7. In some cultures a man who is **hirsute** is considered masculine. ____

8. **Statutes** should be periodically reviewed so that they are kept up to date with changes in society. ___

9. Sometimes a particular work of literature really **resonates** with something deep inside you. _____

10. At the beginning of English class one day Professor Jones wrote this statement by the English Romantic poet William Wordsworth on the board and asked us to keep it in mind during our discussion of the concept of greatness in literature: "Every great and original writer, in proportion as he is great and original, must himself create the taste by which he is to be **relished**." ____

Match It

Match each of the following words to its meaning.

1. gesticulate	a. ridiculous
2. stigmatize	b. seemingly magical process of transforming
3. ostracize	c. make gestures
4. preposterous	d. delusion of importance
5. enervating	e. extremely distressing
6. harrowing	f. stopping and starting at intervals
7. alchemy	g. exclude from a group
8. hiatus	h. draining energy
9. megalomania	i. interruption
10. intermittently	j. brand as disgraceful

Axel Speaks

Greetings! I believe that you are now ready for something more intellectual. Choose the *best* word to fill in the blank in each sentence.

1. The Supreme Court is the final arbiter of state and federal _____, ensuring that they are consistent with the Constitution.

(A) machinations

(B) diatribes

(C) domiciles

(D) hierarchies

(E) statutes

2. An important alloy of iron is steel, which is made of iron, a small amount of carbon, and sometimes _____ amounts of other elements to give it the desired properties.

(A) ordinary

(B) preposterous

(C) enervating

(D) minute

(E) spurious

3. The myth of a golden age appears in many cultures, perhaps because of a human _____ to romanticize the past and fear the future.

(A) propensity

(B) methodology

(C) naiveté

(D) hiatus

(E) machination

4. English has a wide range of synonyms for many words; thus a speaker can select the one with the exact _____ he or she is trying to convey.

(A) metaphor

(B) lexicon

(C) nuance

(D) platitude

(E) alchemy

5. Citing its poor treatment of the native peoples of the Americas and Australia, some historians see European civilization as uniquely _____.

(A) rapacious

(B) hirsute

(C) harrowing

(D) profligate

(E) enervating

Answers on pages 468–469.

And now, on with the story.

The Deal Goes Down

These observations are fine, Simon thought, but I'm still worried I won't be able to get all my brilliant observations down on paper. I guess I can alter things a little in the vignette so that Miss Bridget doesn't recognize the setting or any of the characters. He took a sip of the double espresso that the waitress had just brought. He needed a break from observing and trying to **decipher** the behavior of his three charming subjects. It seemed, somehow, that there was something else he was supposed to do. He couldn't put his finger on it. He looked at the three women again. No, whatever it was, it didn't seem to have anything to do with them.

It was a little odd that they were here together having a little party, but that was no doubt just a weird coincidence. Yes, there was something he had to do. Something important. He had been trying to forget about all this alien stuff. That all seemed almost like a crazy dream now, sitting here in DelMonico's eating chili mussels, enjoying an excellent espresso, and looking at three lovely women. Yes, he was getting into it. A fellow could do this all day.

Then he noticed a man. A scrawny, almost **emaciated**, middle-aged man sitting at a table by himself. He was looking intently at the table where Christine, Miss Bridget, and Dr. Beaufort were sitting. Looking closer, Simon saw that he was staring at Christine, who was looking back at him. On her face was a look of **repugnance**. Simon looked at the man again. He seemed oblivious to everything but Christine.

Where is he?

He's at the cafe, Jaz. He's still observing. But he's getting closer.

I'm so worried, Xela.

Don't worry. He'll do fine.

I just feel so bad. He doesn't know what's happening.

He cannot know.

Yes, I realize that.

Remember, he is Lexa—the concentrated power of the four of us.

He's not a killer, Xela. He's so gentle and kind.

I know. But in this case there is no alternative. It has taken human form. If he kills the body suddenly It will be trapped in the corpse for as long as it exists.

Why?

*To project psychic energy so far takes an **astronomical** amount of energy. If the link is suddenly broken, It will be alone, a little entity without the others. We will surround it and **sequester** it.*

Will you kill it?

*No. We can never kill. Even destroying the body will be **reprehensible** to us. However, it won't be killing because it's just a body created by It.*

Simon **quaffed** the rest of his coffee and got up. He walked over to the man's table. He stood in front of him and looked at him.

"Hello," he said to the man.

The man looked up at Simon. He seemed annoyed that Simon had blocked his view of Christine's table. Although the man was looking at Simon, he appeared to be barely aware of him.

Simon picked up a newspaper that was lying on the man's table. It was the sports page. "Jets **Vanquish** Rams" was the headline.

"Hey, did you see that game?" Simon moved up very close to the man.

379

The man looked blankly at Simon. What a **repulsive-**looking guy, Simon thought.

"Yeah, last minute pass," Simon said. "Really something."

He moved even closer to the man. He was right in his face now.

The man looked directly into Simon's eyes. *Now* he was aware of Simon. He seemed nervous. *Who is this big stupid jock,* he was probably saying to himself, Simon thought.

*Target acquired. Simon's got the **quarry** in his sights. The deal's going down? Yes. The deal's going down.*

"I guess you're not a football fan, huh?" Simon said.

The man stared at Simon. He had the look of someone who had been distracted from something he had been engrossed in. He looked away from Simon. Simon followed his gaze. The man was staring fixedly at Christine, totally absorbed.

"Here, let me show you something." Simon came around the man and stood behind him.

"Hey, what are you doing, young fellow?"

Simon reached down and held the man's head like a center gripping a football, ready to snap it back to the quarterback. Simon had never played center, but as a quarterback he had taken thousands of snaps. He knew the drill well. And he was extremely strong. He pulled the man's head back as hard as he could. The man fell backwards. His head hit the cement hard, making the loud "Crack!" you hear when a middle linebacker puts a clean straight-on hit on a really quick halfback who has just turned the corner and hit full stride in all his 4.1-in-the-forty glory. The man lay motionless on the ground. A large pool of blood accumulated around his head.

"Hey, this guy has fallen!" Simon shouted. "I think he's hurt bad." A woman yelled, "Somebody call an ambulance!" Simon walked away from the dead man, toward the street. His head was spinning. The world seemed to be reeling crazily down some vortex in his brain. Surely he was going crazy. What had he just done? Apparently he had acted on some animal instinct deep inside him. A man was dead. He must get home, to Jaz. Maybe she could help. She could phone for help and be there when they came to take him away. He was crying, stumbling in a **stupor**. *He had killed a man.* For absolutely no reason. **Paroxysms** of anguish shook his body. He was a *murderer.*

"Simon, it's all right." It was Miss Bridget. She and Christine were walking by his side. Each had an arm on one of his shoulders. He looked back. Dr. Beaufort was standing by the body, talking on her cell phone. It looked like she was explaining the "accident" to the police. Nobody was paying attention to the three of them leaving the cafe.

"Simon," Christine said. "Dr. Beaufort will take care of everything. Don't worry."

"You knew it was me all the time?" Simon said. He was confused. Terribly confused. Yes, he must be going out of his mind.

"Simon," Miss Bridget said, "that was not a *person* you killed."

"He sure *looks* like a person," Simon said. "And a pretty dead person right now."

Miss Bridget smiled. She has a really scintillating smile, Simon thought. Maybe I'm not completely crazy if I can still appreciate something like that.

He looked at Christine, who was also smiling. Why were they both *smiling*? He had just murdered a man. "Remember?" she said.

Remember. *Remember.* That word. His head was spinning again. The world seemed to disappear. He seemed to be on some other plane of reality. There was a Being. Lexa. It was happy. So happy now. The Being had asked him to do something. Something really important. And he had done it, though it had **wrenched** his soul to do it.

Simon sat on the curb, sobbing.

Miss Bridget was stroking his head. Christine held his hand and was squeezing it gently.

"Simon, it's OK," Christine said. "You have a right to be **distraught** after what you've just been through."

"Simon, you were wonderful," Miss Bridget said. "You followed your heart. None of us thought it could be done, but Xela kept saying you could do it."

"Wow," Simon said. "I'm still a little woozy, but I'm feeling a lot better. The big man may be down, but he's definitely not out."

Christine and Miss Bridget laughed.

"Simon," Christine said, "the Group is a little more **extensive** than you know. You see Xela told us several weeks ago that you would, very soon, have to do something really critical. But you couldn't consciously know about it. She asked a few of us to kind of play dumb for a while. So when the deal went down you would have some people around to help you out, people who are part of the Group and who will do anything to protect you." Christine smiled at Simon. "Sort of your guardian angels," she added.

Simon felt that the world was returning to normal. No, *more* than normal. The world was clearer. More real. Simply *nicer*. It reminded him of something else. A memory came to him. Xela placing her hand over his heart: In that moment he had glimpsed a purer realm of being. This was something like that.

"You guys were watching, weren't you? You were there to protect me, covering me in case something went wrong. Some gabfest."

Christine laughed. "We had to give you something to focus on so your mind was distracted. It could not be allowed to get into your mind. We rehearsed that get-together for days. Just for you. I sure hope you enjoyed it."

"I guess it taught me a lot about women," Simon said.

"I can't *wait* to read your vignette," Christine said. "I especially liked it when you seemed to be reading my lips." She *winked* at Simon.

"Simon," Miss Bridget said, "we swore we would die, if necessary, to protect you. You see, the three of us formed a kind of entity for a while there in the cafe."

"I thought it was pretty intense. But I just figured you guys were really into it."

"Oh, we were. We were drawing Its energy, Its attention, away from you."

"With a little help from my friends," Simon murmured.

Miss Bridget whispered something to Simon.

"She did? My God."

Simon took Christine's hands and held them in his. "Thank you," he said. Christine was crying. He leaned toward her and gently kissed her on the forehead.

"You almost died to save me—to save the mission?" Simon said.

Christine nodded. "Just before you found It, It looked like it was getting close to you. So I let It have me. It was horrible. The only way I can describe it is to say that It had my soul and was squeezing it, trying to make me part of It."

For some reason a line from a poem by John Donne he had studied in English crossed Simon's mind: "Nor ever chaste, except You ravish me."

"And," Miss Bridget said, "in that moment It let its guard down just the slightest bit. You moved immediately. You were a total hero. However, young man, do not be under any illusions about that vignette. Do not for one moment think that this means you'll get more time to get your assignment in. Extension denied. *In advance.*"

"Miss Bridget, with due respect, this time I think I have a *really* good excuse. If there was ever a time that you could cut a fellow just a little bit of slack, this surely must be it."

"I hope, Simon, that you are not suggesting that I ... ."

Christine was laughing.

"OK," Miss Bridget said. "Listen. I don't know what's come over me. It must be all the excitement. Or maybe that I can't refuse a hero's request. I want you all to witness this unprecedented event. I am officially granting Simon an extension. One week. But it better be *bad!* It better tell me things about women nobody's ever even *thought* of, let alone written. I want to see writing that will take me to the stars. Simon's 'The Gabfest' will be the best vignette ever written. Or else."

They all laughed.

Christine whispered in Simon's ear.

Miss Bridget looked at Christine. "No dear," she said. "That's sweet of you, but you cannot help him. He's got to write it by himself."

"Anyway," Simon said, "I may be the big hero, but it seems to me that there were three heroes today besides me. All females too. So I'd better make that 'heroines'."

"We're always talking about sex stereotyping in class, aren't we Simon?" Miss Bridget said.

"Well, in this case, Miss Bridget," he said, "it looks like the females were as brave as the males."

Christine looked at Simon. "But you know, Simon, the guy thing is important too," she said. "Sometimes physical action is the most important thing of all. Like Xela always says, 'Everything has its place.' *Remember*?" She smiled.

"My two angels," Simon said. He looked into the cafe. An ambulance had come. The corpse was being lifted into it. Dr. Beaufort waved. No, my *three* angels, Simon thought.

*****

Back at Simon's house, Jaz had felt a jolt when Simon had killed the Observer. She looked at Xela.

"Yes, he has done it. It's over," Xela said.

Everything seemed so much clearer, Jaz thought. Different. It was hard to describe. Just *nicer*. "What *was* that?"

"That was something like evil leaving this plane of reality," Xela said.

"Can it come back? Can it harm others? I mean, can it flee to another plane?"

"It really is over," Axel said. "It has been neutralized. Simon has destroyed the body It was using. Lexa has now **quarantined** It."

384

"Like a computer virus you can't destroy, so you just quarantine it?"

"Yes, something like that. We have pursued it for eons through thousands of planes of existence. It has **eluded** us. Until today. Now it will forever be **innocuous**."

"Can it be helped?"

"Slowly," Xela said, "we will **rehabilitate** it. Nothing is evil. It is only confused. It needs to be cared for."

"When will you start to rehabilitate it?"

"Jaz, you're **insatiable**. You and your boyfriend have just saved the world, freed it from some really nasty aliens controlling it—some seriously *not nice* customers—and you're already worried about *helping* that thing?"

"I guess what Simon said about me is true," Jaz said. "I do seem to be an inveterate do-gooder. How did Simon describe me? Oh yes, 'the original Good Samaritan.'"

"Yeah. Well, Xela—*no, Lexa*—has a flash for you, Miss Good Samaritan Gotta-Save-the-World-Because-No-One-Else-Will-If-I-Don't. Listen up. Big time."

"*What?*" Jaz was looking at Xela like she had lost her mind.

"Chill," Xela said.

"*What?*"

"Just chill, girl."

Jaz smiled. "You know what?" she said.

"What?"

"I think I will."

Xela laughed.

1. **decipher** v. to interpret; decode
2. **emaciated** ADJ. thin and wasted
3. **repugnance** N. disgust
4. **astronomical** ADJ. immense
5. **sequester** v. to set apart
6. **reprehensible** ADJ. deserving of condemnation
7. **quaff** v. to drink with relish
8. **vanquish** v. to defeat
9. **repulsive** ADJ. causing extreme dislike; disgusting
10. **quarry** N. object of a hunt
11. **stupor** N. daze; state of mental confusion
12. **paroxysm** N. spasm; convulsion
13. **wrench** v. to pull at the emotions; pain
14. **distraught** ADJ. distressed
15. **extensive** ADJ. large in extent and number
16. **quarantine** v. to place in enforced isolation
17. **elude** v. to evade; avoid the grasp of
18. **innocuous** ADJ. harmless
19. **rehabilitate** v. to restore to normal life through education and therapy
20. **insatiable** ADJ. never satisfied

Simply Simon

Think you know the words? Then prove it! Choose the *best* word to fill in the blank in each of the sentences below.

sequester   quaff   eluded   vanquishing

paroxysms   astronomical   repulsive   quarry

extensive   insatiable

1. The countries of the world spend a/an _____ amount of money on weapons that could be far better spent to improve the lives of their people.

2. Many societies _____ individuals who can't fit into society until their behavior improves.

3. After I finish writing this story I'm going over to Pete's Place with Jaz to have an excellent dinner and then _____ an espresso or two.

4. After _____ the Pleiadesians, solving the social, economic, and political problems of Earth should be a breeze.

5. Jaz has a/an _____ desire to discover the truth.

6. Being a quarterback is usually pretty cool, but when your pass protection breaks down you feel sort of like the _____ of the hounds on a foxhunt.

7. Think of the nastiest-looking guy you've ever seen, multiply that picture by ten, and you'll have a pretty good idea of how _____ the Observer looked.

8. I have to tell you, I was really lucky to have those wonderful women comfort me when I was having _____ of anguish about having killed the Observer.

9. The Group has become so _____ that Jaz and I are thinking of creating an official body called the "One World Institute."

10. Jaz and I both pray that the world can now move forward and achieve the social justice and economic equality that has so far _____ it.

Making Sense

Indicate whether or not each of the words in **bold** makes sense in the sentence. If it makes sense, put Y (Yes); if it doesn't make sense, put N (No).

1. For relaxation Axel enjoys **deciphering** Morse code sent to him by other amateur radio operators and then sending them replies. ____

2. It's sad to see the **emaciated** bodies of people nearing starvation, especially in a world with an excess of food. ____

3. From what I learned in religion class about the great saints, I would say that they looked at their fellow humans not with **repugnance** for their wrongdoing, but with forgiveness and confidence that they will become better in time. ____

4. We have a high-security laboratory on campus that allows scientists to study **innocuous** bacteria that would cause outbreaks of disease in humans if they were released. ____

5. In criminology class we learned that efforts to **rehabilitate** criminals often are not very successful. ____

6. One thing I've learned in life is that the world is full of both bad and **reprehensible** people; you just have to find the good ones. ____

7. When I really want to concentrate I go into such a **stupor** that everything becomes crystal clear. ____

8. My teammates and I were so **distraught** about our big victory over State that we had a humongous party. ____

9. Dr. James is concerned that terrorists could **quarantine** a powerful new virus that people wouldn't have acquired a resistance against. ____

10. There's nothing more **wrenching** than coming to the end of the adventure and finding that everything is completely groovy and so you can finally get in some serious down time. ____

Match It

Match each of the following words to its meaning.

1. decipher	a. daze
2. repugnance	b. distressed
3. reprehensible	c. interpret
4. stupor	d. restore to normal life through education and therapy
5. wrench	e. large in extent and number
6. distraught	f. never satisfied
7. extensive	g. deserving of condemnation
8. elude	h. avoid the grasp of
9. rehabilitate	i. disgust
10. insatiable	j. pull at the emotions

Axel Speaks

Greetings! I believe that you are now ready for something more intellectual. Choose the *best* word to fill in the blank in each sentence.

1. The main attraction of America for immigrants in the nineteenth century was the tremendous industrial boom, which created a/an _____ demand for well-paid labor.

(A) equitable

(B) profligate

(C) insatiable

(D) insuperable

(E) lavish

2. To the casual observer, the workings of the natural world can seem _____; however, beneath this appearance there is a dynamic and often violent process through which balance is maintained.

(A) innocuous

(B) staid

(C) reprehensible

(D) nefarious

(E) discouraging

3. The Christian writer C. S. Lewis speculated that God might have separated worlds by extremely vast distances in order to _____ each form of life from others in the universe.

(A) wrench

(B) emulate

(C) decipher

(D) quarantine

(E) engender

4. One of the problematic aspects of the concept of war crimes is that what is to be considered unacceptable behavior in war is defined by the victors, who are both the accusers and the judges of the _____.

(A) quarry

(B) vanquished

(C) emaciated

(D) distraught

(E) apostates

5. Since, according to the theory of relativity, space is curved by mass, one would expect space around a black hole to curve dramatically because of the huge concentration of mass; this is indeed what happens, as space curves and _____ the star, preventing light from leaving it and rendering it unobservable.

(A) assimilates

(B) undermines

(C) stigmatizes

(D) rehabilitates

(E) sequesters

Answers on page 469.

And now, on with the story.

I'm Out of Here

Hi. It's Simon, your personal mentor at your service again. That was a pretty cool story, wasn't it? It got kind of intense toward the end there. Those Pleiadesians are rough customers. But we took care of business. So, everything is excellent now.

Before I go any further, I've got some good news for you—there are no vocabulary words to learn in this episode. That's right. None of those **words in bold**. No exercises to do. It's clear sailing from here to the end of the saga.

Well, pretty clear sailing. I wouldn't feel right if there wasn't some didactic component to this episode. So, what I've done is I've taken a sample of the 820 words you learned in the context of the story and used them in this episode. The sample is 121 words. If you have a predilection for mathematics, you'll know that's exactly 14.76 percent of the words—a statistically valid sample, according to Jaz. This means that you can run your own little reality check: If you can understand these words, it means you've been doing your homework and have assimilated the words. So, you've taken a prodigious step toward being an erudite person with a sophisticated vocabulary.

But before you say, "So long, Simon, it's been real," I must inform you that it is imperative that you postpone your imminent departure. Yes. Hang with me for a while.

Here's a flash. Before you become too complacent, I've got some more news for you. Yes. I'm afraid it's bad news. How can there be good news without bad news? It wouldn't be right. It would violate the inherent equilibrium of our universe. How bad? Pretty bad, I fear. In fact, it's verging on diabolical. A test. A FINAL TEST on all 820 words. And you will not be allowed to refer to the word lists—under pain of stigmatization, ostracism, and all things punitive. (*Punitive?* Just testing. Don't worry, I haven't taught you that word yet; it means "inflicting punishment.")

You say you have all the words down cold already? You advance the hypothesis that there is no need for a Final Test? Tough! I haven't gotten where I am by acquiescing to the trivial and inconsequential requests of high school students. I'm not a martinet like Dr. Beaufort, but I've learned one fundamental verity from the fanatical but sagacious and altruistic Miss Bridget—it is imperative that *each and every* student (do you discern redundancy? some linguistic experts believe we should totally eschew such constructions, whereas others believe they are legitimate uses of language; it's a nebulous area of grammar) develop his or her aptitudes to the fullest. And the only way to do this entails hard work and long hours. There is no other way. No student is going to achieve anything less than what he or she is capable of. Not on my watch.

So sharpen your pencils and clear your schedule for the next several days. Tell your friends you'll have to repress your innate gregarious propensities and become reclusive for a while. Get ready to bust a gut. Don't even *think* about asking for mercy. Request for cancellation of Final Test denied. *In advance.*

You say that Miss Bridget cut me some slack and gave me more time to complete my vignette? Yes, a reasonable point. There is an issue of equitable treatment and fair play here, I suppose.

You say that Jaz would want me to give you a break after all the work you've done because too much work can have a deleterious effect on a young person's delicate psyche and is considered unsound pedagogy? Although I'm a bit dubious about some of its underlying presuppositions, that's a fairly cogent argument, I must admit.

You advance the thesis that Xela would appreciate and applaud a major act of clemency on my part at this juncture? That she would regard such benevolence not as a sign of weakness but as the mark of a truly virile, self-assured man? That she would censure me and never forgive me if I inflicted such pain on you, an innocuous, guileless, completely innocent young being?

Listen. I don't know what's come over me. Maybe it's because you're such an awesome student for getting all the way through this mammoth tome and doing all the exercises so indefatigably. Maybe it's because I can't refuse the request of a savant in a nascent stage of development. Most likely it's because I still have a touch of vertigo from finishing off the Observer. That really was harrowing. Whatever it is, I want you to appreciate this unprecedented event: I am officially granting you a holiday. No Final Test. That's right. It really is over. No more work. You're free to party.

No Final. Pretty cool, huh? But listen up. Big time. After what I've just done for you, you'd better *ace* your SAT. You better do so well I'll hear cherubs singing their sublime songs in the celestial realms. And to do that, you'll have to do a lot more than this one book. I want you to promise me that you'll conscientiously peruse other high-quality SAT preparation books such as *Barron's How to Prepare for the SAT* and *Barron's Verbal Workbook for SAT I*. And pledge that you'll keep augmenting your lexicon by becoming a bibliophile and reading every book in sight. And maybe even take a peek at a dictionary once in a while. (Warning: Do this with some circumspection; teachers have been known to keel over at the rare sight of a student opening a dictionary.)

Yes. I've just cut you a colossal break. Now I'd like you to do a little favor for me. First, relax. That's right, just kick back for a while and think about nothing at all. Now, concentrate. Think about your future. You are clairvoyant—totally prescient. You're in the kitchen with your mom and dad one fine afternoon several months from now. A missive has arrived from Princeton, New Jersey. Yes, your SAT results have come. They're in an envelope lying on the table. Your father is getting ready to pick up the envelope. An image of you studying at one of America's better colleges is powerfully exercising his mind. Your mother is at his side, waiting for the verdict on your future. In her mind is a lucid vision of you happily ensconced at a prestigious institution with ivy-covered walls. Your father is now holding the envelope in his hand. He is looking at your mother, who is gazing entreatingly toward the heavens. Your father is opening the envelope. A revelation is at hand. Soon the occult secret of your destiny will be revealed.

Your father is holding a piece of paper in his hand.

Worry. Anxiety.

Your father is looking at the piece of paper he is holding in his hand.

Fear. Dread.

You are looking at your father's face. You have never seen that expression before. Usually he is the most affable and imperturbable man around. But not now.

Anguish. Pain. Searing pain. So much pain. The world seems to be spinning.

Your normally garrulous father is speechless. Now you recognize his expression. He looks like he did when you were in ninth grade and you told him there was a possibility, however minute, that you might fail French. Except this is worse. Much, much worse. He looks, in fact, like he is about to go completely ballistic.

Terror. Palpable fear for your corporeal well-being.

Your mother is looking at your father, her eyes importuning him to divulge what he has beheld. He looks at her, and in that brief glance tells all. Your mother now looks completely forlorn. Her countenance is transfixed by a look of utter bemusement and melancholy. It is a look that transcends shock. She is in a complete stupor; so far gone, in truth, that she is no longer a functioning part of this plane of existence.

You are running. Fleeing the inevitable wrath of your parents. Your world has ended. Your dreams are shattered. You've just *killed* your chance of getting into a good college. Just like that. Through negligence—through sheer unadulterated carelessness. Because you thought you could play it cool and not study hard for the SAT.

Not a pretty scenario, huh? Plausible, maybe, but not pretty.

Now imagine something different. Concentrate. Really focus. Remember what Xela said: "The future will be what you want it to be, so try to think about it clearly."

Your SAT results have come. Once again, your father is opening the envelope. He's reading the results. But this time it's different. There's a smile as wide as the cosmos on his face. Your mother is elated, truly enraptured, transported to some supernal realm of ineffable bliss.

The world seems so much clearer. Different somehow. It's hard to describe. It's just a lot nicer now. There is a Being. The Parental Unit. It is happy. So happy now. All because you had foresight and studied diligently.

Well, it's been great hanging with you, but I've got to get ready to roll. I've got an astronomical amount of stuff to take care of. I seem to have undergone a transmogrification into a total bureaucrat recently. The Group has become the One World Institute and it's gotten really big. There's a pile of paperwork on my desk from the Institute *a mile high*. (A cliché and hyperbole in one shot. *Yes.* I still have my touch with language.) And there's a pretty critical play-off game coming on the tube soon. Maybe we'll meet up again some day and I'll help you learn some more words. By that time you'll probably be thinking about graduate school, law school, medical school, or something like that. So, the words will have to be even more obscure than the ones you've learned in this book. Maybe I'll try to locate the ultimate Renaissance dude (yes, good old Axel) to see if he could pay us a visit and help us out.

If we do meet up again, I'll fill you in on how the Institute has been going. But for now, don't worry about the fate of our species and all that heavy-duty stuff. It's in pretty good hands. All I want you to do is study hard in school and for the SAT. Then I'll be happy. *So happy.*

Best of luck. Stay cool. *Everything will work out just great.* I'm out of here.

Double Trouble by Axel

Greetings. Remember Simon told you how I helped him learn all those difficult words back in high school? Well, I wrote a special set of really tough review exercises for him to do the day before he took the SAT. These are the exercises that drove him *crazy.* But I didn't want to leave anything to chance. I wanted to make sure he knew all the words perfectly. He moaned a lot when I made him do them, but he certainly thanked me after he aced the test.

Simon doesn't know it, but for some reason I saved that set of exercises. And now I'd like to share them with you. They're an SAT-style review of the words Simon has taught you in this book. As I said, they're tough. But if you can handle them, you will be—as Simon would no doubt say— "Ready to rock and roll." I call them "Double Trouble" in honor of one of my favorite bands, Stevie Ray Vaughan's "Double Trouble." *Check it out.*

Round 1

1. Based on the laws of physics as understood by the leading scientists of the 1940s, it was _____ that it would be impossible for an airplane to exceed the speed of sound since that was considered at the time to be a/an _____ barrier.

(A) extrapolated.....feasible

(B) inferred....infinitesimal

(C) hypothesized.....fictitious

(D) conjectured..... indelible

(E) surmised.....insuperable

2. In *The Republic* the Greek philosopher Plato advocated the principle that for a society to be governed justly and wisely it must have rulers who have received a rigorous intellectual training so that they are _____ and free of _____.

(A) dispassionate.....fanaticism

(B) acquiescent.....pragmatism

(C) cherubic.....empathy

(D) apostate.....presuppositions

(E) amenable.....animosity

3. Many antibiotics have become less _____ than they were previously because resistant strains of microorganisms have evolved as a result of mankind's efforts to _____ them.

(A) benign.....augment

(B) discerning.....intimidate

(C) innocuous.....circumvent

(D) efficacious.....eradicate

(E) enticing.....ameliorate

4. Modern taste generally demands that works of art not be purely _____ and that they convey an underlying truth in a manner that is not obviously _____.

(A) contemporary.....sententious

(B) ephemeral.....prosaic

(C) aesthetic.....didactic

(D) compelling.....polemical

(E) autonomous.....hedonistic

5. Research by psychologists has found that romantic love lasts an average of 30 months, after which a relationship becomes more oriented toward companionship; from the _____ of people in love, however, love is not reducible to a scientific observation, but is a real and very meaningful, perhaps even _____, experience.

(A) speculation.....sublime

(B) vantage.....mundane

(C) camaraderie....inane

(D) perspective.....transcendent

(E) legacy.....mystical

6. Among the approximately 25,000 known asteroids with well-_____ orbits, one—with the _____ KY26— has been found to contain reservoirs of water in the form of ice that could be used by future space explorers.

(A) corroborated.....appellation

(B) circumscribed.....jargon

(C) substantiated.....analogy

(D) fabricated.....idiom

(E) divulged.....circumlocution

7. In his book *Beyond Freedom and Dignity* the psychologist B. F. Skinner defends an approach to the study of humankind based on behaviorism; Skinner argues that it is more important to learn the truth than to maintain the pleasant _____ that people are _____ agents who act as a result of their own will.

(A) anomaly........rational

(B) delusion........autonomous

(C) ideology....... intrepid

(D) anecdote........omnipotent

(E) affirmation........indomitable

8. When asked to _____ about humanity's future based on her vast knowledge of the past, the distinguished historian sighed and said, "I am not prescient; I see vast vistas, glorious summits, and depressing troughs, but the end remains _____."

(A) intimate.....ambiguous

(B) extrapolate.....implausible

(C) speculate.....opaque

(D) conjecture.....extravagant

(E) ruminate.....obtuse

9. The quotation from Shakespeare's *Hamlet*, "There are more things in heaven and Earth, Horatio, / Than are dreamt of in your philosophy," reminds us that it is _____ to reserve judgment on the _____ nature of reality.

(A) judicious.....ultimate

(B) cerebral.....provincial

(C) sophisticated.....peripheral

(D) preposterous.....conceivable

(E) prudent.....dogmatic

10. The French writer Alexis de Tocqueville noted in *Democracy in America,* published in 1835, that there seems to be a paradox in American society: that _____ of individualism produces a _____ of public institutions requiring a great collective effort to create.

(A) paragon.....parody

(B) edifice.....motif

(C) citadel.....myriad

(D) titan.....multiplicity

(E) exemplar .....legacy

Answers to *Double Trouble* are on page 470.

Round 2

1. One of the most influential heresies that the early Christians confronted was Gnosticism, a movement that had as its central _____ the belief that human beings are a/an_____ of the spiritual and the physical, and must attain knowledge of the divine nature to return to God.

(A) enigma.....mélange

(B) predicament.....amalgam

(C) inkling.....juncture

(D) premonition.... pastiche

(E) tenet.....fusion

2. Alexander Fleming's discovery of penicillin in 1929 was _____, but it required _____ as well: In the course of an experiment, Fleming noticed that around a mold he was using staphylococcus colonies were decomposing.

(A) serendipitous.....astuteness

(B) inadvertent.....machinations

(C) fortuitous.....repression

(D) inevitable.....foresight

(E) ephemeral.....acumen

3. One of the prominent leaders of the civil rights movement in America was Martin Luther King, Jr., a Protestant clergyman who was greatly influenced by the _____ and example of the _____ Indian political and spiritual leader Mohandas Gandhi, who sought justice through *ahimsa*, or nonviolence.

(A) exhortations.....ethereal

(B) tenets.....pedantic

(C) accolades.....indomitable

(D) precepts.....eminent

(E) expertise.....nebulous

4. The so-called "strong anthropic principle" states that the existence of so many coincidences favorable to the development of life means that intelligence is a/an _____ part of the universe, and that therefore the emergence of intelligence is _____ .

(A) inherent.....inevitable

(B) innate.....redundant

(C) distinctive.....ironic

(D) congenital.....ominous

(E) irrefutable.....fortuitous

5. Every culture possesses its own unique view of the world based on the _____ of previous generations as to which beliefs are fundamental and _____ .

(A) ambivalence.....chimerical

(B) antithesis.....efficacious

(C) consensus......controversial

(D) assessment.....immutable

(E) legacy.....anachronistic

6. In Greek mythology the god Dionysus was attended by a _____ of devotees, among them nymphs—beautiful young girls who were deities associated with various _____ of nature.

(A) mélange.....prerogatives

(B) lobby.....formulations

(C) pantheon......scenarios

(D) colloquy.....sensibilities

(E) retinue.....attributes

7. In the Renaissance, the spirit of free inquiry, which had been _____ for centuries, emerged like a phoenix, bursting into life triumphantly, and reaching its _____ in figures such as Leonardo da Vinci and Galileo.

(A) embellished.....culmination

(B) quiescent.....epiphany

(C) inert.....anachronism

(D) aloof.....zenith

(E) dormant.....acme

8. The story of Odysseus' journey is told in *The Odyssey,* a long _____ poem that some scholars believe to be the work of a solitary writer and others believe to be the result of the _____ of a long tradition of poems in the style.

(A) narrative......culmination

(B) didactic.........concomitant

(C) facile........ amalgam

(D) iconoclastic.........ideology

(E) interminable.........fusing

9. The existence of _____ has been explained by scientists as a trait that was favored in human evolution because it _____ the ability of people to work together, thus increasing their chances of survival.

(A) beneficence.....mollified

(B) autonomy .....augmented

(C) altruism.....enhanced

(D) bureaucracy ......exploited

(E) ennui.....entailed

10. The characteristic class structure of modern industrial society _____ people into groups based, predominantly, on economic _____.

(A) coerces.....karma

(B) stratifies.....criteria

(C) ensconces.....affluence

(D) orchestrates.....debacles

(E) sequesters.....faculties

Answers to *Double Trouble* are on page 470.

Round 3

1. After Confucianism became the _____ belief system of China in the tenth century A.D., educated Confucians have been predominantly atheistic, believing in a supreme moral law but not a/an _____ personal deity.

(A) posthumous.....ultimate

(B) abortive.....transcendental

(C) preeminent.....virile

(D) preposterous.....prescient

(E) paramount.....omnipotent

2. One's position on the use of live animals in experiments is dependent on one's _____ regarding the rights that animals are entitled to; if one believes that animals have a right to _____ treatment, then one might have difficulty in justifying any form of vivisection (that is, experimentation on living animals).

(A) karma......beneficent

(B) presuppositions....humane

(C) dogma ......bellicose

(D) inkling........cavalier

(E) creed.......diabolical

3. A problem that has puzzled astronomers is how a presumably _____ early universe _____ into one with such large and varied structures as clusters of galaxies that are separated by vast distances.

(A) monolithic .....transpired

(B) homogenous.....transmogrified

(C) anomalous .....coalesced

(D) superfluous.....metamorphosed

(E) hybrid.....mesmerized

4. Some observers believe the American system of checks and balances is a/an _____, in that power is dispersed so widely that government cannot act _____ to meet quickly changing circumstances in the modern world.

(A) rationalization.....efficaciously

(B) bureaucracy...furtively

(C) ritual.....resolutely

(D) conundrum.....judiciously

(E) anachronism.....decisively

5. A majority of historians would probably agree with the view that, although their discipline has come increasingly to rely on _____ methods, there still exists a need for a subjective and personal _____ of historical data.

(A) tangible.....inveigling

(B) reductionistic.....plumbing

(C) speculative.....embellishing

(D) empirical.....assessment

(E) pragmatic.....fabrication

6. The term "global village" draws a/an _____ between a village in which people know each other through _____, and modern technological society in which people know each other through radio, television, publications, and the Internet.

(A) anomaly....proximity

(B) abstraction.....accessibility

(C) analogy.....propinquity

(D) disparity.....gregariousness

(E) methodology.....congruity

7. In his Barchestershire novels, the English Victorian writer Anthony Trollope succeeded brilliantly in creating a tone of affectionate satire in which he combines fondness for his characters with _____ criticism of their _____.

(A) facetious.....altruism

(B) amiable.....travesties

(C) poignant.....incarnations

(D) droll.....foibles

(E) rapacious.....altercations

8. Perhaps the myth of the phoenix—a bird that is consumed in fire but rises from its ashes—is a/an _____ of the hope that out of death can come new life, a renewal of the old that, _____ , can sometimes come out only of destruction.

(A) manifestation.....paradoxically

(B) incarnation.....nebulously

(C) amalgam.....ironically

(D) exemplar.....redundantly

(E) replicate.....remorselessly

9. Anthropologists vary in their views on race from those who believe the differences between races are so slight as to be _____ , to those who _____ a number of distinctly different races.

(A) negligible.....discern

(B) trivial....eschew

(C) miniscule.....engender

(D) peripheral.....exude

(E) compelling.....surmise

10. One of the first _____ of the _____ of intelligence tests were the results of tests given to United States Army recruits in World War II: Test scores were very accurate predictors of the rank subsequently attained by soldiers.

(A) queries.....efficacy

(B) corroborations.....validity

(C) rationalizations.....potency

(D) inklings......premonition

(E) precepts......pervasiveness

Answers to *Double Trouble* are on page 470.

Round 4

1. A number of studies have suggested that violence in the media is _____; rather than increasing the tendency toward aggression, it might actually dampen it by allowing viewers to experience violence_____.

(A) discerning......remorselessly

(B) cathartic....vicariously

(C) figurative........sporadically

(D) credible .....inadvertently

(E) orchestrated.....retrospectively

2. Wicca, a religion with its origins in pre-Christian times, has great reverence for nature and believes in _____ rather than _____ .

(A) annihilation.....ritual

(B) legerdemain.....dogma

(C) revelation .....hierarchy

(D) hedonism.....asceticism

(E) skepticism.....karma

3. _____ for slavery in America contend that, historically, slavery is the norm rather than a/an _____, and that it took a relatively harmless form in this country, as slaves generally were well treated.

(A) Pundits....stereotype

(B) Rationalizations......stratagem

(C) Apologists.....aberration

(D) Curators.....anomaly

(E) Hypocrites......euphemism

4. In his book *The Case for Mars,* former NASA engineer Robert Zubrin argues _____ for *direct* manned missions to Mars that would make use of existing technology and facilities, making unnecessary way stations in earth orbit or on the moon that would require _____ expenditures to build.

(A) affably ....provisional

(B) coyly....redundant

(C) astutely.....subterranean

(D) dubiously....repugnant

(E) cogently.....lavish

5. In the ancient world the wisdom of the sphinx—a mythical creature with the head of a woman and the body of a lion—was _____; some people even believed she was _____.

(A) acerbic .....sagacious

(B) onerous.....omnipotent

(C) anecdotal.....opaque

(D) proverbial.....omniscient

(E) colossal.....circumspect

6. The past decade has seen a/an_____ amount of agonizing in Western societies over the decline of the family as a/an _____ institution.

(A) anachronistic.....feasible

(B) discreet.....precocious

(C) prodigious.....gregarious

(D) minute.....enervated

(E) unprecedented....viable

7. One of the primary aims of education is the _____ examination of our prejudices so that our beliefs become more _____ with reality.

(A) judicious.....obsessed

(B) dispassionate.....efficacious

(C) objective.....congruent

(D) implicit.....compatible

(E) explicit.....concomitant

8. The psychologist Abraham Maslow believed that there exists a/an _____ of human needs, ranging from basic physical needs to _____ ones, such as the need for self-expression; when the more basic needs are met, a person can move toward what he termed "self-actualization."

(A) cacophony.....mundane

(B) critique.....esoteric

(C) mélange.....immutable

(D) hierarchy.....intangible

(E) lineage.....obscure

9. Some people believe that Buddha was an agnostic, but the _____ of scholars is that he believed in God but thought speculation on His nature was _____.

(A) consensus.....futile

(B) vantage.....redundant

(C) cognition......dubious

(D) connivance.....ineffectual

(E) perspective .....cavalier

10. Language is not entirely a logical system, and thus redundancy sometimes can be used _____ for emphasis or other _____ effects.

(A) resolutely.....linguistic

(B) fundamentally.....erudite

(C) legitimately.....rhetorical

(D) lucidly.....voluble

(E) sporadically.....expeditious

Answers to *Double Trouble* are on page 470.

Round 5

1. The American writer H. L. Mencken was a/an _____ atheist, as illustrated by this _____ comment: "God is the immemorial refuge of the incompetent, the helpless, the miserable. They find not only sanctuary in His arms but also a kind of superiority, soothing to their macerated egos; He will set them above their betters."

(A) credible.....ineffable

(B) unadulterated.....demure

(C) inveterate.....scathing

(D) iconoclastic.....laconic

(E) controversial.....sanguine

2. It will be interesting to see if—given the natural _____ of the human species—many people in the future will want to work at home rather than the office or factory, foregoing the _____ of the workplace.

(A) hierarchy.....rationalizations

(B) empathy.....equilibrium

(C) megalomania.....ennui

(D) gregariousness.....camaraderie

(E) amiability.....benevolence

3. The militaristic nature of Norse culture is _____ in the idea of Valhalla, a place in which warriors who were killed in battle live eternally in a palace in which day after day they enjoy _____ and fighting battles against one another.

(A) presumed.....regaling

(B) depicted.....revelry

(C) enthralled.....ogling

(D) deployed.....metamorphosing

(E) stigmatized...ruminating

4. The artist René Magritte incorporated elements in his work that appear _____ to the ordinary sensibility because they do not _____ to conventional ideas of reality.

(A) obtuse.....coalesce

(B) bizarre.....conform

(C) cacophonous.....respire

(D) alluring.....adhere

(E) anomalous.....resolve

5. People in the civilized world hope that anti-Semitism has become a/an _____; unfortunately, however, there have been _____ incidents motivated by anti-Semitism in Europe and the United States in recent years.

(A) anachronism.....sporadic

(B) artifact .....cavalier

(C) enigma.....conspicuous

(D) chimera.....corroborating

(E) legacy.....recurring

6. The ancient Greek philosopher Socrates believed that truth is _____ and that the duty of a philosopher is to take a/an _____ view in striving by every means possible to find it.

(A) elusive.....detached

(B) ephemeral.....ambiguous

(C) enigmatic.....anecdotal

(D) ineffable .....comprehensive

(E) subjective.....cynical

7. The spectacular collision of comet Shoemaker-Levy 9 with Jupiter between July 16 and July 22, 1994, was the most violent event humans have ever witnessed in the solar system, and made _____ heed the warnings of astronomers that comets pose a real hazard; it is now agreed that there is a significant chance of the earth being struck by a similar large comet, an event that would _____ virtually all life on the planet.

(A) hedonists.....neutralize

(B) pragmatists.....coerce

(C) cynics.....ostracize

(D) ornithologists.....obliterate

(E) skeptics.....annihilate

8. Some historians contend that the industrial revolution did not happen in China during the period in which it was the world's most technologically advanced country because of _____ inertia, and a desire on the part of the elite to preserve their _____.

(A) congenital.....creed

(B) rampant.....duplicity

(C) provincial.....disparity

(D) futile.....affluence

(E) bureaucratic.....prerogatives

9. It is interesting to use myths as a basis for understanding the human _____, but it is wise to be_____ about such interpretations since myths can be viewed in many different ways.

(A) propensity.....conservative

(B) alchemy .....doctrinaire

(C) saga.....uninhibited

(D) psyche.....circumspect

(E) agenda......condescending

10. Although at the time it seemed to many Americans to be a/an _____ amount of money to spend on helping foreign countries, in _____ the Marshall Plan that helped to rebuild Europe after World War II was a bargain for the United States, since it helped make Western Europe a fortress against the Soviet Union and provided a rich market for American goods.

(A) gargantuan.....reminiscing

(B) controversial.....replicating

(C) prodigious.....retrospect

(D) colossal.....syncopation

(E) inconsequential....hindsight

Answers to *Double Trouble* are on page 470.

Round 6

1. People sometimes become frustrated by the workings of _____, but it is helpful to remember that each of them functions according to its own set of complex regulations that usually ensure that a task is performed correctly, if not _____.

(A) analogies.....efficaciously

(B) despotisms.....extravagantly

(C) bureaucracies....expeditiously

(D) hierarchies .....intangibly

(E) factions.....sheepishly

2. Some critics and poets argue that poetry should have a/an _____ distinct from that of _____, whereas others, following William Wordsworth's belief that the traditional language of poetry is artificial, maintain that first-rate poetry is more likely to be expressed in language closer to ordinary speech.

(A) syncopation....monologues

(B) facet....jargon

(C) nuance.....irony

(D) diction....prose

(E) potency.....discourse

3. Society must find a proper balance between too much _____, on the one hand, and, on the other hand, excessive individualism; the former discourages individual expression, whereas the latter _____ people from one another.

(A) benevolence.....sequesters

(B) pragmatism.......ostracizes

(C) conformity.....alienates

(D) empathy.....adulterates

(E) equilibrium ....estranges

4. The historian of science Thomas Kuhn believes that scientists are inclined to accept as correct information that fits into the prevailing _____ of science and reject information that challenges _____ thinking.

(A) paradigms.....orthodox

(B) hypotheses.....convoluted

(C) pantheon...conventional

(D) clichés.....insipid

(E) agenda.....iconoclastic

5. In trance a shaman (a holy person) projects his soul into the spirit world in order to seek the help of _____ spirits in _____ bad spirits that have taken a person's soul.

(A) beneficent.....procuring

(B) innocuous.....ogling

(C) disaffected....eschewing

(D) distinctive.....neutralizing

(E) benevolent.....exorcising

6. The _____ Alfred Adler maintained that psychological problems have their origin in a feeling of inferiority that occurs when a person's inborn need to assert his or her abilities is _____.

(A) savant....scrutinized

(B) lobbyist...piqued

(C) psychiatrist.....circumscribed

(D) martinet.....quarantined

(E) maverick.....mollified

7. It is _____ that the launching of *Sputnik 1* (the first object to be put into Earth orbit) by the USSR in 1957 was the _____ for a reevaluation of American scientific education that resulted in vast resources being devoted to improving standards in that area; these improvements contributed significantly to the technological superiority of the United States over the Soviet Union.

(A) paradoxical....query

(B) ominous....ruse

(C) ironic....... catalyst

(D) credible....travesty

(E) diabolical....hybrid

8. Humanity seems to become _____ to the horror of weapons of warfare quite easily: When gunpowder was first used, it was considered barbaric; when dynamite was introduced, it was imagined by some that it would make war unthinkable; napalm and land mines are two of the twentieth century's more _____ contributions to warfare.

(A) enhanced.....inveterate

(B) oblivious....vapid

(C) indigenous.....malignant

(D) impervious.....diabolical

(E) obtuse.....precocious

9. _____, a device frequently employed by satirists, uses _____ to distort its subject and make it appear ridiculous.

(A) Subterfuge....sarcasm

(B) Caricature.....hyperbole

(C) Irony.....jocularity

(D) Hypocrisy.....stratagems

(E) Jargon.....rhetoric

10. Sigmund Freud believed that myths, like dreams, often express psychological truths in symbolic language that, though _____ with some extraneous details, provide insight into the processes of the human _____.

(A) ameliorated....perspective

(B) imbued.....motif

(C) embellished.....psyche

(D) enervated....formulation

(E) saturated ....nomenclature

Answers to *Double Trouble* are on page 470.

Round 7

1. Some _____ remarked that America is indeed a "melting pot" of many different groups of people but that the soup is very lumpy, with different groups retaining their _____ and cultural identities.

(A) apologist....indigenous

(B) hypocrite.....homogenized

(C) bureaucrat....derivative

(D) charlatan....fabricated

(E) pundit...ethnic

2. Astrologers claim that data gathered over the centuries has produced a body of information and a/an _____ capable of telling people something meaningful about their _____ tendencies.

(A) expertise....insular

(B) paradigm....ephemeral

(C) edifice......empirical

(D) dogma.....cordial

(E) methodology.....inherent

3. Within the Hindu religion there are three main types of yoga: *jnana yoga,* the path of _____ ; *bhakti yoga,* the path of love and devotion to a personal God; and *karma yoga,* the path of _____ action.

(A) affirmation.....trivial

(B) pontificating....nefarious

(C) sagacity.....altruistic

(D) beneficence.....enervating

(E) euphemism.....extensive

4. The Church tried to depict the Crusades as motivated entirely by religious belief, but there was often a/an _____ motive present: Noblemen _____ lands and goods of the Middle East.

(A) sublime....undermined

(B) altruistic....ogled

(C) spurious.....disdained

(D) ambiguous....squandered

(E) mercenary.....coveted

5. A number of scientists believe that Mars underwent global warming millions of years ago; if this is true, it is possible that the current situation on our planet is _____, and that by studying Mars' climate scientists may be able to gain an understanding into the _____ of the greenhouse effect for earth's climate.

(A) reminiscent.....speculation

(B) feasible....nuances

(C) recurring.....facets

(D) analogous.....implications

(E) unprecedented.....ramifications

6. Despite progress in improving race relations in America, many people believe that the problem of the racial "divide" remains _____ because of cultural factors such as prejudice that new _____ can do little to change.

(A) incorrigible....precepts

(B) inevitable....quarantines

(C) intractable.....statutes

(D) inconsequential...rebukes

(E) inimitable.....methodology

7. In Herman Melville's great novel *Moby Dick,* seemingly _____ details about whaling accumulate in the reader's mind, helping to create _____.

(A) esoteric.....pulchritude

(B) peripheral.....legerdemain

(C) superfluous.....verisimilitude

(D) ephemeral.....criteria

(E) insipid.....revelry

8. _____ predictions in the 1960s of _____ mass starvation as a result of the inability of the world's food supply to meet the needs of the population proved, happily, to be inaccurate.

(A) Pessimistic.....humane

(B) Melancholy.....imminent

(C) Exotic.....inevitable

(D) Omniscient....unprecedented

(E) Prescient.....subterranean

9. Martin Luther, the leader of the Protestant Reformation, became a/an _____ due to his deep differences with the Church over _____ and practices and was excommunicated in 1521.

(A) maverick.....nuances

(B) apologist .....dictates

(C) charlatan.....orthodoxy

(D) apostate.....dogma

(E) liberal.....chicanery

10. In the twentieth century women came closer to equality with men; unfortunately, however, this advance _____ their becoming more _____ to stress-related diseases that were previously associated with men.

(A) engendered....demeaning

(B) enthralled.....cordial

(C) assailed.....compatible

(D) entailed.....susceptible

(E) divulged ....enticing

Answers to *Double Trouble* are on page 470.

Round 8

1. A difficulty with giving psychological treatment to a person who is believed to be poorly adjusted to society is that the individual may be _____ as a result of officially being labeled as deviant, and consequently may act to _____ society's expectations.

(A) quarantined.....bedevil

(B) stigmatized....corroborate

(C) insular.....stipulate

(D) agitated....squander

(E) sequestered....debunk

2. Some _____ believe the world is now undergoing a second major phase of industrialization that they term an "information revolution," in which the advanced economies are moving away from the production of products such as steel, cars, and electrical appliances to the providing of _____ in "information" areas such as computing and the media.

(A) fundamentalists...aptitudes

(B) savants.....platitudes

(C) pedants.....faculties

(D) pundits.....expertise

(E) liberals.....megalomania

3. Most of the professional astronomers searching for asteroids that come close to earth in their highly _____ orbit around the sun work in the United States; thus, humanity is essentially _____ to asteroids that are visible when the United States is in daylight, or that are visible only from the Southern Hemisphere.

(A) eccentric.....oblivious

(B) anomalous....aloof

(C) surreptitious....impervious

(D) convoluted....complementary

(E) meandering....superfluous

4. The _____ of the Renaissance man—a humanist of remarkably _____ learning and genius—was Leonardo da Vinci.

(A) travesty......esoteric

(B) paragon....puerile

(C) exemplar.....eclectic

(D) antithesis.....diverse

(E) quintessence...peripheral

5. One of the _____ of the American system of government is that power tends to corrupt those who have it, and so structures to _____ the effects of this tendency must be incorporated into government.

(A) presumptions....avenge

(B) motifs.....mesmerize

(C) presuppositions.....mitigate

(D) hypotheses.....engender

(E) impediments.....orchestrate

6. A good rule of thumb for writers is to be as concise and _____ as possible and avoid _____ rhetorical devices.

(A) lucid.....extravagant

(B) redundant....lavish

(C) cogent.....viable

(D) meandering.....hackneyed

(E) ambiguous.....defunct

7. Justification of vivisection (experimentation on living animals) is frequently _____ on the belief that drugs and medical procedures that benefit humans could not be developed without it; however, opponents of vivisection regard this as mere _____.

(A) buttressed .....quibbling

(B) debunked .....naiveté

(C) concocted.....skepticism

(D) predicated......rationalization

(E) posited.....pragmatism

8. The _____ of the Internet has been compared in importance to the development of movable type in the fifteenth century that made books available to the masses, an event that _____ great changes in society.

(A) genesis....entreated

(B) enigma.....divulged

(C) serendipity.....presumed

(D) alchemy.....enunciated

(E) advent.....engendered

9. It is possible that an observer from another civilization would be able to learn of the existence of a technological civilization on earth from radio and television broadcasts _____ from the planet and, upon closer inspection, from the transformation of the natural landscape through the presence of gigantic _____, such as the Great Wall of China and the Egyptian pyramids.

(A) deducing.... despotisms

(B) respiring......euphemisms

(C) emanating.....edifices

(D) exuding...fiascos

(E) enervating.....paragons

10. Artificial intelligence enables computers to _____ some of the _____ processes of the human brain.

(A) eschew....soporific

(B) emulate......cognitive

(C) synthesize...clandestine

(D) assimilate...concomitant

(E) intimate....cerebral

Answers to *Double Trouble* are on page 470.

Round 9

1. The history of _____ has seen humanity's view of its place in the universe go from the geocentric Ptolemaic System to the currently accepted view in which Earth is seen as a planet orbiting a rather _____ star on the outskirts of a galaxy containing approximately 200 billion stars.

(A) cosmology......prosaic

(B) karma ....mundane

(C) terminology...pervasive

(D) millennium ....inconsequential

(E) cartography.....moribund

2. The framers of the U.S. Constitution were _____ that the system of government that they had devised was predisposed toward the formation of _____, each supporting its special interest.

(A) circumspect......monologues

(B) enraptured.....bourgeoisie

(C) judicious.....citadels

(D) cognizant.....factions

(E) prudent.....clichés

3. Thinkers as different in their intellectual outlook as the English Romantic poet William Wordsworth and the American philosopher William James reported _____ states of mind in which they experienced a/an _____ with nature and a sense of the world as a uniform reality.

(A) banal....empathy

(B) eccentric....alchemy

(C) macabre....fusion

(D) mystical....rapport

(E) psychic....ennui

4. Both irony and _____ involve saying the opposite of what you mean, however in the latter the meaning is unambiguous and _____, whereas in the case of irony it is subtle.

(A) antithesis....vitriolic

(B) hyperbole....fictitious

(C) paradox.... figurative

(D) oxymorons....extemporaneous

(E) sarcasm....acerbic

5. In the social sciences it is often difficult to find _____ evidence to prove a/an _____ because of the great number of interrelated factors that play a part in any phenomenon being studied.

(A) ambiguous.....theorem

(B) conclusive.....hypothesis

(C) tenable.....litany

(D) credible.....platitude

(E) figurative....extrapolation

6. In his classic book *Civilization and Its Discontents,* Sigmund Freud argued that human civilization is largely an outcome of sublimation, a process in which people _____ their _____ and other drives, thereby sacrificing their pleasure, and substitute social attainments for them.

(A) suppress....superfluous

(B) undermine..... antithetical

(C) repress.......libidinal

(D) stigmatize...... virile

(E) stifle...... risqué

7. Some experts predict that in the twenty-first century multinational companies will displace the nation-state as the world's _____ political _____ .

(A) provisional.....tomes

(B) pretentious....titans

(C) predominant.....entities

(D) ubiquitous.....ruses

(E) innumerable.....verities

8. An argument against genetic engineering is that it interferes in the natural process of evolution; however, defenders of genetic engineering _____ this by pointing out that humankind has been altering nature for thousands of years through domestication and selection of plants and animals, as well as by grafting and _____ plants.

(A) renege.....debilitating

(B) revile.....fusing

(C) rebut.....hybridizing

(D) refute.....conceptualizing

(E) profane.....homogenizing

9. Although only the United States has built a commercially _____ space shuttle, the European Space Agency and several individual countries have built reliable launch vehicles that have challenged American _____ in space.

(A) consummate.....orthodoxy

(B) feasible.....bureaucracy

(C) superfluous.....omnipotence

(D) viable.....preeminence

(E) loathsome.....rhetoric

10. Few people in the 1980s foresaw that personal computers would become _____ and be used for such _____ purposes.

(A) ephemeral.....diverse

(B) beguiling.....quibbling

(C) ubiquitous.....multifarious

(D) prodigious.....cerebral

(E) alluring.....explicit

Answers to *Double Trouble* are on page 470.

Round 10

1. Myths often provide people with a/an _____ explanation for things that _____ them, such as the apparent capriciousness of nature.

(A) fictitious...mollify

(B) figurative.....peruse

(C) plausible.....bemuse

(D) exotic.....pique

(E) metaphorical....assail

2. It is conceivable that Mars colonists could _____ many of their electronic and other devices from _____ elements, such as zinc, lead, and potassium, and some day perhaps even conduct a flourishing trade with earth, exchanging their plentiful minerals for those they lack.

(A) evince .....ubiquitous

(B) enhance.....pedestrian

(C) fabricate.....ebullient

(D) emulate.....obsolete

(E) synthesize.....indigenous

3. A/an _____ of companies is working to create an electrically driven automobile that would cause far less pollution than gasoline-driven automobiles and not _____ reserves of petroleum.

(A) mélange.....ameliorate

(B) paradigm.....enervate

(C) amalgam.....suppress

(D) cacophony....extrapolate

(E) consortium....deplete

4. In 1831, when the young Charles Darwin began his momentous voyage to South America (a trip immortalized in his account of the journey, *The Voyage of the Beagle*), he still believed in the Creationist view that was the _____ view of the time; as the journey proceeded, however, he began to have doubts about the truth of his views as he saw evidence of geological and biological processes that must have occurred over _____. of time.

(A) orthodox.....eons

(B) fundamental.....impediments

(C) conservative.....amulets

(D) conventional....myriads

(E) dogmatic....narratives

5. The _____ between communist theory and reality was evident in the Soviet Union, a supposedly communist country that was in reality a nation in which both economic and political power was in the hands of a ruling _____.

(A) congruity....multiplicity

(B) camaraderie....lineage

(C) hiatus.....fundamentalist

(D) disparity.....elite

(E) nuance .....retinue

6. It is _____ that oil companies take _____ precautions to avoid oil spills when they are drilling offshore because such spills would have a calamitous effect on many coastal habitats such as estuaries, which are delicately balanced environments for waterfowl and other wildlife.

(A) advantageous....superfluous

(B) proverbial....comprehensive

(C) inconsequential...scrupulous

(D) judicious....ineffectual

(E) imperative.....stringent

7. Controlled fission reactors have been providing electric power since the 1950s, but controlled fusion has proved a/an _____ goal since the _____ amount of heat generated is difficult to contain even with the use of powerful magnetic fields.

(A) ephemeral.....infinitesimal

(B) orthodox.....prodigious

(C) chimerical....inconsequential

(D) elusive.....gargantuan

(E) fortuitous.....minute

8. The philosopher Peter Singer's _____ *Animal Rights* is the bible of many animal rights activists, and has _____ a lively debate about the moral status of animals.

(A) pastiche.....rectified

(B) tome.....engendered

(C) monologue .....concocted

(D) vignette.....obscured

(E) domicile....revivified

9. Some people maintain that Albert Einstein's theory of relativity _____ the clockwork universe of the Enlightenment, with its belief in absolute laws of nature; Einstein himself, however, saw his work as restoring order to our understanding of the universe by explaining _____ for which classical Newtonian physics could not account.

(A) obliterates .....caricatures

(B) undermines.....anomalies

(C) neutralizes.....oxymorons

(D) posits....prerogatives

(E) contravenes....nomenclature

10. _____ may appear to be a fairly _____ activity, but it is an historical fact that those who draw the maps have considerable political power in that they can dictate their view of how the world is perceived.

(A) Bureaucracy....tedious

(B) Iconoclasm....futile

(C) Cartography......innocuous

(D) Hedonism....alluring

(E) Cosmology....esoteric

Answers to *Double Trouble* are on page 470.

ANSWERS TO EXERCISES

ANSWERS: Episode 1

Simply Simon

1. morose
2. chicanery
3. mundane
4. unadulterated
5. arcane
6. mentor
7. bizarre
8. aberration
9. sporadically
10. lexicon

Making Sense

1. N   2. N   3. Y   4. Y   5. N   6. Y   7. N   8. Y
9. N   10. N

Match It

1. d   2. i   3. f   4. c   5. h   6. g   7. e   8. a
9. j   10. b

Axel Speaks

1. C   2. B   3. A   4. D   5. E

Answers: Episode 2

Simply Simon

1. predilection	2. foresight	3. novel
4. missive	5. revelry	6. perusing
7. squander	8. expounds	9. quiescent
10. sustain		

Making Sense

1. Y   2. N   3. Y   4. Y   5. Y   6. Y   7. N   8. N
9. Y   10. N

Match It

1. b   2. e   3. h   4. f   5. a   6. d   7. i   8. c
9. g   10. j

Axel Speaks

1. E   2. C   3. A   4. A   5. E

Answers: Episode 3

Simply Simon

1. cardinal	2. sensibility	3. inopportune
4. inexplicable	5. circumspect	6. embellishes
7. admonished	8. gambits	9. affable
10. pedantic		

Making Sense

1. Y   2. N 3. N   4. Y   5. N   6. N   7. Y   8. N
9. Y   10. Y

Match It

1. c   2. f 3. a   4. j   5. h   6. d   7. i   8. b
9. e   10. g

Axel Speaks

1. D   2. D   3. B   4. C   5. D

Answers: Episode 4

Simply Simon

1. deploy   2. enigmatic   3. comprehensive
4. engenders   5. charismatic   6. verdict
7. alluring   8. disdain   9. countenance
10. sarcasm

Making Sense

1. Y   2. Y 3. Y   4. N   5. N   6. N   7. Y   8. Y
9. N   10. Y

Match It

1. h   2. e 3. a   4. i   5. b   6. j   7. f   8. c
9. d   10. g

Axel Speaks

1. B 2. B 3. A 4. D 5. A

Answers: Episode 5

Simply Simon

1. queries
2. scrupulous
3. ravine
4. perspectives
5. Renaissance
6. ebullient
7. scathing
8. assessment
9. reclusive
10. mollified

Making Sense

1. Y 2. Y 3. Y 4. N 5. Y 6. N 7. N 8. Y
9. N 10. Y

Match It

1. d 2. f 3. i 4. h 5. j 6. b 7. g 8. a
9. c 10. e

Axel Speaks

1. D 2. B 3. C 4. E 5. B

Answers: Episode 6

Simply Simon

1. idioms	2. sojourn	3. appellation
4. verbatim	5. soporific	6. undaunted
7. replicate	8. paramount	9. mélange
10. revivify		

Making Sense

1. N   2. N   3. Y   4. Y   5. Y   6. N   7. Y   8. Y
9. N   10. Y

Match It

1. f   2. c   3. h   4. a   5. d   6. j   7. i   8. b
9. e   10. g

Axel Speaks

1. A   2. B   3. E   4. B   5. C

Answers: Episode 7

Simply Simon

1. tenet	2. uninhibited	3. chimerical
4. empathize	5. unprecedented	6. predominant
7. cryptic	8. atrophy	9. miniscule
10. validity		

Making Sense

1. Y   2. Y   3. N   4. N   5. N   6. N   7. N   8. N
9. Y   10. Y

Match It

1. h   2. c   3. j   4. i   5. a   6. b   7. e   8. g
9. d   10. f

Axel Speaks

1. E   2. E   3. E   4. B   5. D

Answers: Episode 8

Simply Simon

1. amiable
2. criterion
3. conform
4. immersed
5. discourses
6. acme
7. synthesis
8. acumen
9. pulchritude
10. ponder

Making Sense

1. N   2. Y   3. N   4. N   5. N   6. Y   7. Y   8. Y
9. N   10. Y

Match It

1. c   2. h   3. f   4. a   5. i   6. b   7. e   8. j
9. g   10. d

Axel Speaks

1. A   2. E   3. E   4. C   5. E

Answers: Episode 9

Simply Simon

1. impediments
2. succinctly
3. confounding
4. retrospect
5. chides
6. unbiased
7. lethargic
8. empirical
9. perturbed
10. eschew

Making Sense

1. N   2. N   3. Y   4. N   5. Y   6. N   7. N   8. Y
9. Y   10. N

Match It

1. c   2. f   3. i   4. h   5. j   6. a   7. d   8. g
9. b   10. e

Axel Speaks

1. A   2. E   3. C   4. B   5. A

Answers: Episode 10

Simply Simon

1. gregarious
2. advantageous
3. innumerable
4. reproachfully
5. enunciate
6. incalculably
7. multifarious
8. theorem
9. rallied
10. interlocutor

Making Sense

1. Y 2. Y 3. Y 4. Y 5. N 6. Y 7. N 8. N
9. Y 10. Y

Match It

1. e 2. i 3. b 4. h 5. a 6. j 7. g 8. c
9. d 10. f

Axel Speaks

1. A 2. D 3. E 4. C 5. C

Answers: Episode 11

Simply Simon

1. expostulation
2. coerces
3. formulation
4. insipid
5. emulate
6. ramifications
7. ornithology
8. interminable
9. incessantly
10. droll

Making Sense

1. N   2. Y   3. Y   4. Y   5. N   6. Y   7. N   8. Y
9. Y   10. N

Match It

1. h   2. f   3. c   4. d   5. g   6. b   7. e   8. a
9. j   10. i

Axel Speaks

1. A   2. C   3. C   4. E   5. D

Answers: Episode 12

Simply Simon

1. repasts
2. resolve
3. fracas
4. succumb
5. peripheral
6. connotations
7. suave
8. onerous
9. embroiled
10. dispassionate

Making Sense

1. Y   2. Y   3. Y   4. N   5. N   6. Y   7. Y   8. Y
9. Y   10. N

Match It

1. b   2. g   3. f   4. j   5. a   6. c   7. i   8. d
9. h   10. e

Axel Speaks

1. C   2. E   3. C   4. B   5. D

Answers: Episode 13

Simply Simon

1. saturated   2. nirvana   3. perpetual
4. unmitigated   5. lineage   6. syncopation
7. fiasco   8. humane   9. intrepid
10. susceptible

Making Sense

1. N   2. Y   3. Y   4. N   5. Y   6. N   7. Y   8. N
9. Y   10. Y

Match It

1. c   2. h   3. e   4. g   5. i   6. a   7. j   8. d
9. b   10. f

Axel Speaks

1. B   2. A   3. C   4. C   5. B

Simply Simon

1. cajole	2. hypotheses	3. gravity
4. oblivious	5. stolidly	6. dour
7. myopically	8. intimate	9. debacle
10. vicissitudes		

Making Sense

1. N   2. Y   3. Y   4. N   5. Y   6. N   7. Y   8. Y
9. Y   10. N

Match It

1. g   2. d   3. i   4. e   5. a   6. j   7. b   8. f
9. c   10. h

Axel Speaks

1. A   2. C   3. B   4. A   5. A

ANSWERS: Episode 15

Simply Simon

1. millennium	2. coquette	3. ubiquitous
4. congenital	5. pluck	6. connivers
7. pithy	8. propinquity	9. overtly
10. delusional		

Making Sense

1. Y   2. Y   3. N   4. N   5. Y   6. Y   7. Y   8. N
9. Y   10. N

Match It

1. d   2. j   3. h   4. a   5. i   6. g   7. b   8. e
9. c   10. f

Axel Speaks

1. B   2. E   3. D   4. C   5. C

Answers: Episode 16

Simply Simon

1. inveigle	2. loathsome	3. wily
4. ploy	5. curator	6. exercised
7. anachronisms	8. escapades	9. provincial
10. discreet		

Making Sense

1. Y   2. Y   3. Y   4. N   5. N   6. N   7. Y   8. Y
9. N   10. Y

Match It

1. c   2. j   3. b   4. f   5. h   6. a   7. i   8. d
9. e   10. g

Axel Speaks

1. E   2. A   3. A   4. D   5. B

Answers: Episode 17

Simply Simon

1. render   2. poignant   3. clamber
4. tableau   5. potency   6. macabre
7. entreating   8. sensual   9. benevolent
10. pervasive

Making Sense

1. Y   2. Y   3. N   4. N   5. Y   6. N   7. N   8. N
9. Y   10. Y

Match It

1. e   2. f   3. j   4. b   5. d   6. i   7. g   8. a
9. h   10. c

Axel Speaks

1. A   2. B   3. A   4. C   5. C

Answers: Episode 18

Simply Simon

1. covertly	2. entails	3. incorrigible
4. unsullied	5. inevitable	6. ethnic
7. inimitable	8. innate	9. elaborating
10. uncanny		

Making Sense

1. N   2. Y   3. N   4. Y   5. Y   6. N   7. N   8. N
9. N   10. Y

Match It

1. e   2. a   3. g   4. b   5. h   6. c   7. j   8. d
9. f   10. i

Axel Speaks

1. B   2. C   3. B   4. B   5. D

Answers: Episode 19

Simply Simon

1. inkling	2. metamorphose	3. depictions
4. untainted	5. transfixed	6. cavalier
7. serendipity	8. eons	9. turbulence
10. luminous		

Making Sense

1. Y   2. N   3. Y   4. N   5. Y   6. Y   7. Y   8. N
9. N   10. Y

Match It

1. d   2. h   3. a   4. f   5. b   6. i   7. j   8. c
9. e   10. g

Axel Speaks

1. E   2. A   3. B   4. A   5. D

Answers: Episode 20

Simply Simon

1. cognizant   2. corroborated   3. spurious
4. motif   5. objective   6. contravened
7. dogma   8. irrefutable   9. vestigial
10. suppress

Making Sense

1. Y   2. N   3. N   4. Y   5. Y   6. N   7. Y   8. N
9. Y   10. N

Match It

1. d   2. g   3. i   4. b   5. h   6. j   7. e   8. a
9. c   10. f

Axel Speaks

1. E   2. B   3. D   4. A   5. B

Answers: Episode 21

Simply Simon

1. rationality   2. recondite   3. expertise
4. candid   5. verifiable   6. fuse
7. diverse   8. ultimate   9. bemused
10. vertigo

Making Sense

1. N   2. Y   3. N   4. N   5. Y   6. N   7. N   8. Y
9. Y   10. Y

Match It

1. h   2. a   3. i   4. f   5. b   6. g   7. d   8. j
9. e   10. c

Axel Speaks

1. E   2. A   3. C   4. A   5. D

Answers: Episode 22

Simply Simon

1. ruses
2. mesmerized
3. ballad
4. melancholy
5. paradoxical
6. dulcet
7. tremulous
8. lyrical
9. infer
10. doleful

Making Sense

1. N   2. N   3. Y   4. Y   5. N   6. N   7. Y   8. Y
9. N   10. Y

Match It

1. g   2. d   3. h   4. b   5. i   6. j   7. a   8. e
9. f   10. c

Axel Speaks

1. C   2. E   3. A   4. B   5. C

Answers: Episode 23

Simply Simon

1. pensive
2. epiphany
3. artifacts
4. mysticism
5. prosaic
6. duplicity
7. disarms
8. retinue
9. demurely
10. conspicuously

Making Sense

1. Y   2. Y   3. N   4. Y   5. N   6. Y   7. Y   8. N
9. Y   10. Y

Match It

1. c   2. b   3. f   4. j   5. a   6. i   7. e   8. d
9. g   10. h

Axel Speaks

1. A   2. D   3. B   4. B   5. C

Answers: Episode 24

Simply Simon

1. proficient   2. tranquility   3. amalgams
4. scintillating   5. dais   6. imperative
7. coheres   8. juncture   9. renouncing
10. guileless

Making Sense

1. Y   2. Y   3. N   4. N   5. Y   6. Y   7. Y   8. N
9. N   10. N

Match It

1. e   2. d   3. j   4. i   5. b   6. c   7. a   8. g
9. f   10. h

Axel Speaks

1. C   2. C   3. B   4. A   5. B

Answers: Episode 25

Simply Simon

1. lavish
2. fazes
3. factions
4. altercations
5. liberals
6. apologist
7. ameliorated
8. consortium
9. lobbyists
10. intractable

Making Sense

1. N   2. N 3. Y   4. N   5. Y   6. Y   7. N   8. N
9. Y   10. N

Match It

1. b   2. d 3. h   4. e   5. a   6. c   7. i   8. j
9. f   10. g

Axel Speaks

1. A   2. C   3. A   4. C   5. D

Simply Simon

1. catalyst	2. imperturbable	3. agitated
4. diabolical	5. monologues	6. animosities
7. divulge	8. surpassingly	9. tinge
10. karma		

Making Sense

1. N   2. Y   3. Y   4. N   5. Y   6. Y   7. N   8. Y
9. N   10. Y

Match It

1. h   2. d   3. g   4. j   5. f   6. a   7. c   8. i
9. b   10. e

Axel Speaks

1. D   2. A   3. B   4. E   5. C

Answers: Episode 27

Simply Simon

1. ominous	2. vantage	3. homogenized
4. doctrinaire	5. hindsight	6. reductionistic
7. rampant	8. insular	9. sententious
10. reactionary		

Making Sense

1. N   2. Y   3. N   4. Y   5. Y   6. Y   7. Y   8. N
9. N   10. Y

Match It

1. c   2. i   3. j   4. f   5. h   6. a   7. e   8. b
9. g   10. d

Axel Speaks

1. C   2. D   3. E   4. C   5. A

Answers: Episode 28

Simply Simon

1. autonomous   2. ironic   3. inconsequential
4. thermal   5. creed   6. stasis
7. proximity   8. filial   9. debilitating
10. edifice

Making Sense

1. N   2. Y   3. N   4. N   5. N   6. Y   7. N   8. Y
9. N   10. N

Match It

1. b   2. f   3. a   4. h   5. i   6. c   7. j   8. d
9. e   10. g

Axel Speaks

1. B   2. C   3. D   4. D   5. C

Answers: Episode 29

Simply Simon

1. eminent   2. litany   3. depleted
4. oxymoron   5. maverick   6. alienated
7. provisionally 8. undermine   9. mammoth
10. cogent

Making Sense

1. N   2. N   3. N   4. Y   5. Y   6. N   7. Y   8. Y
9. N   10. Y

Match It

1. j   2. h   3. e   4. g   5. i   6. b   7. a   8. d
9. f   10. c

Axel Speaks

1. A   2. E   3. A   4. D   5. B

Simply Simon

1. preeminent	2. utilitarian	3. futile
4. zenith	5. omniscient	6. agenda
7. maudlin	8. legacy	9. lucre
10. exorcise		

Making Sense

1. Y   2. N   3. Y   4. Y   5. Y   6. N   7. N   8. Y
9. Y   10. Y

Match It

1. b   2. e   3. g   4. a   5. j   6. c   7. i   8. d
9. f   10. h

Axel Speaks

1. D   2. B   3. D   4. C   5. D

ANSWERS: Episode 31

Simply Simon

1. diatribes	2. concomitant	3. prestigious
4. intricate	5. pugilism	6. pinnacle
7. gauche	8. wrath	9. genesis
10. winsome		

Making Sense

1. Y   2. N   3. Y   4. N   5. Y   6. N   7. Y   8. N
9. Y   10. N

Match It

1. f   2. a   3. j   4. b   5. g   6. i   7. c   8. d
9. h   10. e

Axel Speaks

1. E   2. C   3. A   4. B   5. E

Answers: Episode 32

Simply Simon

1. impermeable
2. terminology
3. distinctive
4. protrudes
5. insuperable
6. feasible
7. exude
8. cosmic
9. conceivable
10. presumption

Making Sense

1. Y   2. Y   3. N   4. Y   5. N   6. N   7. Y   8. Y
9. Y   10. N

Match It

1. d   2. i   3. a   4. b   5. e   6. h   7. j   8. c
9. f   10. g

Axel Speaks

1. C   2. D   3. A   4. E   5. D

Answers: Episode 33

Simply Simon

1. engrossed	2. avenging	3. apex
4. bedeviled	5. decisively	6. hierarchies
7. keynotes	8. tyro	9. imminent
10. tutelary		

Making Sense

1. N   2. Y   3. Y   4. N   5. Y   6. Y   7. Y   8. Y
9. Y   10. N

Match It

1. d   2. g   3. a   4. i   5. b   6. j   7. h   8. c
9. f   10. e

Axel Speaks

1. D   2. B   3. B   4. C   5. E

Answers: Episode 34

Simply Simon

1. banal	2. extenuating	3. devoid
4. pastiche	5. subterranean	6. opine
7. context	8. prose	9. posthumously
10. archetype		

Making Sense

1. N   2. Y   3. Y   4. N   5. N   6. Y   7. Y   8. N

9. N   10. Y

Match It

1. d   2. h   3. f   4. a   5. g   6. i   7. e   8. j

9. b   10. c

Axel Speaks

1. D   2. C   3. B   4. A   5. E

Answers: Episode 35

Simply Simon

1. ogle	2. efficaciously	3. impartially
4. rapture	5. olfactory	6. burly
7. quantify	8. incognito	9. cuisines
10. trepidation		

Making Sense

1. Y   2. Y   3. N   4. N   5. Y   6. N   7. N   8. Y
9. Y   10. N

Match It

1. h   2. e   3. j   4. b   5. g   6. a   7. i   8. c
9. f   10. d

Axel Speaks

1. D   2. C   3. D   4. C   5. D

Answers: Episode 36

Simply Simon

1. gesticulating
2. nuance
3. megalomania
4. alchemy
5. hiatus
6. ostracized
7. inconspicuously
8. rapacious
9. intermittently
10. din

Making Sense

1. N   2. Y   3. Y   4. N   5. N   6. N   7. Y   8. Y
9. Y   10. Y

Match It

1. c   2. j   3. g   4. a   5. h   6. e   7. b   8. i
9. d   10. f

Axel Speaks

1. E   2. D   3. A   4. C   5. A

Answers: Episode 37

Simply Simon

1. astronomical
2. sequester
3. quaff
4. vanquishing
5. insatiable
6. quarry
7. repulsive
8. paroxysms
9. extensive
10. eluded

Making Sense

1. Y   2. Y   3. Y   4. N   5. Y   6. N   7. N   8. N
9. N   10. N

Match It

1. c   2. i   3. g   4. a   5. j   6. b   7. e   8. h
9. d   10. f

Axel Speaks

1. C   2. A   3. D   4. B   5. E

Round 1
1. **E**   2. **A**   3. **D**   4. **C**   5. **D**   6. **A**   7. **B**   8. **C**
9. **A**   10. **C**

Round 2
1. **E**   2. **A**   3. **D**   4. **A**   5. **D**   6. **E**   7. **E**   8. **A**
9. **C**   10. **B**

Round 3
1. **E**   2. **B**   3. **B**   4. **E**   5. **D**   6. **C**   7. **D**   8. **A**
9. **A**   10. **B**

Round 4
1. **B**   2. **D**   3. **C**   4. **E**   5. **D**   6. **E**   7. **C**   8. **D**
9. **A**   10. **C**

Round 5
1. **C**   2. **D**   3. **B**   4. **B**   5. **A**   6. **A**   7. **E**   8. **E**
9. **D**   10. **C**

Round 6
1. **C**   2. **D**   3. **C**   4. **A**   5. **E**   6. **C**   7. **C**   8. **D**
9. **B**   10. **C**

Round 7
1. **E**   2. **E**   3. **C**   4. **E**   5. **D**   6. **C**   7. **C**   8. **B**
9. **D**   10. **D**

Round 8
1. **B**   2. **D**   3. **A**   4. **C**   5. **C**   6. **A**   7. **D**   8. **E**
9. **C**   10. **B**

Round 9
1. **A**   2. **D**   3. **D**   4. **E**   5. **B**   6. **C**   7. **C**   8. **C**
9. **D**   10. **C**

Round 10
1. **C**   2. **E**   3. **E**   4. **A**   5. **D**   6. **E**   7. **D**   8. **B**
9. **B**   10. **C**

Simon's Glossary

The **bold-faced** number after each entry indicates the location of the word's first usage in context.

aberration N. something different from the normal or usual **2**
abortive ADJ. interrupted while incomplete **49**
abstract ADJ. complex **186**
abstruse ADJ. difficult to comprehend **205**
acerbic ADJ. sharp tempered **39**
acme N. highest point **65**
acquiesce V. to agree without protesting **148**
acronym N. word formed from the initial letters of a name or series of words **290**
acumen N. keenness of insight **66**
adherent N. follower **259**
admonish V. to reprimand **23**
advantageous ADJ. having benefit; useful **83**
advent N. arrival or coming **168**
aesthetic ADJ. pertaining to beauty or art **22**
affable ADJ. friendly **21**
affective ADJ. relating to the emotions **57**
affirm V. to maintain to be true **259**
affluent ADJ. wealthy **231**
agenda N. list or program of things to be done **291**
agitated ADJ. disturbed **247**
alacrity N. speed (also: cheerful willingness) **39**
alchemy N. seemingly magical process of transforming **368**
alienated ADJ. feeling separated from others **280**
alluring ADJ. very attractive **32**
aloof ADJ. detached **113**
altercation N. noisy dispute **238**
altruistic ADJ. unselfishly generous (N. altruism) **187**
amalgam N. mixture; combination **228**
ambiguous ADJ. unclear in meaning **48**
ameliorate V. to improve **238**
amenable ADJ. agreeable **49**
amiable ADJ. friendly; pleasant; likable **64**
amulet N. ornament worn as a charm against evil spirits **216**
anachronism N. something out of its proper time **145**
analogy N. correspondence in some way between two otherwise dissimilar things **259**
anecdote N. short account of an event **247**
animated ADJ. lively **32**
animosity N. hostility **247**
annihilate V. to destroy completely **335**
anomaly N. deviation from the norm **56**

antithesis N. the opposite of **64**

apex N. highest point **333**

apologist N. person who defends or justifies a cause, a program, and so on **239**

apostate N. one who abandons his or her beliefs or principles **286**

appease V. to calm; pacify **39**

appellation N. name **49**

aptitude N. ability **346**

aptly ADV. expressed in a precisely suitable manner **92**

arcane ADJ. known only by a few; obscure **3**

archetype N. original model after which others are patterned **346**

arduous ADJ. extremely difficult **159**

articulate ADJ. speaking in clear and expressive language **13**

artifact N. item made by human craft **216**

ascetic N. person who renounces the comforts of society to lead a life of self-discipline **82**

assail V. to attack **157**

assessment N. appraisal **40**

assimilate V. to absorb **228**

astronomical ADJ. immense **379**

astute ADJ. keen in judgment; shrewd **22**

atrophy V. to waste away **57**

attributes N. qualities **64**

augment V. to increase **331**

autonomous ADJ. independent (N. autonomy) **268**

avenging ADJ. taking vengeance **335**

ballad N. narrative poem intended to be sung **206**

banal ADJ. lacking originality; commonplace **349**

bedevil V. to plague **333**

beguiling ADJ. charming **157**

bellicose ADJ. aggressive **39**

bemused ADJ. confused **196**

beneficence N. kindness **249**

benevolent ADJ. kindly **159**

benign ADJ. harmless (also: kind) **31**

bibliophile N. book lover **12**

bizarre ADJ. strikingly unusual; fantastic **1**

bourgeoisie N. middle class (ADJ. bourgeois) **238**

bureaucracy N. government administration **240**

burly ADJ. husky **359**

buttress V. to support **72**

cacophony N. jarring, unpleasant noise **113**

cajole V. to persuade **122**

camaraderie N. good will and rapport among friends **73**

candid ADJ. without pretense or reserve; straightforward **197**

cardinal ADJ. of foremost importance **22**

caricature N. exaggerated portrait **13**

cartography N. science of making maps **289**

473

deduce V. to draw a conclusion by reasoning **83**
deleterious ADJ. harmful **1**
delusional ADJ. having a false belief **136**
demeaning ADJ. degrading **124**
demurely ADV. in a reserved and modest manner **218**
denotation N. direct meaning of a word **2**
depiction N. portrayal **178**
depleted ADJ. reduced in quantity; exhausted **279**
deploy V. to station systematically over an area **30**
derivative ADJ. unoriginal; derived from another source **346**
despotism N. absolute power **260**
detachment N. feeling of being emotionally removed; aloofness **318**
devoid ADJ. totally lacking **348**
diabolical ADJ. wicked **247**
diatribe N. bitter verbal attack **300**
dictate N. guiding principle **250**
diction N. choice of words **217**
didactic ADJ. instructional; teaching **2**
digress V. to stray from the main topic **12**
dilapidated ADJ. ruined because of neglect **123**
diligent ADJ. making a persistent and painstaking effort **21**
din N. ongoing loud noise **370**
disaffected ADJ. no longer contented **238**
disarm V. to overcome or allay suspicion; win the confidence of **218**
discerning ADJ. perceptive; showing insight and judgment **1**
discourse N. formal, lengthy discussion (also: conversation; verbal expression)
   65
discreet ADJ. prudent **146**
disdain V. to treat with scorn or contempt **31**
disparity N. difference **293**
dispassionate ADJ. impartial **102**
dissemble V. to disguise; conceal **57**
distinctive ADJ. characteristic **314**
distraught ADJ. distressed **382**
diverse ADJ. various **195**
divulge V. to reveal; make a secret known **249**
doctrinaire ADJ. rigidly devoted to beliefs **257**
dogma N. belief asserted on authority **187**
doleful ADJ. sad; mournful **207**
domicile N. home **216**
dormant ADJ. inactive **187**
dour ADJ. sullen and gloomy **123**
droll ADJ. amusing in an odd, a wry way **92**
dubious ADJ. doubtful **219**
dulcet ADJ. pleasant sounding **207**
duplicity N. deception; dishonesty **219**
ebullient ADJ. overflowing with enthusiasm **39**
eccentric ADJ. odd; deviating from the normal **3**

eclectic ADJ. selecting from various sources **40**
edifice N. structure **271**
efficaciously ADV. effectively **360**
elaborate V. to add details **170**
elated ADJ. very happy; jubilant; in high spirits **169**
elite N. most skilled members of a social group (also: a privileged group) **248**
elude V. to evade; avoid the grasp of **385**
elusive ADJ. hard to grasp **205**
emaciated ADJ. thin and wasted **378**
emanate V. to issue forth **318**
emancipate V. to free **291**
embellish V. to add details to make more attractive (also: adorn) **22**
embroil V. to involve in **102**
eminent ADJ. distinguished **278**
empathize V. to put oneself in another's place **57**
empirical ADJ. derived from observation or experiment **73**
emulate V. to imitate **92**
enamored ADJ. captivated **290**
enervating ADJ. draining energy; weakening **369**
engender V. to cause; produce **31**
engrossed ADJ. occupied fully; absorb **330**
enhance V. to improve **328**
enigmatic ADJ. deeply puzzling; mysterious **32**
ennui N. boredom and dissatisfaction **279**
enraptured ADJ. filled with delight **317**
ensconced V. to settle comfortably; settled **358**
entailed V. caused or involved by necessity **168**
enthralled V. enchanted **169**
enticingly ADV. temptingly; attractively **101**
entity N. something that exists **314**
entreat V. to plead **159**
enunciate V. to pronounce clearly **83**
eon N. indefinitely long period of time **179**
ephemeral ADJ. short-lived **180**
epicurean ADJ. suited to the tastes of an epicure (that is, a person devoted to the pleasure of the senses) **359**
epiphany N. comprehension of reality through a sudden intuitive realization **220**
equilibrium N. stable, balanced state **269**
equitable ADJ. just; fair **231**
eradicated V. wiped out **293**
erudition N. deep learning **13**
escapade N. prank; adventurous action violating conventional conduct **146**
eschew V. to avoid **74**
esoteric ADJ. hard to understand; known only to a few **179**
estranged ADJ. alienated **280**
ethereal ADJ. highly refined; spiritual **205**
ethnic ADJ. relating to cultures or races **169**

ethnocentric ADJ. based on the belief that one's group is superior **257**
euphemisms N. inoffensive language used in place of unpleasant language **102**
evince V. to show clearly **73**
evocative ADJ. calling forth ideas or feelings **205**
exemplar N. model to be imitated **170**
exercise V. to absorb the attention **145**
exorcise V. to drive out evil spirit; free from bad influence **290**
exotic ADJ. strikingly unusual **23**
expeditiously ADV. quickly and efficiently **330**
expertise N. specialized knowledge **195**
explicit ADJ. very clear; definite **3**
exploit V. to make use of selfishly or unjustly **333**
expostulation N. scolding; reproof **91**
expound V. to explain by presenting in detail **12**
extemporaneous ADJ. unrehearsed **332**
extensive ADJ. large in extent and number **382**
extenuating ADJ. reducing in severity by providing a partial excuse; mitigating **347**
extrapolate V. to estimate by projecting known information **81**
extravagant ADJ. excessive; beyond reasonable limits **239**
exude V. to give off **317**
fabricate V. to construct **316**
facet N. aspect (also: side) **147**
facetious ADJ. playfully humorous **111**
facile ADJ. superficial (also: done with little effort; easy) **57**
faction N. group of people within a larger group **240**
faculty N. ability; power **328**
fanatically ADV. with excessive enthusiasm or zeal **346**
fastidious ADJ. very fussy **227**
faze V. to bother; disconcert **238**
feasible ADJ. possible **316**
federal ADJ. constituting the central government of a nation as opposed to states or other smaller governing units **239**
fiasco N. disaster **112**
fictitious ADJ. imaginary **292**
figurative ADJ. using figures of speech; metaphorical **350**
filial ADJ. pertaining to a son or daughter **268**
flustered ADJ. nervous; upset; confused **304**
foibles N. minor weaknesses **100**
foresight N. concern with respect to the future (also: the ability to foresee) **12**
forlorn ADJ. nearly hopeless (also: sad and lonely; destitute) **23**
formulation N. something prepared in a specified way **92**
forte N. strong point or special talent **219**
fortuitously ADV. occurring by chance **179**
founder V. to fail; collapse **125**
fracas N. loud dispute **103**
fundamental ADJ. forming an essential part of something; basic; central **186**
fundamentalist N. person who rigidly follows fundamental principles **258**

furtively ADV. sneakily; stealthily **32**
fuse V. to combine into one **196**
futile ADJ. fruitless **291**
gambit N. carefully considered strategy **22**
gamut N. entire range **333**
gargantuan ADJ. huge **3**
garrulous ADJ. very talkative **12**
gauche ADJ. lacking social grace **304**
genesis N. origin **305**
gesticulate V. to make gestures **368**
glutton N. one who eats and drinks excessively **358**
gravity N. seriousness **126**
gregarious ADJ. sociable **82**
guileless ADJ. without deceit **230**
gustatory ADJ. pertaining to the sense of taste **358**
hackneyed ADJ. worn out by overuse **137**
harrowing ADJ. extremely distressing; terrifying **369**
hedonistic ADJ. believing that pleasure is the chief good in life
   (N. hedonist) **358**
Herculean ADJ. calling for great strength **291**
hiatus N. interruption; break **370**
hierarchy N. body of persons organized according to authority **333**
hindsight N. perception of the significance of events after they
   have occurred **257**
hirsute ADJ. hairy **370**
histrionics N. exaggerated behavior for effect (also: theatrical arts) **301**
homogenized ADJ. similar or the same **259**
humane ADJ. merciful; kind **112**
hybrid N. something of mixed composition **259**
hyperbole N. exaggeration **270**
hypocrite N. person who claims to have virtues he or she does
   not have **137**
hypothesis N. provisional explanation of facts (*pl.* hypotheses) **122**
iconoclastic ADJ. attacking cherished beliefs **288**
ideology N. set of beliefs that are the basis of a political or economic
   system **259**
idiom N. expression whose meaning differs from the meaning of its
   individual words **49**
ignominy N. great personal dishonor or humiliation **3**
imbued V. filled **257**
immersed ADJ. deeply involved; absorbed **65**
imminent ADJ. about to happen **331**
immutable ADJ. unchangeable **271**
impaired ADJ. diminished in strength **102**
impartially ADV. fairly; without bias **360**
impassive ADJ. showing no emotion **39**
impeccable ADJ. flawless **112**
impediment N. obstacle **72**

intermittently ADV. stopping and starting at intervals **370**
intimate ADJ. very personal; private **126**
intimate V. to communicate indirectly; imply **83**
intimidate V. to make fearful or timid **249**
intractable ADJ. not easily managed **238**
intrepid ADJ. fearless and bold **114**
intricate ADJ. complex **303**
intuition N. power of knowing without reasoning **127**
inveigle V. to win over by persuasion; cajole **148**
inveterate ADJ. deeply rooted; confirmed **100**
iota N. very tiny amount **186**
ironic ADJ. constituting a difference between what might be expected and
    what actually occurs **268**
irrefutable ADJ. impossible to disprove **187**
jargon N. specialized language **48**
jocularity N. jest; joke **81**
judiciously ADV. wisely **347**
juncture N. turning point **231**
karma N. person's life force that determines his or her destiny
    in the next life **250**
keenly ADV. perceptively **350**
keynote N. main underlying theme **332**
laconic ADJ. using few words **126**
lavish ADJ. spending liberally or abundantly **238**
legacy N. something handed down **292**
legerdemain N. slight of hand; trickery **358**
legitimate ADJ. in accordance with established standards; reasonable **30**
lethargic ADJ. sluggish; dull **72**
lexicon N. vocabulary **2**
liberal ADJ. person favoring civil liberties and the use of government
    to promote social programs **238**
lineage N. ancestry **112**
linear ADJ. like a straight line **315**
linguistics N. study of language **216**
litany N. repetitive recital **279**
loathsome ADJ. abhorrent; disgusting **145**
lobbyist N. private person who tries to influence legislators in favor
    of a special interest **240**
lofty ADJ. elevated in nature; noble **13**
loquaciousness ADJ. talkativeness **126**
lucid ADJ. clear **123**
lucre N. money **290**
lugubrious ADJ. sorrowful; mournful **280**
luminary N. notable person in a specific field **348**
luminous ADJ. glowing **178**
lyrical ADJ. expressing feeling or emotion in an affecting manner **206**
macabre ADJ. suggesting death and decay **158**
machinations N. crafty plots **114**

malignant ADJ. highly injurious **31**
mammoth ADJ. gigantic **280**
manifestation N. one of the forms in which something is revealed **91**
martinet N. strict disciplinarian **147**
maudlin ADJ. overly sentimental **291**
maverick N. rebel; nonconformist **280**
maxim N. concise statement of a fundamental principle **137**
meandering ADJ. winding back and forth **248**
megalomania N. delusion of importance **370**
melancholy ADJ. sad; tending to promote sadness or gloom **208**
mélange N. mixture **49**
mentor N. wise advisor **1**
mercenary ADJ. interested in money or gain **290**
mesmerize V. to hypnotize **209**
metamorphose V. to transform **178**
metaphor N. figure of speech that compares two different things **288**
metaphysical ADJ. pertaining to speculative philosophy **305**
methodology N. set of procedures and principles applied in a specific brand
    of knowledge **57**
millennium N. thousand-year period **136**
miniscule ADJ. very small **57**
minute ADJ. tiny **368**
minutia N. petty details **229**
mirth N. merriment; laughter **103**
missive N. letter **12**
mitigate V. to make less severe; moderate **316**
modicum N. limited quality **170**
mollify V. to soothe **39**
monolithic ADJ. constituting a single, unified whole **258**
monologue N. long speech by one person **247**
moribund ADJ. about to die **305**
morose ADJ. ill-humored; sullen **2**
motif N. dominant theme **188**
multifarious ADJ. diverse **83**
multiplicity N. large number **347**
mundane ADJ. typical of the ordinary (also: worldly as opposed to spiritual) **1**
muse V. to consider something at length; ponder **82**
myopically ADV. in a near-sighted manner **123**
myriad N. large number; innumerable **81**
mysticism N. spiritual practice seeking direct union with ultimate
    reality or God **216**
naiveté N. the quality of being unsophisticated and simple like a child **169**
narcissistic ADJ. excessively admiring oneself **147**
narrative N. story **49**
nascent ADJ. starting to develop **328**
nebulous ADJ. vague **206**
nefarious ADJ. wicked **304**
negligent ADJ. careless; inattentive **65**

negligible ADJ. not significant enough to be worth considering **73**
neophyte N. beginner **103**
neutralize V. to make ineffective **334**
niche N. recess in a wall **157**
nirvana N. ideal condition of rest, harmony, or joy (also: state of absolute blessedness) **113**
nomenclature N. terms used in a particular discipline **360**
nominally ADV. in name only **136**
nonchalantly ADV. in a carefree and casual manner **218**
novel ADJ. new or original **11**
nuance N. shade of meaning **371**
obeisance N. homage **348**
objective ADJ. unbiased **187**
obliterate V. to completely destroy **347**
oblivious ADJ. not aware **123**
obscure ADJ. not easily understood (also: dark; indistinct; not well known) **65**
obsessed ADJ. preoccupied with excessively **135**
obsolescent ADJ. becoming obsolete (no longer used) **12**
obsolete ADJ. outmoded; old-fashioned **56**
obstinate ADJ. stubborn **48**
obtuse ADJ. stupid; dull **49**
occult ADJ. secret **292**
odyssey N. long adventurous voyage **197**
ogle V. to stare at **360**
olfactory ADJ. concerning the sense of smell **358**
ominous ADJ. threatening **259**
omnipotent ADJ. having unlimited power **288**
omniscient ADJ. having infinite knowledge **289**
onerous ADJ. burdensome; troublesome **102**
opaque ADJ. obscure; unintelligible **72**
opine V. to express an opinion **348**
optimistic ADJ. looking on the positive side **100**
orchestrate V. to coordinate **238**
ornithology N. the scientific study of birds **92**
orthodoxy N. traditional belief **270**
ostracize V. to exclude from a group; shun **368**
overtly ADV. openly **136**
oxymoron N. combining of terms not suited to one another **280**
palpable ADJ. capable of being touched; tangible **359**
pantheon N. all the gods of a people; a group of famous persons **156**
paradigm N. model **73**
paradoxical ADJ. contradictory; incongruous **207**
paragon N. model of perfection **64**
paramount ADJ. foremost; primary **48**
paraphrase V. to restate in other words **279**
paroxysm N. spasm; convulsion **381**
pastiche N. imitation of another's style in writing **346**
patent ADJ. obvious; unconcealed **124**

pedagogical ADJ. related to teaching **39**
pedantic ADJ. having a narrow concern for book learning and technicalities **23**
pedestrian ADJ. ordinary; commonplace **3**
pensive ADJ. deeply thoughtful; thoughtful with a hint of sadness **216**
perambulate V. to stroll **11**
peregrinate V. to wander from place to place **12**
peripatetic ADJ. moving from place to place **12**
peripheral ADJ. of minor importance; not central **102**
perpetual ADJ. endless **114**
perspective N. point of view **40**
perspicacious ADJ. able to understand keenly **135**
perturbed ADJ. greatly disturbed **73**
peruse V. to examine **13**
pervasive ADJ. spread throughout every part **155**
pessimist N. person who tends to take the gloomiest possible view of
     a situation **127**
phenomena N. observable occurrences **188**
piety N. devotion and reverence to parents (also: devotion and reverence to
     God) **268**
pinnacle N. peak **303**
pique V. to arouse **41**
pithy ADJ. precisely meaningful; cogent and terse **137**
platitude N. stale, overused expression **137**
platonic ADJ. beyond physical desire (for example, spiritual) **168**
plausible ADJ. apparently likely (also: having a show of truth but
     open to doubt) **147**
ploy N. trick to obtain an advantage **145**
pluck N. courage; spirit **136**
plumb V. to examine deeply (also: determine the depth) **56**
poignant ADJ. emotionally moving **159**
polar ADJ. occupying opposite extremes **239**
polemicist N. person skilled in polemics (for example, the art of argument
     and controversy) **260**
ponder V. to think deeply **65**
pontificate V. to speak with pompous authority **260**
posit V. to assume to be true; postulate **315**
posthumously ADV. occurring after death **346**
potency N. power **160**
pragmatism N. practicality **269**
precept N. rule governing conduct **195**
precocious ADJ. unusually advanced at an early age **228**
predicate V. to base on **198**
predilection N. preference; disposition **13**
predominant ADJ. having greatest importance and authority **56**
preeminent ADJ. notable above all others **288**
premonition N. forewarning **240**
preposterous ADJ. ridiculous **369**
prerogative N. exclusive right or privilege **30**

prescient ADJ. having knowledge of events before they occur **12**
prestigious ADJ. esteemed **304**
presume V. to assume to be true **92**
presumption N. belief based on reasonable evidence **314**
presupposition N. something assumed in advance **270**
pretentious ADJ. making an extravagant show; ostentatious **23**
procrastinate V. to postpone **336**
prodigious ADJ. enormous (also: extraordinary) **2**
prodigy N. highly gifted child **228**
proficient ADJ. skilled in a certain area **228**
profligate ADJ. recklessly wasteful **238**
profound ADJ. deep; not superficial **56**
propensity N. inclination; tendency **370**
propinquity N. nearness **137**
prosaic ADJ. commonplace **216**
prose N. ordinary writing (as opposed to verse) **349**
protrude V. to stick out **314**
proverbial ADJ. widely referred to **238**
provincial ADJ. limited in outlook; unsophisticated **147**
provisionally ADV. for the time being **279**
proximity N. nearness; closeness **270**
psyche N. mind **316**
psychiatrist N. doctor who treats disorders of the mind **316**
psychic ADJ. related to extraordinary mental processes **196**
puerile ADJ. childish; immature **13**
pugilism N. boxing **300**
pulchritude N. beauty **64**
pundit N. authority or critic **12**
quaff V. to drink with relish **379**
quantify V. to express as a quantity **358**
quarantine V. place in enforced isolation **384**
quarry N. object of a hunt **380**
query N. question **39**
quibbling V. finding fault for petty reasons **100**
quiescent ADJ. still; inactive **11**
quintessence N. purest and most concentrated essence of something; defining, essential quality of something (ADJ. quintessential) **178**
rally V. to recover (also: assemble; recuperate) **83**
ramification N. consequence; implication **92**
rampant ADJ. unrestrained **259**
rapacious ADJ. taking by force; greedy **369**
rapport N. a harmonious emotional relationship **169**
rapture N. ecstasy **359**
rationality N. exercise of reason **196**
rationalization N. self-satisfying but incorrect reason (V. rationalize) **346**
ravine N. deep, narrow gorge **39**
reactionary N. opponent of change **258**
rebuke V. to scold; reprimand **49**

rebut v. to present opposing evidence or arguments; refute (N. rebuttal) **72**
reclusive ADJ. seeking seclusion **40**
recondite ADJ. profound **195**
rectify v. to correct **359**
recurring ADJ. happening repeatedly **251**
reductionistic ADJ. attempting to explain complex phenomena by simple principles **258**
redundant ADJ. unnecessarily repetitive; exceeding what is necessary **12**
regale v. to entertain and delight **169**
rehabilitate v. to restore to normal life through education and therapy **385**
reiterate v. to repeat **49**
relish v. to greatly enjoy; savor **371**
reminisce v. to recollect and tell of past experiences **111**
Renaissance N. the humanistic revival of classical art and learning that occurred in 14–16th-century Europe (also: renaissance: rebirth; revival; note: a "Renaissance man" is a man with diverse interests) **40**
render v. to represent; portray (also: provide) **158**
renounce v. to give up; reject **230**
repast N. meal **99**
replicate v. to duplicate; repeat **49**
reprehensible ADJ. deserving of condemnation **379**
repress v. to hold in; restrain (ADJ. repressed) **159**
reproachfully ADV. in a way that expresses blame **81**
repugnance N. disgust **378**
repulsive ADJ. causing extreme dislike; disgusting **380**
resolute ADJ. firmly determined **330**
resolve N. firmness of purpose; determination **102**
resonate v. to vibrate; echo **368**
respire v. to breathe **160**
retinue N. attendants **217**
retort v. to reply (especially in a quick, direct manner) **219**
retrospect N. looking back at the past **73**
revelation N. something revealed **198**
revelry N. boisterous festivity **11**
reverie N. daydream **144**
revivify v. to give new energy **49**
rhetoric N. pretentious language **300**
riposte N. quick reply; retort **179**
ritual N. detailed procedure regularly followed (also: the prescribed form of conducting a ceremony) **11**
rostrum N. platform for speech making **232**
rudimentary ADJ. not developed **229**
rueful ADJ. regretful; sorrowful **125**
ruminate v. to reflect upon; contemplate **206**
ruse N. trick; stratagem **209**
saccharine ADJ. excessively sweet or sentimental **111**
sacrosanct ADJ. beyond criticism **330**
saga N. prose narrative **3**

sagacious ADJ. wise **320**
sanguine ADJ. cheerfully optimistic **100**
sarcasm N. scornful remark **30**
saturated ADJ. soaked **114**
savant N. learned person **40**
scathing ADJ. very severe or harsh **40**
scenario N. possible situation or chain of events (also: outline of the plot of a literary work) **65**
scintillating ADJ. sparkling **231**
scrupulous ADJ. very thorough **40**
scrutinize V. to examine closely **158**
sensibility N. refined awareness and appreciation in feeling **22**
sensual ADJ. suggesting sexuality; voluptuous **157**
sententious ADJ. given to pompous moralizing (also: terse and vigorous in expression) **260**
sentient ADJ. conscious; aware **196**
sequester V. to set apart **379**
seraphic ADJ. like an angel **170**
serendipitously ADV. occurring as a result of a gift for making fortunate discoveries by accident **179**
serene ADJ. calm; peaceful **205**
sheepish ADJ. embarrassed; bashful **31**
skepticism N. doubting or questioning attitude **195**
skewed ADJ. distorted in meaning **65**
sojourn N. visit **49**
somnolent ADJ. sleepy **49**
sophisticated ADJ. having worldly knowledge or refinement (also: complex) **13**
soporific ADJ. sleep producing **49**
speculate V. to conjecture **22**
spontaneously ADV. occurring apparently without cause **23**
sporadically ADV. occurring irregularly **2**
spurious ADJ. false **187**
squalid ADJ. dirty **123**
squander V. to waste **11**
staid ADJ. self-restrained **169**
stasis N. motionless state **269**
statute N. law; rule **368**
stereotype N. oversimplified idea **123**
stifle V. to suppress **126**
stigmatize V. to brand as disgraceful **368**
stipulate V. to specify as an essential condition **209**
stolidly ADV. showing little emotion **123**
strata N. layers (*sing.* stratum) **269**
stratagem N. trick designed to deceive an opponent **125**
stringent ADJ. imposing rigorous standards; severe **112**
stupor N. daze; state of mental confusion **381**
suave ADJ. smoothly gracious or polite **103**
subjective ADJ. particular to a given individual; personal **278**

sublime ADJ. exalted; uplifting **170**
substantiate V. to support with proof **196**
subterfuge N. deceptive strategy; trick **304**
subterranean ADJ. hidden **349**
subtle ADJ. not immediately obvious **48**
succinctly ADV. briefly; concisely **72**
succumb V. to yield; give in **99**
superfluous ADJ. unnecessary; excessive **350**
supernal ADJ. heavenly; celestial **31**
suppress V. to restrain **187**
surmise V. to make an educated guess **64**
surpassingly ADV. exceptionally; exceedingly **249**
surreptitiously ADV. secretly; stealthily **146**
susceptible ADJ. easily influenced; vulnerable **113**
sustain V. to maintain (also: support; uphold; undergo) **12**
syncopation N. temporary irregularity in musical rhythm **113**
synthesis N. combination **64**
tableau N. scene presented by costumed actors who remain silent and
      motionless (also: a striking scene) **158**
taciturn ADJ. not inclined to speak much **125**
tangible ADJ. real; concrete **219**
tedious ADJ. boring; tiring **2**
tenable ADJ. defensible; reasonable **305**
tenet N. belief; doctrine **56**
tentatively ADV. not definitely; provisionally **279**
tenuous ADJ. weak; insubstantial **12**
terminology N. specialized vocabulary **313**
theorem N. idea that is demonstrably true or assumed to be so **82**
thermal ADJ. pertaining to heat **269**
thesis N. proposition put forward for consideration **72**
timorous ADJ. fearful **318**
tinge N. slight amount **249**
titan N. person of great stature or achievement **65**
tome N. book (usually large and scholarly) **12**
tranquility N. peace; calmness **231**
transcendentally ADV. in a way beyond the ordinary; surpassingly **170**
transfix V. to make motionless by awe **178**
transitory ADJ. existing only briefly **125**
transmogrify V. to change into a different form **180**
transpire V. to occur **186**
travesty N. highly inferior imitation (also: exaggerated portrait) **13**
tremulous ADJ. vibrating; quivering **207**
trepidation N. apprehension; dread **359**
trite ADJ. unoriginal **92**
trivial ADJ. unimportant **92**
truism N. self-evident or obvious truth **137**
turbulence N. unrest; agitation **180**
tutelary ADJ. protective **331**

tyro N. beginner **331**
ubiquitous ADJ. being or seeming to be everywhere simultaneously **136**
ultimate ADJ. final; not susceptible to further analysis **196**
unadulterated ADJ. absolutely pure **2**
unbiased ADJ. impartial **93**
uncanny ADJ. mysterious; strange **169**
undaunted ADJ. not discouraged **49**
undermine V. to weaken **280**
uninhibited ADJ. unrepressed **56**
unmitigated ADJ. not lessened or moderated in intensity **112**
unorthodox ADJ. breaking with convention or tradition **125**
unprecedented ADJ. never occurring before; novel **56**
unsullied ADJ. untarnished **170**
untainted ADJ. not contaminated **178**
utilitarian ADJ. stressing the value of practicality (also: functional; useful) **288**
validity N. the state of being well grounded and sound **57**
vanquish V. to defeat **379**
vantage N. position likely to provide superiority or give an overall view **257**
vapid ADJ. dull and uninteresting **292**
vaunted ADJ. boasted about **113**
veracious ADJ. truthful **170**
verbatim ADV. in exactly the same words **49**
verdict N. finding of an authority **31**
verifiable ADJ. capable of being proven true **198**
verisimilitude N. quality of appearing real **92**
verity N. belief viewed as true and enduring **207**
vermin N. small animals or insects that are destructive or injurious to health **348**
vernacular N. everyday language used by ordinary people **49**
vertigo N. dizziness **197**
vestigial ADJ. remaining as a remnant of something that previously existed **187**
viable ADJ. practicable **316**
vicarious ADJ. enjoyed through imagined participation in another's experience **179**
vicissitude N. sudden change in life **123**
vignette N. short literary composition **346**
virile ADJ. manly **169**
virtuoso N. someone with masterly skills **159**
vitriolic ADJ. sharp; bitter; scathing **300**
vivacious ADJ. lively; spirited **99**
vogue N. prevailing fashion or practice **157**
volatile ADJ. tending to vary frequently **39**
voluble ADJ. talking a great deal with ease; fluent **56**
wily ADJ. sly; deceiving **145**
winsome ADJ. charming; engaging **302**
wrath N. anger **301**
wrench V. to pull at the emotions; pain **381**
xenophobia N. fear or hatred of foreigners **258**
zenith N. highest point **292**